3-

Kaleidoscopic Ethnicity

Kaleidoscopic Ethnicity

INTERNATIONAL MIGRATION AND THE RECONSTRUCTION OF COMMUNITY IDENTITIES IN INDIA

PREMA A. KURIEN

Rutgers University Press
New Brunswick, New Jersey, and London

Library of Congress Cataloging-in-Publication Data

Kurien, Prema A., 1963–
    Kaleidoscopic ethnicity : international migration and the reconstruction of community identities in India / Prema A. Kurien.
    p. cm.
    Includes bibliographical references and index.
    ISBN 0-8135-3089-X (cloth : alk. paper)
    1. Return migration—India—Kerala. 2. Ethnicity—India—Kerala. 3. Kerala (India)—Social conditions. I. Title

JV8509.A2 K475 2002
304.8'0954'83—dc21

                                                                    2001058673

British Cataloging-in-Publication information is available from the British Library.

Manufactured in the United States of America

For Appa and Amma

CONTENTS

PREFACE AND ACKNOWLEDGMENTS

During the summer of 1980, immediately after my high school graduation, I spent some time at my ancestral home in Kerala, a coastal state in southwestern India. In the small town where I lived, in the many villages where I visited relatives, indeed, wherever I went in the tiny state, the topic of conversation was invariably the large outmigration to the Middle East. Close relatives on holiday from one of the Persian Gulf countries had many stories to tell of their adventures there. And, of course, they were showing off the latest household gadgets they had brought back.

Nonmigrant relatives talked about the "arrogance," "garish tastes," and "contemptible extravagances" of the newly rich, about the man who had bought himself an elephant with his Gulf wealth since owning a pachyderm had been his long-cherished dream; and about the young upstart who would casually light his cigarette in public with a bank note. Outraged middle-class teachers and government employees told of former servants buying up their land and constructing palatial houses on adjoining properties. In one case, the newly rich migrant even had the temerity to ask if he could marry his former employer's daughter. Common complaints concerned the scarcity of domestic help and agricultural labor as more and more workers were migrating to the Middle East. Another source of resentment was the skyrocketing price of fish (a delicacy of the Keralite cuisine), as the "Gulfans" (as they were called) were paying ridiculously high amounts for it. Christian priests and evangelists put the blame for the migration of their congregants on a lack of interest in the Kingdom of God and an eagerness to enter the Gulf Kingdom! There were also many stories about psychologically disturbed or unfaithful wives, delinquent children, and broken families.

The social consequences of the Gulf migration were so palpable that they left a deep impact on my then sociologically untrained mind. In retrospect I can see that the seeds of the present study were sown during that summer. Subsequent visits to Kerala and accounts from relatives and friends about the dramatic consequences of the migration only heightened my interest in the phenomenon. The stories and media reports painted a picture of a society shaken to the core by the exodus of fortune seekers to the Gulf countries and their return laden with wealth and electronic marvels. The title of one such newspaper article, "Towering Mansions, Crumbling Morals," is illustrative of the way in which many nonmigrant Keralites perceive the consequences of the migration.

As I discuss in chapter 1, the realization that ethnicity, or community differences, was crucial in shaping the migration came much later, only midway during my fieldwork, and forced me to change my research design. I made a trip to Kerala in the summer of 1988 for a preliminary study of the impact of the migration on the state and followed this up with nineteen months of field investigation, from June 1989 to December 1990. Two more trips to southern India in 1993 and 1997 and correspondence with scholars and residents in Kerala helped me keep up with subsequent developments in migration patterns.

Portions of the material presented in this book have been published elsewhere. Chapter 3 is a revised version of "Colonialism and Ethnogenesis: A Study of Kerala, India," *Theory and Society,* 1994, vol. 23, pp. 385–417, reprinted with kind permission from Kluwer Academic Publishers. "Economy in Society: Consumption, Investment and Exchange Patterns among Three Emigrant Communities in Kerala, India," *Development and Change,* 1994, vol. 25, pp. 757–783, and "Sojourner Migration and Gender Roles: A Comparison of Two Ethnic Communities in Kerala, India," in Julia S. Emlen, ed., *Continuity and Change: Women at the Close of the Twentieth Century,* 1994, pp. 43–61, foreshadow some of the arguments presented here.

A book as long in the making as this one accumulates many debts. The largest undoubtedly is to the many, many people who welcomed me into their homes and offices and provided me with valuable information. I have benefited a great deal from what they shared with me, both professionally and personally, but as I am only too aware, they did not and will not gain anything directly from my research.

The fieldwork was supported by a fellowship from the American Institute of Indian Studies and by grants from the Center for the Comparative Study of Development at Brown University, Sigma Xi, Taraknath Das Foundation, and the Indian Council for Social Science Research. Some of the early writing was done while on a fellowship from the Thomas J. Watson Jr. Institute for International Studies, Brown University. The revisions were completed while I was a postdoctoral fellow at the Center for the Study of Religion at Princeton. Funding from the Dean's office at the University of Southern California helped me in the final stages of this project.

My heartfelt gratitude goes to Dietrich Rueschemeyer, who encouraged and mentored me through this long process. Thanks also to the scholars in Kerala who provided valuable information and insight: M. Gangadharan, K.K.N. Kurup, B. A. Prakash, Thomas Issac, P.R.G. Nair, and John Kurien. Paget Henry, Louise Jezierski, David Laitin, Arthur Stinchcombe, Jon Miller, Robert Wuthnow, Kofi Benefo, Calvin Goldscheider, Pierrette Hondagneu-Sotelo, George Lipsitz, Sylvia Vatuk, and several anonymous referees provided important feedback. The support and advice of Robert Wuthnow and Penny Becker helped this project finally see the light of day.

The book could not have been written without the encouragement and assistance of my family. Feedback from Kofi Benefo was crucial in the writing process. Kofi also provided the support and emotional stability that allowed me to focus on my work and cheerfully did more than his share of housework and child care so I could put in long hours in front of the computer. Our son, Roshan, refreshed me with much-needed diversion. Both Kofi and Roshan came into my life after the fieldwork was completed, but my parents were involved in the project from its inception. It is through them that I obtained many of the contacts in Kerala who helped me find information, fieldwork sites, and housing. My periodic trips home to Madras (now Chennai) while I was doing my fieldwork were rejuvenating and helped me keep my perspective and sense of humor even during trying periods. My parents have been veritable mines of information about Kerala, and my father went to great lengths to obtain additional material and documents. Both my father and mother have read, commented on, and corrected several drafts of this book, and I have had many conversations with them in person or over the phone regarding parts of it. They also came all the way to California to help me with housework and child care so I could revise the manuscript. Without my parents' help, this book would not have been written. I dedicate this work to them.

Kaleidoscopic Ethnicity

CHAPTER 1

Ethnicity and International Migration

$\mathcal{E}$thnicity and ethnic conflict are very much in the news these days. In countries like the United States, Great Britain, and France, immigrants have been coming into conflict with more established groups in the battle for public recognition and resources. In other regions of the world like the Middle East, Africa, Eastern Europe, and South Asia, hostilities between communities (generally defined by religious background) have intensified, leading to violence and bloodshed. Both immigrant and nonimmigrant ethnic groups claim legitimacy for themselves and their demands by referring to their peoplehood, culture, or land, on the basis of events that occurred in the distant past.

Ethnic identities and cultures appear to be intransigent because they are rooted in ancient history. Yet, scholarly literature has now shown that ethnicity is not the immutable, primordial essence that it appears to be, but instead is fluid and amorphous and constantly being reinvented (e.g., see Appadurai 1996, 139–157; Conzen et al. 1992). Despite the attention that ethnic identity and conflict have received recently, there is still no clear understanding of what ethnicity is or of how it shapes the behavior of individuals and groups.

Scholars have paid attention to two main types of ethnicity. The literature on ethnic groups in the Western world deals almost exclusively with immigrants and the way immigrants from different nationalities and their descendants develop communities, identities, and political platforms in their countries of residence.[1] Much of the contemporary literature dealing with ethnicity in non-Western countries on the other hand, focuses on ethnic groups as subnationalities and on ethnic conflict.[2] The problem with these approaches is that immigrant ethnicity and ethnic conflict are fairly unusual instances of ethnic behavior. By focusing on such exceptional situations, both perspectives neglect the quotidian aspects that make ethnicity a basic structure undergirding community life. The power of ethnicity lies precisely in the latent way in which it produces and reproduces individuals and groups. Ethnicity is the largely internalized and constantly evolving woof and warp of our community fabric, manifesting itself in the way we build and furnish our houses; feed and clothe ourselves; find and relate to our mates; raise our children; interact with friends, relatives, and strangers; select our occupations, recreations, and politics; practice our religion; conduct our weddings and funerals; and do the hundred other things that constitute the humdrum of everyday life.

India is a good place to study the functioning of the multifaceted dimensions of ethnicity. It is one of the most diverse countries in the world with major, longstanding differences among groups. There are many features that distinguish these groups. The sense of community based on common language and geographical region has been the principle underlying the division of the country into states. Most states have a distinctive culture and cuisine, and many also have unique religious practices and deities as well as caste groups. Caste groups within states may have different marriage and inheritance practices, life-cycle rituals, religious practices and deities, social customs, and food prohibitions. However, the most fundamental cleavage in modern India has been among religious groups. Religious groups in India are not just different in terms of religion. For the most part, they also have divergent marriage, divorce, and inheritance patterns, family and community structures, gender norms and behavior, occupational specializations, economic positions, and educational attainments. Because of these multidimensional differences, Indian religious communities have been described as *ethnic* groups (see Brass 1991; Phadnis 1990; Schermerhorn 1978; Varshney 1998).

The variations among castes and religious groups are recognized not just by the people but also by state and central governments. The state of Kerala, for instance, acknowledges the differences between the major communities through affirmative-action measures for disadvantaged groups and by a system of communal rotation of appointments for the others. The heterogeneity between the major religious groups is respected and institutionalized even at the federal level. India does not have a common civil code for all communities. Instead, each religious group is governed by its own "personal laws" with respect to matters such as marriage, divorce, and inheritance.

Among Indian states, Kerala offers an unparalleled setting to study ethnicity based on religion because of its unusual configuration of religious groups. While India is largely Hindu (83 percent), Kerala has a large proportion of Muslims (23.45 percent) and Christians (19.31 percent) in addition to Hindus (56.90 percent).[3]

This book focuses on the factors that were responsible for the striking differences in migration patterns, remittance use, and migration-induced social change manifested by three communities in Kerala: *Mappila* Muslims, *Ezhava* Hindus, and *Syrian* Christians, in order to understand what ethnicity is and how it operates in everyday situations. A comparative study of the way different ethnic groups react to the same economic opportunity provides a good test of the ability of ethnicity to shape the activities and decisions of its members.

Migration from Kerala to the Middle East is an excellent lens through which to study ethnicity for another reason. The rapid and substantial economic and social transformation brought about in these communities by the short-term migration presents an outstanding case study of ethnic change. Although the culture, structural position, and social practices of groups are always changing, usually such changes are gradual and are visible only after long periods of time. The large-scale migration from Kerala to the Persian Gulf countries provides us the unusual opportunity to witness a greatly accelerated and very visible process of ethnic transformation.

The main argument is that an interacting nexus of three primary elements—religion, gender, and status—shaped the migration and remittance patterns and was in turn transformed by migration. Religion did not shape migration patterns directly, through religious dictates or practices, but indirectly, by determining the social location of the three groups within colonial and postcolonial Kerala. This social location in turn affected the educational and occupational profiles of each of the groups, their family structures, and their social networks, factors which were fundamental in structuring the migration flows. Gender norms and practices influenced which groups migrated from each community, the organization of remittance flows, and the restructuring of migrant households. Concepts of honor and prestige determined the types of "status spending" that migrant households engaged in.

The rapid enrichment made possible by international migration resulted in a reinterpretation and redefinition of religious identity and practice, which was manifested by changes in patterns of gendered behavior and of status in each of the three migrant areas. Thus, the identity and sociocultural practices of Mappila Muslims, Ezhava Hindus, and Syrian Christians were fundamentally transformed as a result of the migration.

Discovering Ethnicity

I did not originally set out to study ethnic variations in migration. The importance of ethnicity in shaping the migration patterns was, in a sense, thrust upon me. When I started my fieldwork in 1989, my focus was on rural and urban differences of the impact of the Middle Eastern migration on sending communities in Kerala. I knew that the migration and rapid enrichment of largely lower-class migrants had fundamentally transformed Kerala and particularly the migrant communities. As a graduate student specializing in the sociology of development, I wanted to examine the socioeconomic changes brought about by migration. I was primarily interested in the effects of the migration on class, caste, and status in migrant communities and on gender and intergenerational relationships in migrant households. Studies of the social impact of migration seemed to indicate that some communities manifested "conservative change"[4] while others "modernized" or manifested "progressive change"[5] as a consequence of international migration. However, there was little understanding of the circumstances under which conservative and progressive changes took place.

Still trapped within the modernization paradigm[6] that, although discredited, had not been replaced within development studies, I hypothesized that rural migrant areas were more likely to be traditional and therefore manifest conservative change, while urban migrant areas would be more modernized and Westernized and thus manifest progressive change. However, I found to my surprise that there were no significant rural-urban variations in migration impact (possible explanations are discussed later in this chapter). Instead, there were striking differences between the patterns of migration, use of remittances, and migration-induced social changes manifested by the Mappila Muslims, Ezhava Hindus, and Syrian Christians. The types of people who migrated, the nature of the jobs and contracts obtained in the Middle East, and the way money was remitted and used varied tremendously among the three communities. The impact of the migration on the caste, class, and status structures of the communities and on the gender and intergenerational relationships of the households also differed. Since these patterns could not easily be classified as "conservative" or "progressive," I abandoned that schema and the associated economic development framework.

The discovery of such fundamental community differences in the economic and social impact of migration within one geographic region was unexpected especially since there was nothing in the literature to indicate that this would be the case. Most of the discussions regarding ethnicity and migration focused on the differences among migrants from different *countries* in the receiving (largely Western) societies. There was little reference to ethnic differences in the literature on migrant sending communities that I had combed assiduously before starting my research. More specifically, the research on the Middle Eastern migration from Kerala did not indicate that there were any systematic community differences. This migration had been studied extensively by both large- and small-scale survey research (mostly in the rural areas which had the largest numbers of migrants). Of the more than dozen studies conducted, only two of the early village-level studies found significant variations between the villages surveyed in the types of jobs that migrants obtained in the Middle East and the way they used their remittances (Kurian 1978; Mathew and Nair 1978).[7] Only one (Mathew and Nair 1978) mentioned that the community backgrounds of the villages were different. None of the large survey studies conducted subsequently indicated any systematic community differences.[8] I spoke also to the economists who had conducted many of the studies before starting my research, and they dismissed the possibility that there might be community variations in the use of remittances. So this was the central question that I sought to answer as I began analyzing the field data. Why were the patterns and impacts of migration so different in the three communities? A related question was why the research on migration had neglected these differences.

The obvious explanation for the variation in the migration patterns of the Mappila Muslims, Ezhava Hindus, and Syrian Christians was that the three communities themselves were so dissimilar. Not only did they practice three different religions, they varied also in their family and community structures, occupational specializations, educational attainments, inheritance systems, and gender ideologies and practices, to name only the most salient of factors.

But what exactly was it about ethnicity that led to such pronounced differences in the migratory behavior of Mappila Muslims, Ezhava Hindus, and Syrian Christians? Was it their distinct worldviews and beliefs? Or did it have to do with the diversity of their social structures? In other words, were the deciding factors in the realm of ideology, of practice, or both? Which particular beliefs and practices were central in bringing about these differences? To understand the phenomenon better and to find the answer to these questions, I turned to the body of work on ethnicity. There was some discussion of culture and structure in the literature on racial and ethnic groups in the United States. It appeared that much of the earlier research attributed the differential success rates of immigrants from different countries to their respective cultural values, while later research used a more structuralist approach.[9] Most contemporary studies (see Portes and Rumbaut 1996), however, seemed to argue that the behavior of immigrant ethnic groups was the outcome of a complex interaction between the two types of factors, an approach that I myself favor. But beyond this rather general point, the literature on immigrants was not of much help for understanding everyday ethnicity. I turned next to the studies of migration to see why the relationship between migration and ethnicity had been neglected in the literature on sending communities.

Migration and Ethnicity

Short-term international migration from poorer to richer countries leads to tremendous social changes at the household and community level in the sending communities. We are now living in what has been called "the age of migration" (Castles and Miller 1993), and it is important to understand the multifaceted consequences of global labor migration flows. Migration to the Middle East represents a distinct type of international movement that is increasingly common and likely to dominate in the future. It is a strictly temporary migration, with no possibility of permanent settlement for most migrants. More and more developed countries facing labor shortages are turning to this model of buying work hours, by hiring a rolling stock of temporary and cheap labor from lower-income countries. They save on social expenditure and also solve the problem of keeping their culture intact. The "H–1 B" (the type of visa granted) contract migration of computer workers to the United States and to countries around the world is a good example of this type of migration. Unskilled and semiskilled workers in particular are subject to a variety of restrictions concerning the length of stay and the admittance of dependants (Appleyard 1989, 28). Thus, labor-importing countries only give such migrants contracts of a few years at a time, and in most cases (through income and visa restrictions) family members are not permitted to join the migrant, causing social, psychological, and economic disruption in the migrant households. Consequently, migrants are oriented toward their home communities, visiting frequently and living frugally so that they can remit a large portion of their income to their families. The migration takes place largely through kin and friendship networks, and thus both the sources and destinations of migrants tend to be geographically concentrated. In the sending countries, there are villages where most households have (or have had) at least one migrant. Together with the income differential between the sending and receiving societies, this type of migration has therefore had major impacts on the home communities of the migrants, bringing about fundamental changes in their physical, social, and economic structures.

International migration facilitates the reconstruction of ethnicity and identity both directly and indirectly.[10] Relocation to a different context frees people from many of the social, cultural, and mental constraints they face at home. Simultaneously, relocation also forces the imagining and articulation of personal and group identity (Appadurai 1996; Eikelman and Piscatori 1990, xi). Perhaps even more important in the case of the Middle Eastern migration where most of the migrants were from the lower classes, international migration introduces a sudden flow of wealth to the home communities, giving rise to attempts by immigrants and their families to reinvent their community identity and practices to obtain a better status.

Most of the literature on international migrants and immigrants focuses on the impact of immigration on receiving societies, particularly those in the West. Since the social consequences of large-scale immigration are of concern to receiving societies, the relationship between ethnicity and migration has been an important topic within this literature. For instance, starting from the turn-of-the-twentieth-century European migration to the United States, several studies document how and why migrants from different countries are tracked into distinct socioeconomic niches in the host society (Bonacich 1972; 1973; Portes and Rumbaut 1996) and why some groups are more successful than others at "assimilating" into these societies—both economically and socially.[11] Studies also examine the transformations in the culture, identity, and practices of immigrants over time.[12]

The focus on receiving societies can be seen even in the case of most of the recent literature on transnationalism. The transnational paradigm recognizes that immigrants do not cut off ties to their countries of origin upon emigration but maintain complex, long-term social, economic, and political relationships with their home societies (Basch, Schiller, and Blanc 1994). However, the focus is still largely on how transnationalism affects the lives of immigrants in their new environment.[13]

Although the literature on the role of ethnicity in shaping migration patterns to Western countries and the adjustment of immigrants within such societies acknowledges the dialectical relationship between ethnicity and migration, it does not address many of the issues relevant to sending societies. Ethnicity in these studies is defined as national background, and many explanations for the differences in the patterns of migration such as the geographical proximity of sending countries, the political relationship between sending and receiving countries, the relative level of development of the two countries, and the racial, linguistic, and cultural (defined as national culture) background of the migrants do not generally differentiate migrant outflows from one country. Again, the transformation of the ethnicity of immigrants in receiving societies is primarily a consequence of having to develop a community and identity in the new country, not a factor in the transformation of the ethnicity of home communities.

Since short-term migration is generally undertaken for economic reasons and the most obvious effect of such migration on sending countries is the outflow of a significant proportion of the workforce and the inflow of large sums of money, most studies have tended to focus on the economic aspects of short-term migration.[14] These studies are framed largely within the neoclassical economic paradigm or the more recent "new economics of migration" and are based on micro-level (the individual or the household) decision models and completely overlook ethnicity or the sociocultural context, as a factor affecting migration. Since the focus is on generalization, group differences are also missed or ignored.

These problems persist even in much of the research employing the "social networks" approach (Hugo 1981; Gurak and Caces 1992; Massey et al. 1987; Taylor 1986) since this perspective is generally still within the "cost-benefit" economic framework. *Return to Aztlan* (Massey et al. 1987) is based on a study of the U.S. migration from Mexico on four "diverse communities with contrasting patterns of socioeconomic organization" (1987, 321). According to the authors, social networks are important in initiating and sustaining migration flows because *they reduce the costs and risks of international movement.* Several propositions follow from this initial assumption. The authors argue that the social networks gradually expand to encompass all classes and sections of the community, then migration is institutionalized and becomes a routine, mass phenomenon. Consequently, the internal logic of migration irons out any of the initial community differences in patterns of migration. They conclude that "despite the differences in community structure and socioeconomic organization, the social process of migration unfolded in a remarkably consistent and predictable fashion over time" in each of the four communities (Massey et al. 1987, 321; see also Massey et al. 1993, 449–450).

While the social networks approach is a big advance over the micro-level models, the economic framework that it adopts is limiting because it focuses only on *one* of the ways that social networks work. What is important to understand is that the friendship and kin networks that are mobilized for migration were formed prior to the migration and were developed as an integral part of group membership. As such, the primary tasks of networks are usually socialization, social support, and *boundary maintenance.* Consequently, these other functions of social networks might override or interfere with the economic aspects. For instance, since social networks are an important community resource, there may be mechanisms to ensure only group members can access them, thereby preventing their expansion beyond the community. The norms governing the nature of networks are also likely to vary from group to group. In short, the characteristics of the community shape the effectiveness, the strength, and the beneficiaries of social networks.

This was clear from my research. Although the large-scale migration to the Middle East was only about two to three decades old at the time of my fieldwork, there had been prior internal and international migration from the Mappila Muslim, Ezhava Hindu, and Syrian Christian communities from at least the 1930s. Despite this long history of migration, and its prevalence, the three groups showed substantial variations in migration patterns. Many of these variations were evident even at the inception of the migration. The migration had spread over time, but precisely *because* of the operation of social networks, the initial differences had only become intensified. The social networks limited the range of subgroups that migrated within each community and the type of jobs they were able to obtain in the Middle East. The operation of these networks was affected also by the cohesiveness and solidarity of the communities.

Even the literature on the Mexican migration to the United States does not support the claim that social networks have expanded to include all groups in society. In fact, study after study has shown that Mexican immigration continues to be largely from the lower classes, and that due to the operation of the social networks that decades of such migration have put into place, Mexican migrants (even those who are quite well educated) have been pushed into largely unskilled and semiskilled jobs in the United States.[15]

Although community differences in migration patterns are widely recognized by the migrants themselves (see, for instance, Osella and Osella 2000a, 7–8), studies of migration from Kerala missed ethnic differences for much the same reasons as the research on the impact of migration on sending societies discussed above. The Kerala studies focused primarily on the economic consequences of the migration and were almost entirely framed within the neoclassical tradition. According to this perspective, the economy is an autonomous realm, largely unaffected by the social and cultural context. Thus, the Kerala studies were designed on the assumption that there was a generic migrant who went on a legal contract for a particular job and fixed salary, that he or she remitted the entire amount saved to the immediate family in Kerala at regular intervals, and that this amount represented the total monetary benefit gained through the migration. Not only did this design miss crucial variations among groups, but as I will show in the subsequent chapters, few migrants (from any of the groups) fit this model.

Most studies that examine the sociocultural consequences of migration on home communities have been ethnographic and focus only on one community.[16] Comparative studies, however, have generally been guided by economistic paradigms of the type outlined above and have therefore focused largely on household-level impacts.[17] Consequently, the relationship between ethnicity and migration has largely been neglected.

In addition to being both holistic and comparative and thus overcoming the problems of both types of methods, this study contributes to the literature on the impact of migration on home communities by operating under assumptions that differ fundamentally from the approaches that have guided most research on the topic. Unlike approaches that view economic behavior as being relatively unconstrained by social and cultural context, I believe that economic actions are always part of a larger social system. Economic behavior is simultaneously social and symbolic behavior and is therefore shaped by the context within which it is embedded. Several other propositions follow from this approach.

1. It is important to study that context if we are to understand economic behavior.
2. To study the context effectively, we cannot simply focus on the individual or the household. Even if economic decisions are made by individuals or jointly by members of the household, these decisions are affected by the context, and the unit of analysis should be the community.
3. Social and cultural factors have an independent effect on economic behavior. Social identities and cultural beliefs may facilitate or constrain the ability of individuals to obtain access to and benefit from economic opportunities.
4. Economic behavior has an independent effect on society and culture. Economic behavior may reinforce existing social and cultural patterns or may reshape them.

In short, this study focuses on the ways in which the community context within which migration takes place shapes the migration and is in turn reshaped by it.

Ethnicity and Migration in Kerala

While the Mappila Muslims dominated the outflow to the Middle East, Ezhava Hindus and Syrian Christians also participated in large numbers. I wanted to focus on the differences in migration patterns and consequences resulting from ethnicity, so I chose to study three high-migrant villages in different parts of the state that were dominated by each of these three groups. Like most of the other states in India, Kerala constitutes a unique linguistic and cultural entity. Although the three communities were parts of three different subcultural units, they shared a common language and the broader regional history and culture. The contrasting profiles of the communities are described below.

At the time that I did my fieldwork, the Mappila Muslims of Veni village in northern Kerala manifested a strong corporate identity and a high degree of group solidarity. They had a joint family structure that was patrilineal, patrilocal, and strongly patriarchal. Women were secluded and married very early, and gender differentials were sharply marked. Fertility rates were high. The community as a whole had low levels of education.

The Ezhava Hindus of Cherur village in southern Kerala seemed to have a low degree of group solidarity and a great deal of intragroup competition and conflict. Traditionally matrilocal and matrilineal, many of these elements were retained despite a shift to a bilateral system. Households were smaller than those of the Mappila Muslims, and women married later, had fewer children, and had greater autonomy and freedom. Educational levels were also higher.

Although the Syrian Christians in Kembu in south-central Kerala had a strong sense of ethnic exclusivity and identity, they tended to be more individualistic and had fewer community ties. They had a nuclear family structure that was patrilineal and patrilocal in character. Gender relationships were more egalitarian than in the other two communities and marriages were later. A large proportion of the younger women had white-collar and professional or semiprofessional occupations.

The ethnicity of these three groups fundamentally shaped the patterns of migration and its economic impacts. Mappila Muslim migrants from Veni went to the Middle East largely through the help of relatives and friends or illegally on visas granted to make religious pilgrimages such as the Haj. Almost all the migrants were male, and they specialized in trade, petty business, and unskilled or semiskilled jobs. Ezhava Hindu migrants from Cherur migrated by using professional agents who charged a hefty fee to procure jobs and visas. This migration stream was entirely male, and the migrants obtained jobs as technicians or skilled workers. Syrian Christian migrants from Kembu largely were recruited directly by companies who arranged for their visas and paid for their trips. Many of these migrants were female nurses. In general, male and female migrants from this area were employed as clerks, semiprofessionals, and professionals in the Middle East, and in most cases the immediate family migrated as well.

Remittances were used in different ways in the three areas. In the Mappila Muslim village, a great deal of emphasis was given to distributing money earned to the largest circle of people within the community and to supporting religious activities. The Ezhava Hindus spent large sums of money on elaborations of life-cycle rituals during which there was lavish gift giving and entertaining. Thus, there was a smaller circle of exchange than in the Mappila village. In the Syrian Christian village, the gains of migration were largely confined to the immediate family. Some amount went to religious causes, but for the most part the emphasis was on saving the money earned, to be used later for dowries for daughters and for professional education for sons. The major forms of economic investment in the three communities varied also, from business activities in the Mappila Muslim community, to usurious lending in the Ezhava Hindu village, to fixed deposits and bonds in the Syrian Christian locality.

Migration and remittance flows led to the transformation of the socioeconomic structure and culture of all three communities, but again in very different ways. For instance, caste cleavages were eroded in the Muslim localities, redefined in the Hindu areas, and strengthened in the Christian regions. Migrants introduced new patterns of status in all three areas to symbolize their changed socioeconomic position within the communities. The changes in the economic locus of control necessitated by the migration resulted in the reinforcement of patrilinearity and patriarchy in Veni, the revitalization of female inheritance and matrilinearity in Cherur, and the nuclearization of households as well as the empowerment of women in Kembu.

Background to the Migration

Beginning with the dramatic increase in oil prices in the early 1970s, there has been a large outmigration from Asian countries (particularly India and Pakistan) to the Middle East. Gulf countries undertook a massive infrastructural reconstruction and in a relatively short period of time were able to transform themselves from seminomadic societies to some of the most technologically advanced nations of the world. Foreign labor was central to this transformation. By 1980, 69.8 percent of the workforce in the region were foreigners. In some countries like the United Arab Emirates (U.A.E.), the percentage was as high as 82.5 (Owen 1985, 18).

While most of the imported labor consisted of unskilled and semiskilled workers, given a very small and (at the time) relatively uneducated and unqualified population in the region, there was also the need for a variety of other types of migrant skills. There were opportunities for some entrepreneurial activities and clerical workers of different types. Hospital staff from orderlies to lab technicians, nurses, doctors, and administrators were in great demand. Engineers were needed to design and execute the many projects that were being undertaken.

By 1980, Asians constituted around one-third of the foreign workforce in the Gulf countries. Indians and Pakistanis alone accounted for more than 18 percent. A World Bank estimate had projected that the number of Indians in the region would grow to 25.6 percent of the workforce in 1985 (Choucri 1983, 23). In terms of numbers, it was estimated that there were between 1.5 to 1.7 million

Indians in the Middle East in 1990–1991 (Nayyar 1994, 32; Isaac 1993, 60). According to B. A. Prakash (1998), the figure had increased to 2.8 million by 1998. Nazli Choucri (1983, 17) indicates that "both politics and markets played a role in the new inter-regional flow." Asian workers were preferred by Middle Eastern countries since they were willing to work for lower wages than Arabs and because they were believed to be docile and therefore not likely to make political demands. For the Asian countries facing a crisis of high levels of unemployment and poverty, the opening up of the Middle East was a godsend, an opportunity to siphon off excess workers and to earn badly needed foreign exchange.

For the migrants themselves, the arduous work and the far-from-ideal conditions notwithstanding, Gulf countries represented the modern-day El Dorado, with unprecedented opportunities for quick wealth, together with the glamor of foreign travel and experience. Migrants generally earned from five to fifteen times as much as they would have locally. Thus migration provided the income to clear household debts, to take care of household expenditures, and to see family members well settled.[18]

Migrant areas in India have generally been rural and dependent on agriculture or other primary industries such as fishing (Gogate 1986; Nair 1986). Kerala, a small state, has been a major labor exporter to the Middle East. Although the state's population of around thirty million comprises only 3.43 percent of the population of the country (Prakash 1994, 43), 35 to 50 percent of the migrants from India have been from this state.[19] By 1998 the proportion had reached over 50 percent or over 1.4 million (Prakash 1998). Another study has a slightly lower estimate of 1.36 million for the second half of 1998 (Zachariah, Mathew, and Rajan 1999, 5).

These estimates of the stock of migrants at a point in time, however, are grossly inadequate in capturing the magnitude of the phenomenon. Since individual migrants went on short-term contracts, there was a rapid turnover of migrants. Thus, the number of people who were involved in the exodus are several times larger than static figures convey. A statewide survey conducted in 1992–1993 found that 23 percent of households reported having at least one member who had worked outside the country at one time or another.[20] Another survey conducted in 1998 estimated that there were thirty-three international migrants for every one hundred households (Zachariah, Mathew, and Rajan 1999, 4). Ninety-six percent of these international migrants were probably in the Middle East (Banerjee, Jayachandran, and Roy 1997, 3).

There were migrants from Kerala in the Persian Gulf region as early as the 1930s when the oil industry in the region began to be developed, but the large-scale migration began only after the oil boom of the early 1970s. Demand and wages escalated until 1983, when the oil prices crashed. Subsequently, massive retrenchments took place, and wage levels were sharply reduced.[21] In the immediate post-1983 period, there was some decline in migration flows, but they picked up once again, although not to the pre–1983 levels.[22] The war in the Gulf in the early 1990s caused a temporary disruption, but migration resumed as soon as the situation stabilized.[23] Since 1996, Gulf countries have been tightening up their immigration policies, and as a consequence, a large number of illegal immigrants have had to leave. An economist who studied the phenomenon, P.R.G. Nair, estimates that the return migration from the United Arab Emirates (the first country in the region to implement such policies) to Kerala from June to October 1996 must have been around thirty thousand (Nair 1996, 4). Another estimate puts the figure at over forty thousand (Prakash 1998).

Estimates of remittances to Kerala from the Middle East are even more difficult to obtain than figures on the number of migrants from the state. The figures vary from 5 billion rupees per year in the 1975–1986 period (Nair 1987a, 20) to between 7.3 billion to 9.2 billion rupees for 1980–1981 (ESCAP 1987, 81) to 10.14 billion rupees for 1987–1988 (Nair 1994, 109). These remittances contributed a whopping 22 to 28 percent of the state domestic product in 1980–1981 (ESCAP 1987, 81). Since 1996, migration and remittances registered a slump. The Kerala migration study conducted in 1998 estimated that the remittances were around 4.1 billion or 10.7 percent of the state domestic product, but the authors acknowledge that this number is probably an underestimate due to the tendency of households to underreport remittances and the fact that the remittances might not always be sent directly to the household (Zachariah, Mathew, and Rajan 2000, 21–22). Within Kerala, the Gulf migrants were concentrated in a few areas known locally as "Gulf pockets." It is estimated that remittances contributed up to 50 percent of the gross domestic prouct (GDP) of the high-migrant districts (ESCAP 1987, 74).

Methodology

I present an overview of my fieldwork in this section. My experiences and specific fieldwork strategies varied in the three villages because of the distinct features of the communities, but also because my identity as a Malayalee,[24] a woman, and a researcher were perceived in strikingly dissimilar ways, making it necessary for me to adopt different data-collection procedures in each area. These details are discussed in the chapters dealing with the three villages.

The implications of being a native as opposed to a foreign ethnographer have been the subject of some discussion in the past decade, as more and more ethnographers have returned home to conduct their studies.[25] As Kirin Narayan (1993, 672–673) has pointed out, however, globalization and mass migration have greatly complicated such binary categorizations, as what is home is frequently ambiguous. In my case in particular, this was often an issue that I (and the people I encountered) pondered. I am a Syrian Christian, from central Kerala by ancestry. Malayalam (the language spoken in Kerala) is my native language, and almost all of the conversations I conducted during my fieldwork were in

Malayalam. However, until the time of my fieldwork, except for occasional summer visits of a few weeks' duration, I had never lived in Kerala. I grew up in the larger Madras (now Chennai) region of the neighboring Tamil Nadu state. In 1989, when I began my fieldwork, I had been living in the United States for almost three years. All of this muddled my identity and confused many villagers.

I conducted an exploratory study of the migration in the summer of 1988 and then did the fieldwork over a nineteen-month period, between June 1989 and December 1990. Veni, Cherur, and Kembu and the names of the people I discuss in these pages are pseudonyms, to protect the privacy of the communities and the individuals concerned. I lived in, or near, each of the three villages for between three and five months during my period of fieldwork. I made two subsequent trips to southern India in 1993 and 1997 and maintained sporadic correspondence with scholars and residents in Kerala to keep up with the consequences of migration in the state.

As mentioned, I had originally designed the study as a comparison of rural-urban differences in the impact of the Gulf migration and had planned to study a rural community and an urban area. I arrived in Kerala in June of 1989.[26] After an initial period of library work and discussions with the various scholars who had studied the Gulf migration, I went on brief visits to some rural Gulf pockets in different parts of the state and finally selected Veni, a village in the heartland of the predominantly Muslim district Malappuram. I decided to focus on Muslim migrants for three primary reasons. Firstly, Muslims seemed to be overrepresented among Gulf migrants, and secondly, of the three religious groups in Kerala, there were (and still are) relatively fewer contemporary studies of Muslims.[27] Again, both lay people and researchers assured me that there were major differences between the rural Muslim population in northern Kerala and the urban Muslims in and around the capital city of Trivandrum in the south.

In early August, I set off for my first field experience. Bravado quickly turned to despair and frustration as I was confronted by the numerous and varied problems in Veni, both as an outsider and as a woman. (This is discussed in greater detail in chapter 5.) I was finally able to talk to people in seventy-nine households in this area—some for just a few minutes but others for several hours over repeated visits. In addition to my fieldwork in Veni, I did a brief study of a coastal Muslim village where caste divisions were prominent and of a nonmigrant village[28] which was to serve as a control group, so that the general changes affecting the region at large could be separated from the changes brought about as a result of the migration.[29] I completed my work in the Malappuram area in December.[30]

In January 1990, I began my search for a comparable, high-migrant Muslim community (so that ethnicity would not be introduced as an extraneous variable), in or around the capital city of Trivandrum in southern Kerala. Such a community proved surprisingly difficult to find because there were no large Muslim settlements near Trivandrum. After weeks of travel through the whole district, I finally settled on Kuttur, a little outside Trivandrum city. This was a satellite area of Trivandrum, and there was regular movement to and from the city. There was a cluster of around four to five hundred Muslim houses on either side of the national highway, and this community was to be the focus of my research.

Here again, I had several initial problems of entree which were overcome only after the *panchayat* (local government) representative—a dynamic and outgoing Muslim woman—accompanied me on a whirlwind visit to the different houses.[31] She assured her constituents that I was trustworthy and instructed them to tell me what I wanted to know. That worked like magic, and on subsequent house visits I was received cordially. I began my fieldwork in the area in February 1990 and studied thirty-one households, but found to my dismay that there were only minimal differences, more of degree than of kind, between Kuttur and Veni in rural Malappuram.[32] These differences were certainly not large enough or striking enough to warrant selection of Kuttur as an alternate area for a comparative study.

By then I had come to realize that a distinctive feature of Kerala was that there were no sharp rural-urban differences and that it was more of a continuum. Even in Trivandrum, the capital city, many areas were visually, culturally, and socially quite similar to rural villages. The villages in turn were generally quite developed and often presented the appearance and some of the characteristics of small towns. I had also come across a range of direct and indirect evidence suggesting that ethnicity was probably a more significant variable than rural-urban variation. So I decided to change my focus and examine ethnicity as a mediator of the response to migration. This meant that I then had to study a Hindu and a Christian migrant area. I decided to look for areas which were predominantly Hindu and Christian, respectively, since I wanted to study migrant communities. On the basis of my research, I felt that differences between the three groups which were often nascent or muted in ethnically mixed settings would be elaborated and magnified in ethnic enclaves.

By April I had settled on a suitable Hindu migrant village: Cherur, in the northern portion of Trivandrum district. My fieldwork in this area was far easier than it had been in the two earlier communities. People were friendly and cooperative. I visited eighty-nine houses in the predominantly Ezhava area, thirty-six houses in the predominantly Nayar (upper-caste Hindu) area, and nine houses in the *Harijan* (castes formerly considered "untouchable") colony. Here again, these represented a range of migrant and nonmigrant households. I left the area after three months, at the end of June, and later went back for another three-week visit in November.[33]

I lived in the Christian village of Kembu, in south-central Kerala, from mid-July to October 1990 and gathered information about the community and the households. Here, too, people were cooperative. A variety of villagers, a few schoolteachers, a politician, a social worker, and some returned migrants assisted me in various ways. I visited a total of forty-five Syrian (upper-caste Kerala Christian) houses and sixteen Backward Class Christian (lower-caste Christian) houses in this area for the household survey. The last one and a half months of my stay in Kerala were spent collecting material on the historical and cultural evolution of the three communities.

My aim while conducting the fieldwork was to have data of three kinds:

1. community-level information;
2. general household-level information;
3. case studies of representative households of different types such as long-term, short-term, and returned migrant as well as nonmigrant households.

As far as possible, I collected these data for the major classes and castes in the three areas. I had a detailed schedule of questions, for both community-level and household-level information. I used that as a guide, but the focus and the way I asked the questions varied, depending on the situation and the response of the people.

In each of the areas, my method was to first have broad, exploratory talks with a range of people in the initial period and to make careful observations as I walked through the village. After a few weeks, the broad patterns of migration impacts began to emerge. In the next stage, I tried to refine and verify the initial observations, this time with a more purposive sample of households and interviewees, chosen to provide me with the particular information I required. The discussions in this stage were more intensive and focused. I talked to a range of people in the village and *panchayat* offices, travel agencies, banks, schools, creches, shops, hospitals, and police stations, in addition to the women, men, and adolescents that I met in the different households. In the final stage, I concentrated on getting a rough idea of the frequency of the patterns through more extensive household visits and a briefer repertoire of questions.[34]

Although I relied more heavily on the information given to me by some people, who became my key informants and confidants (such as preschool teachers, nurses, travel agents, and teachers), this was only after a certain period of acquaintanceship during which I continuously cross-checked the information for reliability. By staying in or near each of the areas and spending most of the daytime hours with the villagers, I gained an understanding of the social context, which helped me assess the new information.[35]

Yet another way in which I tried to check the validity of my general conclusions regarding the role of ethnicity on migration, as well as the more specific hypotheses about the causal sequence giving rise to particular migration outcomes, was by studying a range of communities. Besides Veni, Cherur, and Kembu, I did shorter studies (of around a week each) in seven other areas. In each case, I assessed and accounted for the similarities and differences between these areas and my primary communities. In this way, I was able to discern the importance and role of several factors that I might have missed or taken for granted if I had restricted myself exclusively to Veni, Cherur, and Kembu.

I was able to understand the importance of doing comparative studies only after I had started visiting other villages besides Veni, particularly ones that were very different. Only then did the ethos and the characteristic features of each area become clear to me. When I went to Cherur I was able to understand Veni better and vice versa; because of my experience in Veni, the distinctness of Cherur was more starkly evident. With my fieldwork in Kembu, the patterns of social organization of the three areas and some of the reasons for those differences became even clearer.

I had started my fieldwork with the expectation that I would supplement my qualitative study with a survey of households in each of the areas. This did not work out as planned. In chapter 5, I discuss some of the problems I faced in Veni which made a proper survey impossible. Although household visits were much easier in the other two communities, there were still several factors which hindered the collection of data that would have permitted a quantitative analysis, even of the most elementary nature. Firstly, my samples were too small to present statistically sufficient cases of each type of household. Secondly, a random sample was not possible as the members of households not included would have felt slighted, or those studied would have been suspicious about why I was selecting them over their neighbors. Thirdly, and most important, I found that most villagers were very uneasy when I started writing down their responses so I generally conducted the interviews in the form of informal conversations and did the writing after I had left the houses.[36] Thus, the information collected through my house visits was more in the form of descriptive case material rather than tabulatable statistics. Instead of tabulations, I noted recurring themes in the accounts and collapsed them into ideal-type descriptions of the areas somewhat in the sense that Max Weber used the term. Weber has defined the ideal type in the following way: "An ideal type is formed by the one-sided accentuation of one or more points of view and by the synthesis of a great many diffuse, discrete, more or less present and occasionally absent concrete individual phenomena which are arranged according to those one-sidedly emphasized viewpoints into a unified . . . construct" (Shils and Finch 1949, 90). What I present, therefore, is not a description of the communities based on averages, but instead is an accentuation of the distinguishing features of the villages.

Interspersed with my stints in the villages, I made trips to libraries to examine the newspapers, magazines, journals, and books that had any bearing on the Gulf phenomenon in particular and the state of Kerala in general. In addition, I looked at several types of primary data such as records from the district, panchayat, and village offices and from the emigration and census bureaus. From these sources I obtained information about the occupational background, size of households, type of housing, literacy of the population, changes in housing, infrastructural facilities, area under crops, livestock, some figures regarding migration and the destinations of the migrants, as well as figures indicating the proportions of people below the poverty line, the number of land transactions that took place over a period of time, and the registered price of the land.

I have used very few of these figures directly in the ensuing pages for a variety of reasons. As the officials themselves admitted candidly, many of these figures were far from accurate since they were often estimated or adjusted. For instance, the reported figures dealing with the price of land, and to some extent even the type of housing, were grossly undervalued so as to reduce the amount of taxes being paid. The poverty figures, on the other hand, were gross overestimations (particularly in the migrant areas) since the amount of government money sanctioned for welfare schemes depended on these proportions. The determination of literacy was based on the ability of the person to write his or her name, and this usually had little to do with the ability to read and write. Government data-collection officers in the Veni region told me that due to the social characteristics of the Veni region, most of the official surveys tended to rely on guesstimates. Also, the figures were usually at least a few years old, and because the changes taking place as a result of the Gulf migration were so rapid, they were not very useful for the period that I was studying.

One of the biggest problems, however, was that the areas for which the information was provided were so large that such aggregate figures had little relevance for the tiny subunits that I studied. For example, at the district offices information was available for the "block," which could be anywhere from ninety to five hundred square kilometers in area. Panchayats usually consisted of two to three villages covering from fifteen to seventy-five square kilometers. Even the administrative village was a huge geographical entity of between ten to twenty square kilometers with between one thousand to eight thousand houses.

Villages in Kerala are far from being the typical small, nucleated, rural Indian settlements that have been so much discussed in the literature (e.g., Marriott 1955; Srinivas 1960). In Kerala, the administrative village is not a social or even a geographical entity. Towns merge into villages and villages into one another. Social interaction and community life spill over messily across government-drawn borders, all of which pose a major headache to the social science researcher who wants to capture a natural social unit but yet would like the backing of official statistics as well. In all three areas, my study was confined to one or more small areas (of one or two hundred houses), each of which could be said to comprise a social village. These areas often did not fit neatly into any one of the official subunits of the village called *kara* (between two to four square kilometers and between one hundred to one thousand houses). For this reason, and because the villages were in three different districts, it was impossible to obtain equivalent data for Veni, Cherur, and Kembu, which made the figures meaningless as a basis for comparison. In a few cases, I was able to find relevant data from village-level studies, and I refer to them in the subsequent chapters.

In the next chapter, I discuss the concept of ethnicity and the constituent elements of the ethnic kaleidoscope and then provide a theoretical model of ethnic development as an outcome of colonialism and ethnic change as a consequence of migration. In chapter 3, I present a historical background to the three groups and focus on the process by which religion became the defining feature of group identity and the three groups became "ethnicized," in other words, developed into autonomous, distinct, competing social units. The following chapter is a brief overview of the socioeconomic characteristics of Kerala and the Gulf migration from the state. In chapters 5, 6, and 7, I provide an account of the migration from the Mappila Muslim, Ezhava Hindu, and Syrian Christian villages, respectively. Each chapter begins with a description of the village in the premigration period, the migration pattern from the community, and how the ethnicity of the community shaped my fieldwork there. This is followed by a detailed discussion of how the Gulf migration and remittance flow affected and transformed religion, status, and gender. In chapter 8, I present a summary of the three patterns and discuss the theoretical and policy implications of the study.

CHAPTER 2

The Kaleidoscope of Ethnicity

RELIGION, STATUS, AND GENDER

$\mathcal{H}$ow are we to explain why Mappila Muslim migrants sent the large sums of money intended to purchase a house to their fathers or brothers, Ezhava Hindus to their fathers-in-law, and Syrian Christians to their wives? Why was there a substantial female migration only from the Syrian Christian community? Why were Hindu migrants more likely to depend on professional agents to obtain jobs and visas? Again, why did Mappila Muslim migrants alone invest in local businesses? Why did migration result in the erosion of caste cleavages among the Mappila Muslims but its strengthening among the Syrian Christians? Although the three groups belonged to three different religious traditions, religious dictates cannot explain the divergent patterns of behavior manifested by the Mappila Muslims, Ezhava Hindus, and Syrian Christian communities. Certainly, there is nothing in Islamic, Hindu, or Christian doctrines that would lead us to predict that communities following these religions would manifest the above-described responses to international migration and the influx of remittances.

Ethnicity is a broader, multidimensional concept that can help us discern the largely internalized and constantly evolving logic underlying the patterns of behavior manifested by different groups. In the case of the three groups under study for instance, an understanding of the ethnicity, or the central defining features of the communities, can explain the patterns of migration, remittance use, and social change adopted by each of the communities and the reasons for the differences between them. Thus, ethnicity allows us to see that the behaviors manifested by the members of a community in different realms of activity share a common principle. In communities defined by religion, like the three groups discussed in this book, the religious beliefs and practices of the community are an important part of its ethnicity, but these beliefs and practices in turn are shaped by history and socioeconomic position, as well as the regional context, and can thus take many different forms.

Ethnicity in the Literature

American readers might be skeptical of this conceptualization since the popular view of ethnicity in the United States is that it refers to the identity and culture of immigrants from different nationalities—those "peculiarities" that set them apart from the mainstream. However, while ethnicity has been defined in a variety of ways in social science literature, it has often been conceptualized as a more general social phenomenon shared by both majority and minority groups, and not merely as the attribute of immigrants.

According to Manning Nash, a theorist of ethnicity, the terms "ethnicity" and "ethnic group" are "among the most complicated, volatile and emotionally charged words and ideas in the lexicon of social science" (Nash 1989, 1). One of the earliest to define ethnicity was Max Weber (1864–1920), who said that ethnic groups are "those human groups that entertain a subjective belief in their common descent because of similarities of physical type or customs or both, or because of memories of colonization and migration; this belief must be important for the propagation of group formation; conversely it does not matter whether or not an objective blood relationship exists" (Weber 1978, 389). ´

Most writers have focused on the content of ethnicity—the shared culture and traditions that create a feeling of community. However, Fredrik Barth (1969) emphasized the importance of boundary mechanisms in the process of group formation and maintenance, pointing out that the cultural content enclosed by the boundaries could and did vary from setting to setting and across time. Following Barth, there have been some attempts to move away from the emphasis on the cultural content of ethnicity to the structural determinants of ethnic culture.[1] Despite this, at present, the core of ethnicity is still seen as comprised of cultural elements such as customs, beliefs, and traditions together with "language, religion, foods . . . folklore, music and residential patterns" (Alba 1992). The structural element, if acknowledged at all, is usually treated as being an incidental and extraneous factor.

A further difficulty with ethnicity as a concept is that definitions of and explanations for ethnicity have changed considerably over the past few decades. While the early assimilationist perspective focused on the cultural content of ethnicity and saw it as a traditional loyalty that would be submerged by economic and social development,[2] the later perspective emphasized the politicized form that ethnicity increasingly seemed to be taking, viewing ethnic movements as an outcome of the modernization process itself.[3] Subsequently it was argued that these two perspectives were actually referring to two different social phenomena. The older, familiar kind of ethnicity (Glazer and Moynihan 1975, 3) was characterized as a natural, objectively definable, geographically bounded group, in contrast to the new ethnicity (Bennett 1975) which was viewed as a group that was artificially created and mobilized to serve a certain purpose.[4] Again, scholars argued that the old ethnicity was based on substantive social and cultural differences while the new ethnicity was symbolic and an identity marker for the individual rather than being a means of differentiating the institutional and behavioral patterns of communities.[5]

Corresponding broadly to (though not overlapping with) this distinction was the debate between primordialists who conceptualized ethnicity as an ineluctable psychological bond, resulting from the "givenness that stems from being born into a particular religious community, speaking a particular language . . . and following particular social patterns" (Geertz 1969, 109) and instrumentalists who claimed that "ethnic loyalties reflect and are maintained by the underlying socioeconomic interests of group members" (Patterson 1975, 306). Of late, however, it is more common to see ethnicity as being an expression of both psychological needs and instrumental interests.

Ethnicity in This Book

Drawing from the above definitions, I use the term *ethnicity* to refer to the identity, culture, and practices of a group of people who feel a sense of connection based on a notion of common heritage.[6] In addition, to be considered an ethnic group, its members should have a sense of being distinct from the rest of society and should have institutionalized boundary marking mechanisms to maintain and emphasize their social separation. Mappila Muslims, Ezhava Hindus, and Syrian Christians each considered themselves to be distinct groups with their own history, culture, and practices, different even from their coreligionists in Kerala. Groups maintained boundaries primarily by a system whereby marriages were arranged between members of the same group or subgroup. Generally, close social interaction was also limited to other members of the group. Ezhava Hindus and Syrian Christians were also a caste and quasicaste group, respectively, and thus caste divisions reinforced their social separateness.

It is important to emphasize that ethnicity is not just created and maintained by group members, but that it is also "constructed by external social, economic and political processes and actors as they shape and reshape ethnic categories and definitions" (Nagel 1994, 152). Group development may arise as a consequence of the attribution (by others) of a common identity to individuals sharing certain characteristics. This was the case particularly with Mappila Muslims and Ezhava Hindus. Mappila Muslims developed a group identity as a consequence of the successive policies of the Portuguese, the Mysorean Muslims, and the British, who controlled northern Kerala from the early sixteenth to the mid-twentieth centuries. As a lower-caste group, Ezhava Hindus did not have much initial freedom in choosing their identity or the rights and obligations their caste status imposed on them. However, from the latter half of the nineteenth century, when commercialization processes introduced by colonialism resulted in the economic mobility of large sections of the group, they actively appropriated their caste label, engaging in a continuous battle to end their caste disabilities and improve their status.

Ethnicity has a powerful social and psychological force binding individual members together.[7] Even in the more individualistic Syrian Christian community and the competitive Ezhava Hindu community, ethnic identity and ethnic obligations were important. Community members rallied around during crisis periods and for major ceremonies and life-cycle events. Although always a social construction, ethnicity exerts its coercive effect through "naturalizing" the ethnic tie and the particular cultural patterns that are part of the ethnic core at any given time. Ethnic bonds and behavioral patterns are therefore perceived as "givens," and deviants are strongly censured by the conscience keepers of the community. In general, the central institutions such as the religious, educational, cultural, or political organizations and their spokespersons tend to take on the role of defining, expressing, and maintaining ethnicity within the community. Some examples from Veni, the Mappila Muslim village and Kembu, the Syrian Christian village, show the way community deviants are coerced into conformity with ethnic norms.

Gaffar, a young and unusually outspoken Mappila Muslim man in Veni, candidly admitted that he was "not at all religious" and felt that religion was a "waste of time." His family and the community at large had put up with his errant ways while he was a teenager, but after he got married they mounted a great deal of pressure on him to "show his face" at the local mosque at least occasionally. He finally yielded when his parents tearfully begged him, saying, "Because of your behavior, the *Maulavi* [mosque priest] and others are now turning against us. We are growing old, we need the support of the community and we want to be buried here with all our family [in the cemetery owned by the mosque]." Gaffar had also not wanted to send his children to the *madrasa* (the religious school) but had again capitulated when he realized that they were being harassed and teased by their friends (and their friends' parents) for being "heathens." Gaffar told me that he had seriously thought of moving to the "city" so that he could escape these demands.

In Kembu, I was told of two cases where Syrian Christian girls had fallen in love with Hindu (and in one case, lower-caste) men, with disastrous consequences. One of the girls was Susan, the daughter of the priest of a local church. She had eloped with her (lower-caste) lover and had married him. But Susan's parents tracked her down, forcibly brought her back, and had the marriage annulled. I was told that after much prayer and counseling, Susan was made to see "the error of her ways." In the other case, the parents had given grudging consent, and the couple had married and set up house in a nearby community. Because of the constant barrage of negativity that the couple had to face, however, the marriage eventually broke down (divorces were generally very rare in the area). Community members used these two cases to deter youngsters who might otherwise have entertained the thought of marrying non-Syrian Christians.

The everyday beliefs and practices that make up the content of ethnicity are stabilized and symbolically reproduced through a panoply of codified sayings and ritualized behavior (religious practices as well as the norms and etiquette governing interpersonal conduct between relatives, friends, and strangers). This was true of the Mappila Muslims, Ezhava Hindus, and Syrian Christians as well. All three communities had various patterns of avoidance behavior characterizing the relationship between men and women and ritualized, respectful behavior that was manifested before members of the older generation, although the specific patterns varied among the three groups.

My conception of ethnicity also borrows heavily from Pierre Bourdieu's notion of "habitus." Although Bourdieu developed the concept to refer primarily to the commonalities shared by members of a social class, habitus can just as well be applied to the understanding of ethnicity. Habitus refers to the similarities in the perceptions and practices of the members of a group that is the outcome of a history of shared experiences. Bourdieu defines the habitus as "a system of lasting, transposable dispositions, which, integrating past experiences, functions at every moment as a *matrix of perceptions, appreciations, and actions* and makes possible the achievement of infinitely diversified tasks" (1977, 83, original emphasis). To some degree, this system is shared by members of the group and is based on "the mastery of a common code" (Bourdieu 1977, 81). According to Bourdieu, the most important consequence of the "orchestration" of the habitus of members of a group is the "production of a commonsense world endowed with the *objectivity* secured by consensus on the meaning . . . of practices and the world" (1977, 80, original emphasis).

I came across Bourdieu's description of the habitus sometime after I had completed my fieldwork and was struck by how aptly it captured the central difference between the three villages that I studied—the vast divergence in the *commonsense worlds* of Veni, Cherur, and Kembu. When I got to the Ezhava Hindu village of Cherur, after completing my study of Veni, the Mappila Muslim village, I felt as though I had entered a different world altogether. Although the topography and the houses were quite similar in both areas, people's attitudes, reactions, and behavior were completely different. The households and community were also organized differently. The same thing happened when I went from Cherur to Kembu, the Syrian Christian village.

I found that my understanding of myself as a woman and a researcher were constantly challenged during my stay in each of the three villages as I confronted very different notions of the self, of gender, and of epistemology. Thus, the nineteen months of fieldwork were a period of self-discovery regarding how much my taken-for-granted assumptions had been shaped by my own upbringing and location. Although I am more critical about assuming consensus, similarity, and shared understanding between members of an ethnic group, I feel that Bourdieu's conceptualization helps us understand some of the central features of ethnicity such as the relationship between individual and collective practices.

It was clear to me that being Mappila Muslim, Ezhava Hindu, or Syrian Christian provided a sense of roots, or social location, and fundamentally affected the worldview, beliefs, self-identity, and relationships, as well as the practices, mannerisms, styles of clothing, and grooming, of its members. The system of "internalized dispositions" that guided the behavior of individual members was largely a product of the socialization the person received from members of the group and was therefore developed early in life. These internalized dispositions were continuously ratified through interaction with other members, and over time, ethnicity became reinforced as a public identity. Even boys and girls in their early teens (sometimes even younger), in the three villages seemed to have a fairly clear sense of their ethnic identity and its practical implications.

As Bourdieu (1977, 82) indicates, these differences in the worldview and assumptions of group members are a product of history. But ethnicity, like habitus, also "produces individual and collective practices and hence history" and is thus dynamic, "constantly reproduced and transformed by historical practices" (Bourdieu 1977, 82, 83). The distinct worldview and assumptions that the three groups developed as a consequence of the experience of colonialism shaped their outlook toward migration and the use of remittances and were responsible for the different migrant patterns manifested by Veni, Cherur, and Kembu. The process of migration and the large inflows of remittances in turn transformed the outlook and behavior of high-migrant Mappila Muslim, Ezhava Hindu, and Syrian Christian communities.

I found two other attributes of the habitus discussed by Bourdieu very useful for understanding ethnicity. Firstly, Bourdieu emphasizes the "dialectical relationship between the structure and the dispositions making up the habitus" (1977, 84). He goes on to note that it is through habitus that the objective structures of society reproduce themselves (1977, 85). Bourdieu's conception of the habitus refers to internalized culture, and while he acknowledges the importance of external structures in shaping habitus, he does not include these structures in his definition.

By ethnicity, however, I mean not just internalized culture but also the social and cultural practices of the group. Since it was fairly obvious that differences in the educational and occupational profiles of the three communities were both a cause and consequence of ethnic differences and practices, I realized that it was important to include structural factors in my conceptualization of ethnicity. Specifically, I include some or all of such characteristics as the socioeconomic position of the group, occupational pattern, educational achievements, and family structure in my definition. (Exactly which types of cultural and structural features will be central to the ethnicity of a particular group is difficult to specify a priori since they vary a great deal over time and space.) Thus, I substitute the word *ethnicity* for habitus and argue, like Bourdieu, that it is through the working of ethnicity—the cultural, economic, and educational capital of groups, their families and social networks—that the objective structures of society such as the stratification system and the economy reproduce themselves. In the last chapter, I briefly touched on the differences in the migration patterns of the Mappila Muslims, the Ezhava Hindus, and the Syrian Christians. These differences demonstrate that the filter of ethnicity mediates a group's response to new structures of opportunity. For these reasons an understanding of ethnicity is central to an understanding of social structure and social change.

Secondly, Bourdieu's (1977, 83) conceptualization of habitus as the "unifying principle of practices in different domains . . . or sub-systems" articulates another fundamental attribute of ethnicity. Although typically one or another factor such as language, region, or religion is seen as being the core around which ethnic formation develops, ethnicity is not based on a single characteristic. Minimally, the members of an ethnic group share an assumption of common heritage and one of the kind of ties mentioned, but in practice, the substantive core of ethnicity is multidimensional and involves a clustering of characteristics that are intertwined. Ethnicity functions like a magnet, holding conjunctions of factors together. It is important to point out that while ethnicity is comprised of a variety of factors, it is more than just the result of the interactive effects of these factors. Thus, the differences in orientation and behavior between members of ethnic groups cannot be reduced to any one or even a combination of these factors. Ethnicity is the guiding logic underlying seemingly diverse and unrelated aspects such as the organization of migration and remittance flows, the patterns of consumption, investment, and exchange manifested by the migrants and the reorganization of the status structure, households and gender relations in the Mappila Muslim, Ezhava Hindu, and Syrian Christian areas.

So far, I have discussed what ethnicity is. But why does ethnicity exist? Most scholars now agree that ethnicity combines both psychological need and instrumental interest. For instance, the institutionalization of international migration in the three communities involved a strategic use of ethnic claims and resources, but it was the powerful bond of ethnicity that resulted in ethnic claims being recognized as important (sometimes even binding) obligations.

In this book, I advance the substantive and theoretical understanding of ethnicity by also showing that ethnicity is the way in which groups express and maintain or compensate for their differential access (whether privileged or disprivileged) to resources. (Where these differences are cumulative and groups are ordered in a hierarchy, a caste or racial system exists.) Ethnicity is also one way in which competing groups try to gain access to new resources—social, cultural, economic, or political. Of course, since ethnicity is based on a claim of common ancestry, not all competing groups can or will use the ethnic strategy. Again, ethnicity is more likely to be used as a strategy in situations where such claims have a greater chance of success.

Ethnicity is a powerful force in contemporary society because it dialectically unifies ascription and achievement while concealing the relationship between the two. Members of ethnic groups use ascriptive criteria to obtain and reproduce achievement while describing it in terms of meritocratic attainment. For instance, beginning from the colonial period, Syrian Christians had a lead in education and professional occupations because of the favoritism to Christians shown by the British missionaries who had started schools, colleges, and hospitals. Since most of these institutions continued to be Christian run in the postcolonial period, the advantage and preferential treatment for Christians continued. These "ascriptive" advantages were rarely recognized by members of the community, who preferred to explain their success as being due to their intelligence and hard work, as well as to their culture, which valued education.

The distributional access of different ethnic groups shifts as the socioeconomic and political landscape changes (see Brass 1991, 25). The content of ethnicity and the basis of group differences is constantly being reformulated. Thus, I do not feel that distinctions such as those differentiating old and new, cultural and political, natural and created types of ethnicity help to clarify the nature of the phenomenon. I have indicated that one of the ways in which old, natural, sociocultural groups were differentiated from new, created, and politicized groups in the ethnic literature was by trying to determine whether the ethnicity was based on substantive social and cultural differences or was just symbolic. The chapters describing Veni, Cherur, and Kembu will make clear that there were very major and very real differences (quite apart from religion) between Mappila Muslims, Ezhava Hindus, and Syrian Christians. For the most part, these groups have also had a long tradition of harmonious interethnic relationships in Kerala. However, at different points in time, particularly in the late colonial period and the early postcolonial period when new political resources were being introduced into the society, ethnic leaders from the three groups were able to mobilize sections of their respective communities to stake a militant claim to these resources.

In short, ethnicity is inherently dynamic. Ethnic identities and boundaries are malleable and group members can assert their identities passively and socially, actively and politically, or in both ways at different periods of time. The particular mode of ethnic expression chosen at any particular point in time will depend largely on the larger socioeconomic and political context. Correspondingly, the constellation of ethnicity is not a fixed or static entity. The pieces constituting the ethnic mosaic break up, realign, and reformulate. In fact, ethnicity can be conceptualized as being a kaleidoscopic unity of disintegration and transformation. Although the label is generally retained and the fundamental building blocks remain largely the same, with each turn in the passage of time, the elements are rearranged and reformulated into different patterns, giving the larger structure a completely new appearance.

The Ethnic Kaleidoscope: Religion, Status, and Gender

I argue in chapter 6 that Ezhavas used their newly earned wealth to obtain a better social position through the "decastification of status"—by trying to have status attributed to achieved characteristics such as education and wealth, rather than caste position. Migrant families were frequently able to use their wealth to obtain well-educated spouses for their sons and daughters. Such hypergamous (where the man was from a higher-status background) and hypogamous (where the woman was from a higher-status background) marriages were a departure from the traditional Ezhava practice of isogamy (where both the bride and groom were from families of the same status). Both hypergamous and hypogamous marriages were celebrated on a grand scale, with several new ceremonies and gift-giving rites added to the traditional Hindu rituals. In other words, a change in ethnic identity (a redefinition of the meaning of being Ezhava) was effected through changes in definitions of status (from ascribed to achieved characteristics), gender relations (the relative status of husbands and wives), and religious rituals.

I found many examples that showed that religion, status, and gender were braided together to form the core components of ethnicity in each of the three communities, which in turn shaped other aspects such as the culture, educational profile, socioeconomic position, and family structure of the groups. For this reason, I have conceptualized the ethnic nucleus of the communities under study as being an interacting and changing nexus of the ideology and practice of religion, status, and gender. In the following section, I will look at the relationship between ethnicity and each of its three constituent elements. This will be followed by a discussion of ethnic formation as a product of colonialism and ethnic change as a consequence of migration.

Ethnicity and Religion

Scholars now accept that ethnicity is a more or less fluid and dynamic entity. However, when that ethnic identity is based on religious background, it is frequently seen as fixed and unchanging. Because of this, religious groups are generally distinguished from ethnic groups that are based on language, nationality, or region. Religions and religious identities (particularly of non-Western groups) have long been essentialized in popular and academic literature. The current focus on cases of assertive religiosity has only strengthened the tendency to stereotype and essentialize the social impact of religion. Conventionally, the only real distinction that is made between individuals and communities belonging to a particular religion is with respect to the strength of their religious beliefs.

But religiosity is only one factor distinguishing religious communities. Even in the so-called religions of the book such as Christianity, Islam, and Judaism, where there are single, canonical texts and codified commentaries, there are a range of elements—religious tenets and practices, pronouncements regarding the regulation of individual, family, and community life—to draw upon to construct a blueprint of the normative society. (And of course living societies deviate from the normative models in many ways.) Which particular elements are chosen, how they are interpreted and practiced, and to what extent conformity is enforced depend on a variety of factors.[8] Although religion may be the defining attribute, a religious community is always a multidimensional entity consisting of social, cultural, political, and economic structures. All of these structures, together with its position in, and relationship to, the larger society shape its central defining features. As these conditions change, so does its identity and character. If this identity is defined largely by religion, then the structural modifications usually bring about a reconceptualization of the meaning and significance of that identity, concretely manifested through modifications in rituals and behavioral practices believed to be religiously sanctioned.

Local Factors. Local factors can bring about such changes in the meaning of religious identity. In her discussion of Bangladesh, Santi Rozario (1992) indicates that "the identity quest of the Bengali Muslims has fluctuated between the Bengali and the Muslim with the socioeconomic and political climate of the region" (p. 21). Similarly she argues that Bangladeshi Christians had been strongly influenced by the overarching Bengali Hindu culture prevalent in the region.

During my own fieldwork in Veni, I discovered nearby Mappila Muslim villages that interpreted the Islamic tenets with respect to the position of women very differently from Veni. There were some villages within the same geographical region where Mappilas had adopted the *Mujahid* doctrine from about the 1970s (Veni was largely *Sunni*). These villages were nonmigrant communities that had relied mainly on occupational opportunities in the neighboring town. They had thus taken a different route to development and had manifested a different pattern of social change. In Veni, upward mobility consequent on migration had a negative effect on the higher education of women since it resulted in their seclusion and earlier marriage. In the nonmigrant areas, however, a sequence of developments had resulted in bringing women out of the home, deferring their marriages, stressing their higher education, and to some extent, permitting their employment out of their home. Not coincidentally, the local interpretation of the Mujahid doctrine conferred a higher status to women and, in contrast to the Sunnis of Veni, emphasized the need for their education, later marriage, and attendance at the Friday mosque services (which was forbidden to women in Veni). The Mujahids also allowed women to go out much more freely—the only restriction being that they wore garments that covered their bodies and hair completely. Thus, there is often an "elective affinity" (in Max Weber's terms) between the particular interpretation of religion that is adopted and the social and economic conditions that prevail.

International Factors: Colonialism. Besides local factors, the international situation also plays an important role in shaping the characteristics of particular world religious communities (see also Gardner 1995, 241–242). Historically and cross-culturally, certain traits have frequently been identified with communities of particular world religions even though they may be located in very different parts of the globe. These similarities are usually attributed to the doctrinal essence of the religion, but my argument is that in many cases *such defining traits have as much to do with global historical developments as with doctrine.* Religious groups have been important players on the global stage for millennia and have substantially shaped political history. To take one example, Christian and Islamic polities have been rivals for global religious and political sovereignty since the birth of Islam in the sixth century A.D. In the beginning Islam was the victor, and in its heyday, the Muslim empire spread across much of Europe, Africa, and Asia. During the period of European colonialism, Christian colonizers ventured into many regions that were under Muslim control (North Africa, South Asia, Indonesia, and parts of the Middle East) and which had significant Muslim populations. In most cases (sometimes after protracted battles) the Westerners succeeded in imposing their domination on these regions. Muslim communities which had been favored groups with special privileges under the Islamic rulers were in a short period of time reduced to the status of subjugated adversaries. By the mid-twentieth century when the process of decolonization began, Muslim "societies, their polities, even their self-perception, were transformed almost beyond recognition" (Lewis 1993, 22).

Colonialism, however, had the opposite effect on the spread and characteristics of Christian communities around the globe. Missionary activities often went along with economic and political conquest. This resulted in the implanting and nurturing of Christianity in many areas that came under the direct or indirect control of Westerners. The new converts usually had privileged access to colonial institutions such as schools, colleges, and hospitals (which were often run by the Christian missions) and were generally also able to obtain better jobs as a consequence. Such benefits as well as their alliance and identification with the colonialists went a long way in shaping the characteristics of the Christian communities in the many former colonial regions. These arguments are elaborated upon in the next chapter which focuses on the sequence of events that led to the fundamental transformations in the socioeconomic and cultural profiles of the Muslims, Christians, and Hindus in Kerala. Mappila Muslims who had been relatively prosperous spice traders on the Kerala coast lost their trade under the Portuguese and were discriminated against under the British, resulting in an "inward turn" and a withdrawal from participation in Western identified institutions such as the educational system, the colonial bureaucracy, and modern medicine. Syrian Christians, on the other hand, were favored by the British and therefore participated heavily in these same institutions.

International Factors: Postcolonialism.   International factors have continued to play an important role in the self-definitions of religious communities in the postcolonial world. The discovery of oil in the Middle East, the oil boom of the seventies, and the embargo of 1973 which demonstrated the power of the Middle Eastern countries to themselves and also to the rest of the world set the stage for the next period in the relationship between the West and the Islamic nations. The nascent "fundamentalist" religious movements and nationalist Muslim movements in the Gulf countries were strengthened and revitalized, and in the postcommunist world, Islam has again emerged as the "new" enemy of the West. The economic and political salience of the Middle East, now considered to be the center of Islam, has given a psychological (and not infrequently financial) boost to Muslim communities in other parts of the world as well. The villagers in Veni and other Muslim communities in Kerala have had a longstanding connection and identification with Muslim Arabs in the Middle East. Over the past two decades, there has been a tremendous increase in the number of mosques and Arabic schools in the Muslim areas in Kerala, several of which have been financially supported by Middle Eastern Arabs.

Many of the Christian churches in non-Western countries maintain ties with the parent organizations in the United States and Great Britain (which include frequent visits back and forth by officials on both sides). Access to the West is also facilitated for congregational members. In the recent past, Kembu, the Christian community, has had a fairly high rate of emigration to the United States (which neither of the other two communities manifested). In many cases the emigration was initiated and facilitated through church contacts. For instance, many of the first-generation migrants obtained admission in Bible colleges through the help of visiting missionaries and church leaders and then managed to stay on and sponsor the emigration of their relatives. Such ties had the effect of reinforcing the sense of difference that Christian minorities felt from the rest of society and also promoted some degree of identification with the Christian West. Thus, Rozario (1992) argues that despite being relatively powerless in relation to the local Muslims, Christians in the village of Dorian in Bangladesh felt a sense of cultural superiority because of their identification with Western culture. "The logic is that Christianity is a religion of the West, whose members are 'superior' to the Muslims of Bangladesh." She goes on to state that this identification "is expressed by the value they place on education, Western style clothing, modern housing and alcohol" as well as the greater freedom of Christian women (Rozario 1992, 76).

Further evidence for the role of global factors in influencing the expression and interpretation of religious identities is provided by the literature analyzing and explaining the rise of religious movements around the world.[9] This literature has shown clearly that the worldwide religious resurgence has developed in the context of the anxieties created by the economic, social, and cultural dislocations resulting from postindustrialism and globalization. Large-scale internal and international migration, the dominance and penetration of electronic media (cinema, television, computers), and the corresponding decline of the power of nation-states, have all made religion an effective and powerful source of group mobilization at the end of the twentieth century. Since we see similar transformations in religions around the world with very different doctrinal principles, it is clear that these changes have more to do with global developments than the nature of the particular religions involved.

By demonstrating that the manner in which religion is defined and interpreted depends on local and global circumstances, my point is that ethnicity based on a religious bond is as likely to be fluid and dynamic as ethnicity based on any other group attribute. Thus there is no justification for making a conceptual distinction between "religious" and "ethnic" communities. In fact, over the period of history, religion has been the most widely used and most enduring means of carving out and maintaining a separate identity. It is for this reason that many symbolic markers of community such as prescriptive endogamy, dress styles, bodily inscription (circumcision, piercing, regulations regarding hair length and facial hair), special foods, and the celebration of festivals (which are largely communal) are regarded as being part of religious practice.

In this book, I focus on the ways in which local and global factors led to the development and transformation of the identities and practices of Mappila Muslims, Ezhava Hindus, and Syrian Christians and argue that the significance and practical implications of a particular religious label are potentially multifarious. Using these three groups as case studies, one of the central aims of the book is to deessentialize the nature of religious communities by focusing on the conditions under which transformations in defining religious attributes and group identities take place.

Status and Ethnicity

Status is central in defining ethnic identity and in maintaining community. Status manifests what the group considers to be important and prestigious, and these values give the group unity and coherence. Such behavior is closely related to codes of honor and shame. As such, my argument is that different ethnic groups often have very distinct ideas about what is "honorable." Having distinctive ideas and symbols of honor are ways of drawing boundaries between ethnic groups and of demonstrating the exclusivity of the community. Thus, a change in group identity is often accompanied by the ostentatious adoption of new symbols that serve to distinguish group members from others. I have mentioned that upwardly mobile Ezhava Hindus had introduced new rituals and ceremonies to celebrate marriage. All of this does not mean that ethnic groups are homogenous. Ethnic groups are internally stratified, but this stratification is generally based on the differential ability of families and subgroups to appropriate (or manufacture) symbols of honor. As such, upward mobility often requires such appropriation or manufacture of honor through the redefinition of identity or "passing" (Milner 1994, 31).

According to Murray Milner, the first source of status "is the approval received for *conformity* to social norms" (1994, 35, original emphasis). Honor is thus obtained through practicing codes of conduct and patterns of behavior (including consumption) that are seen as being "right" or "good"—usually ones that are legitimated with reference to a supracommunal entity such as a divine being, custom, or nature. Since religion presents a transcendental basis of locating communities, ideas of prestige are often presented as based on religion. In other words, there is a close relationship between the way the religious identity of a group is constructed and what is seen as prestigious or honorable. Correspondingly, symbols of status or identity are often those associated with religious identity (see Milner 1994).

Milner argues that a second source of status derives from prestigious "associations"—having intimate relationships with people who are of high status (1994, 36). Since marriage is one of the most important of such intimate associations, changes in marriage patterns are a central indicator of shifts in the status positions of different subgroups. In India, marriage is also the most important life-cycle ceremony and the most public (with the most number of invitees) and thus it becomes the occasion when material resources are most conspicuously displayed as a means of demonstrating a change in status.

Gender and Ethnicity

The significance of changing marriage patterns as an indicator of upward mobility underscores the importance of gender for status and group identity. "Proper" gender behavior is generally a crucial component of right conduct; codes of honor and shame provide different virtues for men and women. Because of this, emotional battles about gender are usually central to any social reconstruction. As social constructions, ethnicity and gender are separate but interdependent entities. Gender, the social definition and patterning of the identities of "femaleness" and "maleness" and the behavior and responsibilities of women and men, is shaped by the cultural and social structure of the community and by its real and mythical past. However, the manner in which sexuality and reproduction are organized by a community is an important determinant of its ethnicity.

Boundary-marking maneuvers and mechanisms for the physical and social reproduction of the community are a central component of ethnicity and gender plays a vital role in this respect. The regulation of sexuality, particularly female sexuality, is central to the physical continuation of the group. But women also play central roles in the social reproduction of the societies. As Virginia Sapiro (1993, 47) points out, in most cultures, it is primarily women who create, manifest, and maintain ethnicity through their "day-to-day cultural work" such as child rearing and socialization, cooking, the making and wearing of ethnic clothing, and the preparation for and celebration of ethnic rituals and celebrations. This was definitely the case in the three communities that I studied. It is for all these reasons that "good women" are seen as the moral guardians of the community, who uphold the social order through example and exhortation (see Hardacre 1993 and the chapters in Hawley 1994). The distinction between "good women" and "bad women" is therefore an important component of ideologies describing the normative social order (see Summers 1975) and is thus central to ethnic culture. Gender norms were different in the Mappila Muslim, Ezhava Hindu, and Syrian Christian communities, and these differences were crucial in the construction of ethnic boundaries.

In addition to the behavior of women, there are also notions about the appropriate feminine body—its proportions, adornment, and docility. Feminists have reinterpreted Foucault's general treatise on the body as the site of disciplinary practices to call attention to the gender dimension that he neglected—that women's bodies are often subject to much greater disciplinary control (Bartky 1988). Thus, ethnicity is frequently manifested through the particular styles of clothing or jewelry worn by women as well as the types of movements considered appropriate and manifested by them. During the period of fieldwork, men in the Mappila Muslim, Ezhava Hindu, and Syrian Christian communities all wore similar clothes and sported similar hairstyles, but the women in each of the three communities could be identified by their distinctive clothes and jewelry.

Since religion provides the transcendental legitimation of the gender order, communities and individuals for whom religion is important usually try to align their gender ideology with their interpretation of religion. The close relationship between gender and religion is seen by the fact that religious change—whether conservative or progressive—almost always brings about a concomitant reconstruction of gender ideology and practice.

Thus, with the three components of the ethnic kaleidoscope, and their permutations and combinations the manifestation of ethnicity at any given time can take a variety of forms.

Ethnic Change

In this book, I focus on an important period of ethnic change and transformation in the structure and practices of Mappila Muslims in Veni, Ezhava Hindus in Cherur, and Syrian Christians in Kembu—the decades between 1970 and 1990 when the large-scale migration to countries in the Middle East took place. The sudden increase in wealth due to migration and the temporary absence of predominantly male migrants from the three communities was responsible for bringing about a reconstruction in the social structure, practices, and identity of the communities. However, there was an earlier critical juncture in the histories of the three groups when they experienced a fundamental metamorphosis. This was the period of Western colonialism (1650–1947). It was during this period that religion became the defining feature of group identity and the three communities and their relations with one another were radically altered. Since the ethnicization of the three communities took place largely during the colonial era, it is important to study this process to understand the nature of ethnicity in the three communities. The period of colonialism is also important for the study of migration because the tradition of migration was first established in all three communities during this time. The colonial period is the first historical juncture that is examined in this study.

Colonialism and Ethnicity

Coinciding with the conceptual shift to "bring the state back in" (Rueschemeyer, Skocpol, and Evans 1985), the role of the nation-state in creating and sustaining patterns of racial and ethnic divisions in society has received a great deal of attention in the past two decades (e.g., Greenberg 1980, Omi and Winant 1986). With its greater power, the colonial state has an even more significant role in this regard. Not only does it define and shape the cleavage patterns in the society, but the powerful structural forces unleashed as a consequence of colonialization lead to a fundamental reorganization of the economy, polity, and also the social structure. One outcome is frequently the formation and transformation of ethnic groups in the colonized areas.

Ethnohistorians such as William Sturtevant (1971) and Peter Newcomer (1972) have coined the term "ethnogenesis" to describe the emergence of ethnic identities among colonial populations (see also Roosens 1989). Jay O'Brien (1986) describes the manner in which new ethnic identities were created in the Sudan as a consequence of the capitalist development fostered by colonialism. He also cites Elizabeth Colson (1968) and Talal Asad (1970) as having shown that many African tribes were colonial constructs created to meet the needs of administration through indirect rule. Similarly, Audrey Richards (1969) points out that in East Africa, ethnic and tribal identities attained a salience under colonialism that they previously never had. Paul Brass, a political scientist who has studied ethnic groups such as the Muslims, Sikhs, and Hindus in India, discusses the importance of colonialism in creating and transforming religious identity and ethnicity, focusing particularly on the role of both Indian and British elites in this process (Brass 1991, 25–30).

A detailed discussion of the process of ethnic formation under colonialism follows in the next chapter. Here, I will only provide a brief summary. While precolonial Kerala was socially stratified, early Hinduism, with its syncretism and its all-embracing caste organization, provided the overarching framework for the society. Even the Christians and Muslims were incorporated into the system as quasicastes and had a defined place within the caste hierarchy. Society was organized into a hierarchical system of interdependent castes and religious groups, each with a particular social, economic, ritual role and position in the larger order. Religion was not always the basis for social or political separation. In fact, intermarriages and conversions were frequent, and it was not uncommon for members of the same family to have different religious affiliations.

The colonial state brought about a major economic and social restructuring of the society, which in turn led to the development of new bases of group formation and mobilization. Over the period of colonialism, the global and systemic character of the social structure and most of the earlier ties of dependency that bound the groups together were dissolved, and each of the units of the system began to develop autonomous, ethnic identities. Religious affiliations were reified and transformed into communal cleavages. Both of these processes involved the redrawing and hardening of group boundaries and the redefinitions of the bases of group formation and maintenance. To distinguish themselves from each other, ethnic communities adopted new styles of dress and new codes of social and ritual conduct. Conceptions of appropriate gender conduct were also revised to signify and maintain differences.

Migration and Ethnicity

Two major processes set in motion by international Gulf migration were affected by ethnicity and in turn transformed ethnicity in the three areas. Firstly, the large-scale exodus to the Middle East necessitated the creation of arrangements to cope with the absence of migrants and the inflow of remittances. Since the migrants were generally married men, and as such, the economic and social heads of their families in the social structures of Veni, Cherur, and Kembu, their absence resulted in a shift in the economic and social loci of control within migrant households and extended families. This had a major impact on gender and intergenerational relationships in the communities.

Secondly, the rapid enrichment of the lower classes brought about several major changes in the migrant communities. Besides being able to afford a better lifestyle, migrants and their families also tried to obtain status and recognition in the community commensurate with their newly acquired wealth. The economic and social structures of migrant villages were fundamentally affected due to this process. This will be discussed further below.

The Status Struggle and Its Effect on Ethnicity. The economic behavior of third-world migrants who earn valuable foreign exchange and repatriate a good portion of their income to their low-income home communities is a matter of some consequence for their governments and policy makers. Therefore, it is not surprising that most studies of the Middle Eastern migration (and of migration in general) have been conducted by economists. There are two fundamental assumptions underlying most economic approaches. Conventional neoclassical economists believe that economic behavior is based on the rational choices of individuals and firms, in other words, that economic actors make economically maximizing decisions. There is the assumption that economic behavior is less influenced by cultural values than other types of behavior. Thus, the neoclassical paradigm views the economy as an autonomous realm with its own laws of behavior and "disallow[s] by hypothesis any impact of social structure and social relations on production, distribution or consumption" (Granovetter 1985, 483).

However, studies of international migration conducted in a variety of countries and at different periods of time have shown that migrants frequently work very hard and live frugally in the host country in order to save and remit as much as possible, only to spend their money on lavish hospitality, ostentatious consumer durables, and the building of large, showy houses on their return.[10] These expenditure patterns of the migrants, which are perceived to be manifestly "unproductive" in classical economic terms, have been the despair of policy makers in the countries concerned.[11]

We need a new understanding of economic behavior in general and that of international migrants in particular. Sociologists such as Paul DiMaggio, Pierre Bourdieu, and Viviana Zelizer have argued that economic goods are not merely consumed for their utilitarian benefits. As DiMaggio (1991, 133) points out, they are also "cultural goods," "consumed for what they say about their consumers to themselves and to others as inputs into the production of social relations and identities." In other words, his argument is that economic activities are also expressive and symbolic and that money and wealth have cultural and social meanings in addition to their purely "utility-bearing" characteristics. Much of Bourdieu's work (e.g., 1977; 1984; 1990; Bourdieu and Passeron 1977) details the ways in which people work to convert (and thereby "disguise") their economic capital into symbolic capital because such transformed symbolic capital is more valuable than the equivalent amount of money.

To illustrate the inadequacy of a purely utilitarian conception of money, Zelizer points out that "not all dollars are equal." "Money is . . . routinely differentiated, not just by varying quantities but also by its special diverse qualities. We assign different meanings and designate separate uses for particular kinds of monies." She gives as examples the way we differentiate a housewife's pin money or allowance from a salary, a lottery winning from an ordinary paycheck, an accident compensation from book royalties (Zelizer 1989, 343). Thus, Zelizer makes the case that the meaning that is attributed to income and the use to which it is put depends on the context within which the money is obtained.

From this analysis, I argue that the "unproductive" use of international remittances on conspicuous consumption that we find among migrants from a range of countries and cultures is due to the similar social meanings attributed to such income. The literature on international migration referred to earlier, as well as my own observations of the behavior of the Gulf migrants and the expectations of their community members, seem to indicate that the money earned as a result of working abroad (particularly in the case of lower-class rural migrants going to a more developed country) was seen as being of a different kind from income that was earned locally. Thus, I noticed that the economic behavior and consumption patterns of nonmigrants (even those earning an equivalent amount of money), especially in villages where there was little or no migration, was invariably different from those of the migrants that I studied.[12]

At the outset, I must make clear that I am referring to situations where the migrant is part of a small village community. Such communities are generally characterized by some degree of mutual bonds as well as the obligations of reciprocity. In fact, as the material will demonstrate, the extent to which conspicuous consumption is manifested is often a function of the degree of cohesiveness of the community in question. Different economic patterns are manifested depending on the nature of the social bonds between community members.

Probably the most important attribute of international remittances is that migrant incomes are generally much higher than the amount that would have been earned in a comparable local job. Due to the higher level of technology in the foreign country, those at home perceive the work undertaken by migrants as being less physically arduous. In addition, they also feel that there are the additional compensations gained from the glamor and experiences of life in a foreign (and developed) country. For all of these reasons, foreign income is seen to be serendipitous, "easy money," one which is not fully earned. As such, community members expect that the money will also be disbursed more freely.[13] In other words, it is seen to have some qualities of windfall income. Zelizer (1989, 350) points out that such income is treated very differently from identical sums obtained through other means. An example will make this clear. A young, fashionably dressed Gulf migrant at home on holiday boasted to me: "When I am here, I spend an awful lot of money. Just yesterday, I took out Rs. 1,200 from the bank and see [pulling out the money from his pocket], now I have only Rs. 400 left. I don't know where the rest went. Someone comes and asks me for money and I give it to him. And when I go to buy something, fish, for instance, even if I need only ten rupees worth, I spend fifty or seventy-five rupees, because otherwise what will they think—a Gulfan being so miserly. Yes, people generally increase prices when they see us. And they know we don't like to haggle."

Typically, earning money easily and spending freely is a characteristic of the lifestyle of the upper classes, who because of their affluence, are obliged to act as patrons for the poorer and less fortunate villagers. This in turn secures them status and a following. Status is a value that takes on the greatest significance in a more or less cohesive community. It has to be conferred and recognized by a group, and this is most successfully accomplished in situations where there is a great deal of face-to-face interaction. Largesse may also be distributed to counteract the possibly harmful effects of envious neighbors and relatives.

Thus, economically successful returned migrants from such communities spend their money conspicuously to indicate that it has been earned easily (which is prestigious) and are also lavish in their generosity to fellow villagers as well as to village causes so that they will be able to secure community goodwill and a higher social standing. Both conspicuous consumption and conspicuous generosity involve pronounced changes in the lifestyles of the migrants. The building of a large and showy house is also of high priority since it is the most visible indicator of the change in status of the family and will stand as a permanent emblem of their success. Migrants proudly display consumer durables brought from the foreign country for the same reason. Since material affluence has come to have virtually universal appeal, it is not surprising that these patterns are manifested by migrants around the world.

Particularly since the migrants from Kerala were largely from the lower socioeconomic classes, they wanted to use their newly acquired wealth to obtain status and recognition in their home communities. As Bourdieu points out (see, for instance, 1977, 177–183), the need for and importance of status and the attempts to convert economic capital into symbolic capital are not adequately recognized either in classical economic theory or in Marxian-based theories. Bourdieu's own work shows that "struggles for recognition are a fundamental dimension of social life . . . what is at stake in them is the accumulation of a particular form of capital, honor in the sense of reputation and prestige" (1990, 22). As he points out (1984, 251), these struggles for recognition are always between the "distinguished" possessors of status and the "pretentious" challengers, both groups being characterized by fundamental differences in tastes and styles of consumption. "Where the petit bourgeois or nouveau riche 'overdoes it' . . . bourgeois discretion signals its presence by a sort of ostentatious discretion, sobriety and understatement, a refusal of everything which is 'showy,' 'flashy' and pretentious" (Bourdieu 1984, 249). Thus, in the struggle between the two groups, the possessors of distinction have to constantly find new ways to assert their distinction (1984, 251–252).

Not surprisingly, given the sudden increase in wealth made possible by the Gulf migration and the class background of the migrants, these "struggles for recognition" were magnified and intensified several-fold in the high migrant areas of Kerala. In order to be in a position to put forth claims for incorporation into the higher-status group, the migrants were trying to devise a strategy that would allow them to accumulate the maximum amount of "community points" in the shortest period of time.[14] But particularly since the time period was so short and the gap that had to be bridged was generally large (between manual laborers and middle classes), not surprisingly, this goal was strongly resisted by many of the traditional elite of the communities.[15] In the course of this struggle, each side tried to mobilize the different resources available in the community—material, ideological, political, and social. For instance, newly rich migrants displayed material resources conspicuously as a means of making public the change in economic standing and also used their wealth to recruit supporters and forge alliances. The old rich on their part invested in goods and practices which they felt showed "cultural refinement." Both groups also invoked and reinterpreted ideologies of religion, culture, and gender to the greatest advantage of the parties concerned. Religious, status, and gender practices were also modified. All of this led to fundamental transformations in the social and cultural landscape, or the ethnicities of the communities.

In her study of a Muslim village in the Sylhet district of Bangladesh, an area that had experienced considerable outmigration to Britain and the Middle

East, Katy Gardner argues that international migration led to a reformulation of religious identity. The migrants seemed to be constructing an international version of Islam, one which deemphasized local religious centers and Sufi saints (a claim of descent from such saints had been the traditional basis for status in the community) and instead stressed a purist Islam, where direct access to Allah was possible and where wealth was the reward given to the pious. Instead of repudiating the Sufi saints completely, however, migrants were simultaneously "inventing" claims of descent from such saints as a means to obtain prestige (Gardner 1995). Similarly, Jonathan Addleton (1992, 158–159) discusses the way in which Pakistani Gulf migrants were redefining religious identity and practice.

Gardner also found that the upward mobility made possible by international migration led to changes in gender practices. Families that had become wealthy appropriated upper-class codes of honor and shame and patterns of behavior which they consider befitting their new station and which distinguished them from the average village family. In Sylhet, the upward mobility consequent on migration resulted in the withdrawal of women from the labor force and their seclusion (Gardner 1995). Gardner also found that there was an increase in dowries and marriages to strangers living far away (conventionally marriages had been arranged to relatives within the village). She argues that this was because, "with increased prosperity and prestige, marriage has become a strategy to gain status and useful alliances for the upwardly mobile" (Gardner 1995, 177).

By introducing these new patterns of material and social living, migrants are also cultural entrepreneurs of the society. Since migrant households comprise a large proportion of the high-migrant communities, these changes spread in the society through the "contagion effect." Even migrants who are not able to earn much as a consequence of the migration tend to imitate the behavior of the wealthier returnees so that they can also secure a higher status. Nonmigrants for their part try their best to keep up.

Ethnicity and Differences in the Impact of Migration.   Adopting the modernization paradigm, the earlier literature on the social impact of return migration on emigrant communities was cast in terms of the tradition-modernity axis, and as in the case of social change in general, the initial expectation was that migration would lead to modernization. This was seen as resulting from two types of factors—cultural and structural. Since migration usually took place from less developed to more developed areas, the cultural exposure of the migrant to the more "modern" ethos of the host society was presumed to work against traditional beliefs and practices. In addition, structural factors such as the individualism associated with migration (which uprooted the migrant from the familistic network of the home community) along with the new money and skills they presumably acquired in the new society were expected to encourage the migrants to act like economic and cultural entrepreneurs in their own communities, triggering off modernization as a consequence.

A few studies did seem to indicate that this process was taking place as predicted.[16] But several more recent studies have pointed out that quite to the contrary, precisely due to cultural and structural factors, migration actually resulted in an increase in traditionalism in the emigrant communities.[17] The cultural explanation was that international migration resulted in conservative change since migrants were tired of the anonymity they faced in their host societies and wanted to return to the refuge of their communities where they were not interested in changing the system but in securing high status within it. Structurally, migration frequently increased traditionalism since it depended principally on kin networks which thereby got strengthened. Furthermore, migrants often performed unskilled and menial jobs in the host societies which did not lead to any real transference of skills. Thus the two perspectives came up with opposing interpretations of the same variables. If both progressive and conservative change take place as a consequence of the affluence and exposure gained due to international migration, what is needed is an understanding of the circumstances under which one takes place instead of the other.

My argument is that the type of change that takes place depends on the social organization of the communities in question and on what is defined as prestigious behavior. For instance, the literature has documented different consequences for gender relationships due to predominantly male migration, depending largely on the social structure of the migrant communities.[18] As Jonathan Parry and Maurice Bloch (1989) point out, economic actions such as short-term migration for financial goals must be seen as part of a total social system. In opposition to the neoclassical tradition, they argue that these actions bear the impress of the larger structure of which they are a part and that individual acquisitiveness and freedom are therefore subordinated to larger family and community interests.

Parry and Bloch distinguish between "short cycles" and "long cycles" of economic exchange. The short cycle refers to "the cycle of short-term exchange: which is the legitimate domain of individual—often acquisitive—activity," while the long cycle is "the cycle of long-term exchanges concerned with the reproduction of the social and cosmic order" (Parry and Bloch 1989, 2). The two orders are, of course, interconnected—ideologically and materially—and thus the reproduction of the social order is dependent on individual activities. But what is important to note is their argument that to sustain the balance, at least some of what is "obtained in the short-term individualistic cycle . . . [has to be] converted to serve the reproduction of the long-term cycle" (1989, 26). If this takes place, the social harmony of the community is maintained. According to them the tendency that communities have to constantly guard against is that individuals might become "so embroiled in the short-term cycle that [she]/he will ignore the demands of the long cycle" (1989, 27). It is to prevent this from happening that communities mobilize all their resources of informal social control. Thus, the ethic of generosity is imposed on the migrant through persistent demands from relatives and community members, and deviants are censured through various expressions of individual and community disapproval.

Thus, we should view individual and group responses to migration and remittances within the social cosmos of the particular migrant community. Although the Mappila Muslims of Veni, the Ezhava Hindus of Cherur, and the Syrian Christians of Kembu experienced large-scale migration, the actual responses of the communities at each stage were quite different. This was due to the fact that their ethnic structures—or, in the language of Parry and Bloch, their social and cosmic orders—were fundamentally different. The ethnic structure of the three communities influenced the economic behavior of the migrants—the types of activities into which the money was channeled, the range of people who were the beneficiaries of the migrant remittances, the patterns of reciprocity or charity practiced by the migrants, the selection of the tradeoff point between community status and economic accumulation, and the groups of individuals who gained or lost economic control. It also influenced the impact of the migration on the status stratification of the communities and the gender relationships within the household. At the same time, the economic resources and prestige gained through international migration and the sheer numbers of migrants involved gave the people an opportunity to reformulate their identity and that of the community. Thus, the reconstitution of religious identity, status, and gender was a way in which the bases of difference among the communities were reconstructed as circumstances changed.

CHAPTER 3

Colonialism and Ethnogenesis

$\mathcal{T}$his chapter traces the sequence of events that led to religion forming the basis of group identity, giving rise to ethnic cleavages in colonial Kerala. I introduce material to demonstrate the manner in which political, social, and economic processes shaped the meaning and significance of the religious identities of each of the three groups and show how such meanings were reconstructed as these factors changed. This provides a good illustration of the role of internal and external factors in ethnic formation and transformation and of the dynamic nature of ethnicity.

We also see that groups in precolonial and colonial Kerala were greatly concerned with boundary marking and maintenance, precisely because ethnicity was an important means through which to gain, retain, and express differential access to resources. The nexus between religious identity, conceptions of honor, and appropriate male and female behavior is clear from the way each of these were modified as groups gained or lost social status.

Precolonial Society in Kerala

Early Trade

Kerala's long western coastline and strategic position at the center of the Indian ocean, together with its tremendous natural wealth of spices, teak, and ivory brought foreigners to the shores of the state from as early as the third millennium B.C.E. if not earlier. The Arabs of Oman and the Persian Gulf were probably the first to come to Kerala in search of spices. The Assyrians, the Babylonians, and the Phoenicians followed. King Solomon of Israel is believed to have sent ships to Kerala in 1,000 B.C.E. which returned laden with gold, ivory, apes, and peacocks. In the last few centuries B.C.E., Greeks and Romans carried on an extensive trade with Kerala. Spices such as cardamom, cinnamon, ginger, turmeric, and pepper seem to have been in particular demand. In addition to the

West, Kerala also carried out trade with China and other countries to the East (Menon 1967, 52–57).

Early Kingdoms

For the first five centuries C.E., Kerala was part of Tamilagam—the area inhabited by the Tamil people of the time. During the next three centuries, Kerala was divided into several small kingdoms that constantly feuded with each other. After a few centuries of struggle between the petty principalities, three kingdoms emerged: in the north, the kingdom of Calicut (later to become Malabar province) around the thirteenth century; in the south, the kingdom of Venad (later to become Travancore) in the twelfth century; and in central Kerala, the kingdom of Cochin in the sixteenth century. These three political entities would continue more or less unchanged until the time of independence in 1947 (Menon 1967, 176).

The Religions

At present, Kerala is home to three main religious groups—Hindus, Muslims, and Christians. The Hindus in turn are subdivided into several castes, the most important of which are the Brahmins, Nayars, Ezhavas, and the Harijans. Christians and Muslims also manifest caste-like subdivisions. Kerala Christians are grouped into Syrians, Latins, and the Backward Class. The major divisions among Kerala Muslims are those between the *Tangals* (an elite group that traces its ancestry to the Prophet), *Malabaris* (the mass of Mappilas), and the *Pusalars* (fisherfolk, considered to belong to a lower-status category).[1]

The three religious groups have existed in Kerala for well over a thousand years. In fact, all three religions—Hinduism in its Brahminized form, Christianity, and Islam—were being actively propagated as early as the second half of the first millennium C.E. These groups and their relationships with each other will be treated in more detail below.

Early Hinduism.   According to historians of Kerala, the region experienced a gradual process of "Aryanization" from about the sixth century onward, this being the process by which the cultural hegemony of the "Brahmin dominated Aryan culture, the foundation of which was the . . . varna caste system with occupational, ritual and social differentiations" (Pillai 1987, 46; see also Menon 1979, 66) was established in the society.[2] Aryanization also entailed a gradual reduction in the freedom and status of women (Pillai 1987). The process reached its peak between the eighth and twelfth centuries. The Brahmin priests first gained a foothold in society through royal patronage. They managed to impress the local rulers with their knowledge and mastery of the scriptures and convinced them of the need to conduct *yagas* (complex rites with sacrifices) for the sake of their longevity and political supremacy. The Brahmins also empowered the local chieftains by conferring Aryan titles upon them and by creating the fiction that they were of divine descent. In return for these favors, the kings acknowledged the dominance of the Brahmins and bestowed extensive gifts of lands, hamlets and herds on them, as well as absolute protection.

Next, the groups that were in close contact with the Brahmins and kings (performing personal and military service for them) Aryanized and evolved gradually into a caste—that of the Nayars.[3] The rest of society—namely, the laboring classes—were relegated to the status of "unclean" castes, outside the pale of Aryanic Hinduism. Those groups which carried out the hard physical tasks had the lowest status of all the groups. They were deemed as being outside the pale of society itself. Thus developed a group of agrestic slaves. The caste system was subsequently legitimized by a legend that it was divinely created.[4]

The caste system that evolved in Kerala deviated in significant ways from the ideal typical pan-Indian varna schema. Of the four basic varnas—*Brahmin* (priest), *Kshatriya* (warrior), *Vaisya* (business person), and *Sudra* (service person)— Kshatriyas were rare and Vaisyas nonexistent. The Nayar caste took the place of the Kshatriyas, but they were regarded as Sudras by the local Brahmins. The Ezhavas came below the Nayars, followed by the slave castes. The Christians and the Muslims were the main business and trading communities in Kerala.

The caste system in Kerala also achieved a degree of elaboration and severity not found anywhere else in the country. While untouchability existed in the rest of India, in Kerala, the notion of pollution by contact was taken a step further to include "atmospheric pollution"—pollution from a distance, and, in the case of the lowest castes, even by sight. The specific physical distances to be maintained between the different castes were stipulated, depending on their respective positions in the caste hierarchy. There were other prescriptions and proscriptions imposed on the members of the different castes with the restrictions becoming increasingly severe as one went down the caste hierarchy. Thus there were restrictions on the access to education, to religious, social, and political institutions, and on the occupations a caste could follow. Each caste also had certain types of hairstyles, clothes, jewelry, shoes, and houses that they were allowed. Lower castes were obliged to observe specific demeaning forms of address and posture when talking to a higher caste member. There was also a differential justice system for each of the castes.[5]

The Brahmins (locally known as *Nambudiris*) were ensconced securely at the apex of the hierarchy. The first census that was conducted for the whole of Kerala that had caste data was in 1968, and at that time, Brahmins constituted less than 1 percent of the population. Despite their small numbers, their control over the rest of the community was absolute. Besides being the religious specialists, they were also the largest landowners of the state. However, they were absentee landlords. The actual cultivation was supervised by Nayars and performed by Ezhavas and slaves. In addition, they were the teachers and advisers of the rulers as well as the supreme legal authority in the state. The Brahmins had a family structure and lifestyle evolved so as to prevent the fragmentation of their estates and the dissipation of their wealth. It was a patrilineal joint family system in which only the eldest son was allowed to marry. His children were regarded as the legal issues of the joint family. The rest of the sons contracted liaisons with Nayar women. The Nayar family structure was matrilineal and matrilocal, so the Nambudiris would visit their Nayar wives (polygyny was combined with polyandry) at night in their own homes. The children born of such unions were Nayars and became the full responsibility of the mother's *taravad* (the Nayar joint family).

The Nayars were divided into several subcastes and occupied a range of positions. High-status Nayars were important chieftains and military commanders. Others held high government positions. Both these categories of Nayars were also large landowners. Among the middle-status Nayars were those who rendered services to the Brahmins as accountants and agricultural supervisors. Low-status Nayars were service functionaries like washermen and barbers. It appears from the evidence that the Nayar category was extremely fluid. Since the power of kings depended on the size of their armies, they "created" a lot of Nayar warriors by bestowing the Nayar status on members of other castes.[6] In 1968, the Nayars constituted 15 percent of the population. The Nayars lived in matrilineal and matrilocal joint-families called the taravad, headed by the eldest male member. The property and assets of the taravad were held in common and could be alienated only with the consent of all its members. Prepubescent Nayar girls underwent an expensive mock marriage ceremony after which they were permitted to contract sambandham (agreement) marriages with men of the same or higher-status groups.[7] A woman could have sambandham with several men at the same time. Such marriages were loosely structured and could be dissolved at any time by the wishes of either party.[8] The husband had no rights over the woman and her children and little obligation except to provide small presents.

The Ezhava caste formed the largest section of Hindu society in Kerala, constituting 22 percent of the population in 1968. Their traditional occupation was the tending of the coconut palm—mainly tapping it for toddy and using its husk to make *coir* (coconut fiber) products. Some were also sharecroppers and agricultural laborers of land held by the Nayars. Although this caste performed the tasks of the Sudras, they were classified as an *avarna* (unclean) or "untouchable" caste (Nossiter 1982, 30) and thus had several prohibitions imposed on them. According to A. Aiyappan, who has produced the most detailed historical study of this caste, the Ezhavas were "at the top of the caste group known as *tindal jati;* i.e., castes that pollute from a distance. A member of this caste pollutes a Namputiri [Nambudiri] from a distance of thirty-two feet; he has no access to the houses of Nayars or Namputiris, their temples, tanks and wells and has no freedom to use roads or foot-paths when Nayars or Namputiris are nearby" (Aiyappan 1944, 39). Since they could not approach the regular temples, they had their own temples and priests. They also could not carry an umbrella or cover their upper bodies (not even the women) and could not wear certain types of jewelry and footwear or use metal vessels and finely woven cloth. The family structure of the Ezhavas varied, depending on the region where they lived, but in southern Kerala, the area that I studied, it was matrilocal and matrilineal, and they followed most of the ceremonial practices of the Nayars. However, Ezhava women generally married only within their caste.

The slave castes (who in 1968 constituted 9 percent of the population) were treated like property with no rights over self or family. They carried out the most arduous agricultural tasks in return for a minimum amount of food. There were innumerable restrictions on their behavior, the most onerous of which stemmed from the rules requiring that they maintain a great distance from the rest of the society, particularly the higher castes. It was even inauspicious for them to be spotted on the horizon by a high caste member before any important ritual; if that happened, they could be killed on the spot.

Early Islam. Historical evidence seems to indicate that Islam was brought into Kerala about the middle of the ninth century C.E. by Arab travelers. Many of the Arab traders who visited Kerala gradually settled in the country and married native women or had temporary liaisons with them. Such intermarriages and conversions served to swell their numbers. Thus developed the Mappilas—the term by which Muslims of north Kerala are known. The Zamorin (king) of the kingdom of Calicut, one of the chief patrons of the Arab trade, is said to have directed that in every family of fishermen in his dominion, at least one male member should be brought up as a Muslim in order that there would be enough locals to man the Arab ships (Innes 1951, 186). The Mappilas lived mostly in coastal northern Kerala and were the main traders of the region. Many were very wealthy and owned large tracts of land. The lower classes were fishermen, laborers, and petty cultivators. In this early period, the Mappilas seem to have been considered "honorary Nayars" since they were granted several privileges within the caste system, dressed like Nayars and partly adopted the Nayar matrilineal system.[9] Lower-caste converts could overcome several of their traditional disabilities through conversion, and this encouraged the process.[10]

Early Christianity. The local tradition about the origin of Christianity in Kerala is that Saint Thomas the apostle landed in north Kerala in 52 C.E. and converted many people to Christianity, chiefly from among the Brahmin and other high-caste Hindu families.[11] In the early centuries of the Christian era, the Christians increased in numbers (through conversion and fresh migration) and in prosperity. They were traders, and the foreign trade was almost entirely in their hands. The rulers bestowed several high privileges on them in the eighth and ninth centuries.[12] The *Nazranis* (as they were then called) were accorded a status similar to high-caste Nayars and, like the latter, were adept in the use of arms. In several respects, however, they had more privileges than the Nayars (Ayyar 1926, 55).[13] Susan Bayly gives several examples of the way in which the Nazranis were integrated "within the wider 'Hindu' society of the region— the term 'integration' being used here to convey a position of high status and acceptance within the region's most prestigious social and religious institutions" (Bayly 1989, 250–251). She points out that many of the Christian churches were endowed and protected by Hindu kings. Nazrani rites in this period were very similar to those of the Nayars, and they were "accorded the same position within the region's elaborate gradations of caste rank and ritual purity" (Bayly 1989, 251). The Nazranis also had the right of access to Hindu temples. Many of the early European observers "bracketed" the two groups together, and there is some evidence that Nazranis and Nayars intermarried at least till the end of the sixteenth century (Bayly 1989, 252).

Thus, early Hinduism with its syncretism and its all-embracing caste organization provided the overarching framework for the society. Since the geographical area that now constitutes Kerala was politically fragmented, Pamela Price argues that in southern India it was the caste organizations that "served as major institutions of social integration and control" and that variations in the rules of the different castes "helped to distinguish one from another and to define membership" (Price 1989, 157). Even the Christians and Muslims were incorporated into the system as quasi-castes and had a defined place within the caste hierarchy. Each group also had a defined economic and ecological niche within the system, and thus they shared a symbiotic relationship of mutual dependency with other groups. The boundaries between the groups were porous, as testified by the fact that both the Christians and the Muslims increased their numbers mainly through conversions and intermarriages. The kings were the principal agents of change within the society. They conferred caste membership and honors on some individuals and groups and also withdrew privileges and imposed caste disabilities on others (Dumont 1970, 169).

The three groups and their relationships with one another changed drastically under the influence of colonialism. An outcome of colonialism was that this overarching system was unbundled and the castes and religious groups developed into separate communities, each emphasizing their social and cultural exclusivity.[14] The displacement of the groups from their traditional niches also pitted them into competition with one another.[15] René Lemarchand describes a similar process in southern Chad as being one in which the preexisting "vertical social system of super- and subordination" was transmuted to a pattern of "horizontal ethnic cleavages and competition" (Lemarchand 1983, 49–50). In Kerala, the hierarchical element continued to be informally retained, but except for this modification, Lemarchand's characterization is very apt for this region.

Colonialism and the Transformation of Society

In the last chapter, I referred to the way the state and, in particular, the colonialist state, fostered the ethnicization of society.[16] The hegemonic capacity of the colonial state gave it greater transformative power. Generally, the colonial state also had a tremendous degree of autonomy from the society it was colonizing.[17] The emergence of ethnic groups took place as a result of a complex of factors, but in the final analysis, it was the "consequence of the economic and social transformation dictated by the imperatives of economic viability and administrative efficiency" (Lemarchand 1983, 55).

Colonialism imposed a new economic and political system on the society and usually introduced large-scale commercialization. The consequent disruption of the economic and political structure eventually resulted in a change in the social organization of the society. In addition, colonialism gave rise to religious and cultural proselytization. Often there were attempts to forcibly change many of the traditional practices which were perceived to be "barbaric" or "immoral." Both these processes were at work in Kerala during the period of colonialism and brought about a societal transformation.

Colonialism in Kerala began with the arrival of foreigners wanting to carry on trade with the local population. Vasco Da Gama, the Portuguese explorer, arrived in the port of Calicut in 1498. More of his compatriots followed. Through a combination of coercion and intrigue, the Portuguese soon wrested the spice trade from the hands of the Arabs and the Mappilas. Thus, the Arabs were forced to leave and the Mappilas were driven inland, where they became petty farmers on land controlled by Hindu landlords.

The Portuguese presence also led to tremendous changes in the Christian community in Kerala. The initial welcome they were accorded by the Nazranis (as coreligionists) soon turned to hostility when the Portuguese tried (to some extent forcibly) to purge the native Christians of their Hindu practices and to substitute the Latin liturgy for the Syriac. The Portuguese also wanted the church in Kerala (which until then had been under the Patriarch of Babylon) to come under the control of the Pope of Rome. Meanwhile, several missionaries worked among the lower castes (mainly in the southern regions of Kerala) and succeeded in converting large groups to Christianity. These Christians were called Latin Catholics since they followed the Latin liturgy. Since most of them were lower-caste converts, the Nazranis continued to treat them as such. The Nazranis, or the St. Thomas Christians (as they were then called),[18] strongly resisted the attempts at forced Latinization, and it was this process of confrontation that led them to develop and articulate their distinct self-identity as *Syrian* Christians.

The Portuguese interlude was relatively short lived, ending in 1663. It was the British who were the real colonizers of Kerala (and India as a whole). They arrived in Kerala in the early eighteenth century and entered into a series of skirmishes with local kings and other European powers to gain control. By the end of the century, the northern portions of Kerala (the kingdom of Calicut, which was now called Malabar province) had become part of the British empire, while the central (the kingdom of Cochin) and southern (the kingdom of Travancore) regions came under its indirect rule.

The First Phase of Colonialism

The period of colonialism can, in most cases, be divided into two phases on the basis of the types of transformations that took place.[19] The classic cases of colonialism have most often been situations where colonial rule was imposed on a precapitalist society containing some system of hierarchically arranged, hereditary, occupational groups.[20] In the first phase, the colonialists tried to keep most of the existing socioeconomic structures intact, only adapting them to the exigencies of revenue generation and political control. To achieve the latter, there was an attempt to rationalize and systematize the economic and political system. Cultural factors often played a crucial role at this stage. As foreigners, colonists often did not understand the subtleties of the local system.[21] Consequently, groups and their relationships with one another were viewed through the lens of Western categories or textual descriptions; fluid boundaries perceived as rigid, stereotypes developed and variations missed or ignored (Lemarchand 1983, 53). The usual strategy was to use the elites of the society (or those perceived to be the elites) as social and economic entry points and as colonial agents. This resulted in their position being strengthened. Together with the need for additional revenues, the outcome was often an increase in the degree of exploitation of tenants and agricultural laborers. Since economic and social cleavages generally overlapped, the oppression experienced by this section of the population could initiate a process of ethnic formation and group mobilization, manifesting itself in the form of sporadic rebellions. But as the might of the colonial state was on the side of the upper classes in this period, such revolts were strongly put down. Ethnic formation and revolts could also be initiated by precolonial elites who were displaced from economic, social, or political positions as a consequence of the misperceptions of the colonists (see Brass 1991, 26–27).[22] In this stage it was also not uncommon for the colonists to deliberately foster group cleavages so as to keep the opposition to their rule divided.

Mappila Muslims and Hindus. The homeland of the Mappilas, Malabar in northern Kerala, came under the direct rule of the British. Thus, it was in this region that the "rationalization" of the existing system for revenue production and administrative control was initiated in its characteristic form. In the quarter century before the British conquest, north Kerala (where most of the Mappilas lived) had been under the control of Muslim rulers from Mysore state (a south Indian state to the north of Kerala), who for a combination of economic and religious reasons had undertaken a series of repressive measures against the high-caste landlords and had favored the Mappila peasants. With the coming of the British, the balance of power changed. In the war against the Muslim rulers, the British allied with the higher castes against the Mappilas and won a decisive victory. In return for their support, the British allowed the higher castes to reclaim the lands which for years had been in the hands of the Mappila cultivators.

To make matters worse for the Mappilas, the British misunderstood the customary land relations in the area, which had given security of tenure to tenants. Viewing the land tenure of the area through European ideas of property, the landlords (who were predominantly Hindu) were given absolute control over the land and thus the customary rights of the (Mappila Muslim) tenants were abolished. Property taxes were also very high and were assessed unequally, the Mappila Muslims having a higher tax rate than the Hindus. Thus, the gulf between the Hindus and Mappila Muslims, first created by the Muslim rulers, was even further widened by British policies. The impoverishment of the cultivating classes (the Mappilas) led to a series of peasant uprisings against the landlords and the British state[23] and since the peasants were largely Muslim, it took a religious form and was conducted as a *jihad* (Muslim religious war). Because of this, the early British officials tended to attribute the attacks to the "fanaticism" of the Mappilas, and the economic basis was neglected for a long time. The most serious was the Mappila Rebellion of 1921 which lasted for six months and took a toll of about ten thousand (mostly Mappila) lives (Menon 1967, 340).[24]

The colonial state brutally suppressed the rebellions. It instituted several repressive policies (including deportation and large fines) targeted at the Mappila community as a whole. These measures further impoverished the Mappilas. The dire poverty and the political repression spurred the first large exodus of Mappila men to other parts of India where they worked mainly within the informal economic sector.

The rebellion also widened the chasm between the Hindus and Muslims. Further, since the Hindu-dominated Indian Congress leadership had quickly distanced itself from the revolt, the Mappilas, in the aftermath of the crushing defeat they faced, withdrew from the national political scene and drifted into communal politics. The late thirties saw the rise of the Muslim league in Malabar, which supported the national Muslim League demand for Pakistan. In 1947, the Mappilas made a similar demand for the establishment of "Moplastan"—a separate Muslim majority province in south Malabar. They argued that besides being a much-oppressed community, the Mappilas had a history and culture of their own related to their Arab background, and that they were therefore entirely different from the rest of the communities of Malabar (Menon 1967, 340). The Indian government (which had taken over upon independence in 1947) rejected this demand, but a later demand to create a Muslim majority district was ultimately conceded.

Cultural and religious proselytization generally began in the latter part of the first phase of colonialism. This further contributed to the formation of ethnic groups. When confronted with aggressive missionaries espousing one religion and one culture as the *only* right one, groups not of that religio-cultural orientation tried to explain, justify, and rationalize their own behavior, in the process often redefining themselves and their culture. If the relationship between the proselytizers and the group concerned was antagonistic, the local group was likely to withdraw into themselves to nurture their own culture, which would

then be defined in opposition to that of the dominant group. Thus, rigid boundaries were created and existing differences exaggerated. This process took place
in the case of the Mappilas. For the new converts or existing adherents of the
proselytizing religion, the situation was different. Their alliance and identification with colonialists invariably resulted in attempts by converts to bring their
culture into greater congruity with that of the latter. This pattern was more characteristic of the Syrian Christians.

Syrian Christians. The collapse of the political order brought about by
colonialism and the disbandment of native armies resulted in both the Nayars
and Syrian Christians losing their roles as "privileged warriors and office-
holders" (Bayly 1989, 281). However, the Syrian Christians fared relatively better
and, in fact, thrived under British rule. The British were far less confrontational
than the Portuguese and accorded Syrian Christians favorable treatment, hoping that the alliance with a section of the population would strengthen their political power.[25] Under the British there was a large influx of missionaries into
the region. Besides proselytizing, the missionaries became involved in social
welfare programs and introduced schools, hospitals, and other charitable institutions. They also frequently interceded with the British government on behalf
of the Christians in the population.

The identification and alliance of the Syrian Christians with the British
led to their large-scale participation in the wide range of mission-run institutions. Thus, Syrian Christians led the other groups in English education (Nossiter
1988, 50), and a large proportion of the community secured positions as teachers, lecturers, doctors, nurses, and administrators in the mission schools, colleges, and hospitals. Their English education and British contacts also gave them
entry into the plantation industry as planters, clerks, and supervisors and helped
them migrate to other parts of the British empire (both within India and to other
countries like Ceylon [Sri Lanka], Malaya [Malaysia], Singapore, and the Middle
East) for well-paying white-collar positions.

The missionaries gained several Protestant converts, mostly from the "untouchable" castes such as the Pulayas. These converts continued to be referred
to as "Pulaya Christians" (later officially designated as "Backward-Class Christians") by the upper-caste Christians, who wanted to make sure that this lower-
status group would not be confused either with Syrians or Latin Catholics (who
were accorded a higher status in society than the Pulaya Christians due to their
earlier conversion and better economic position).

The Second Phase of Colonialism

The caste system underwent major changes during the colonial period.
Most of these changes took place after 1850 in what I call the second, capitalist
phase of colonialism. This phase of colonialism generally began with the development of a market economy, the intensification of colonialist capitalism, and

the rise and expansion of the colonialist state. The requirements of such a system were incompatible with the traditional social structure that was prevalent in the society. The need for wage labor meant that laboring classes had to be freed from their ties to individual landlords; the penetration of the market economy also required the liberation of the economic resources from the precapitalistic control of the upper strata. As the state apparatus and the secondary and tertiary sectors developed, the spread of education among the population and the need for educated and trained personnel to occupy the new positions became necessary. All these factors necessitated not just the modification of the traditional system (as in the first phase), but also its overthrow.[26] Thus, it was during this stage that the moral objections to the system were most vehemently expressed.[27] Even if missionary activities were introduced in the previous phase, their numbers and power increased during this period. With or without their efforts, it was generally in this second period of colonialism that slavery was abolished, as were many of the traditional disabilities of the lower sections. The colonists modified customary landownership practices, established schools, and widened the access to education. Several of the other fundamental features of the traditional social system were also generally abolished at this stage.

In Kerala, the second phase of colonialism began in the latter half of the nineteenth century. The public works department was created in southern Kerala in 1863, and the colonists took measures to encourage trade and commerce and to establish large-scale plantations. Both the Brahmins and the Nayars had lost their traditional occupational roles by this period. The colonists and missionaries started to publicly deride many of the central features of the caste system in Kerala such as the polygyny of the Brahmins, the polyandrous and loosely structured sambandham marriage system of the Nayars, and the institution of slavery as being immoral. Stung by the criticism that the matrilineal system was an "abomination" (Jeffrey 1993, 40), young educated Nayars called for family reform. Legislative attempts to reform the matrilineal system began in the 1890s and were largely completed by the 1950s. The Nayars adopted more "respectable" practices such as monogamy, patrilineality, patrilocality, and greater patriarchy. Legislation was also passed which permitted the partitioning of joint family land to the individual members.[28] The alienation of land by the Brahmins and Nayars led to a weakening of their economic position. Thanks to their newfound prosperity (obtained through participation in mission-run institutions), the Syrian Christians bought much of this land. The marriage and land practices of the Nayars and Brahmins had formed the basis for the upper-caste alliance and dominance in society, and their abolition brought the whole edifice down.

At the same time, the commercialization process introduced by colonialism permitted the participation of the lower castes, particularly the Ezhavas, and they were able to improve their situation. With the improvement in their economic position and with the backing of the British missionaries, they sought corresponding improvement in their social position and began to organize and militate against the many disabilities they faced, particularly the restriction against their attending government schools. At the turn of the century, an Ezhava spiritual leader, Sri (an honorific title) Narayana Guru, emerged, who launched a crusade against untouchability and casteism and exhorted the group to pursue education and to start economic enterprises. The Ezhava movement spurred the Syrian Christians and then the Nayars to mobilize to press for a redressal of their grievances and an increase in their share of government jobs and political representation.

The number of British missionaries increased a great deal during the second phase of colonialism, and they gradually began to take an active role in the administrative policies of the state. Since they were rebuffed by the higher castes and welcomed by the ones at the bottom of the hierarchy,[29] they soon adopted the role of being the proponents of the lower castes, particularly of the Christian converts, realizing that the success of their mission depended on such intervention (Jeffrey 1976). Slavery was first abolished in Malabar, north Kerala (in 1843). Responding to the lobbying of the missionaries, the colonists[30] put pressure on the two southern states of Cochin and Travancore to do the same.[31] The differential dress regulations imposed on the castes were withdrawn[32] in this period as were the restrictions on movement of the lower castes in public areas.[33] The missionaries established schools and colleges,[34] and the native governments of the two southern states which had earlier banned lower castes from attending government schools were forced to lift this restriction in the early twentieth century. The establishment of such institutions resulted in the creation of new positions that Indians were recruited for. The Syrian Christians benefited disproportionately from these developments as a consequence of their ties with the missionaries and colonists. More and more Indians also began to be inducted into government service as the state sector expanded, which again increased the opportunities for mobility within the society. Here, however, Brahmins and Nayars with their tradition of serving in the native governments were favored, particularly in Cochin and Travancore.

The dismantling of the traditional system displaced groups from their socioeconomic niches. At the same time, the spread of capitalism, bureaucracy, and the introduction of new institutions generated new economic and social resources. The expansion of the capacity and role of the state created a new landscape of power (see also Frankel 1990, 483–485). These developments gave rise to competition among the groups as they jockeyed for control over the new resources and for a favorable position in the transformed political order.[35] Thus, there was a fundamental erosion of the original socioeconomic and cultural basis of group formation and identity. Ethnic entrepreneurs emerged in this period who carried forward the process of ethnic formation and mobilization.

Thus, the second period of colonialism coincided with one of heightened ethnic consciousness and activity in Kerala. In the north, the large-scale Mappila revolt was launched in 1921, and the demand for a separate province for the Muslims was made in 1947. In the south, ethnic leaders emerged who tried to mobilize their groups to press for the redressal of the grievances of their communities. An Ezhava association was formed in 1903, followed by a Nayar association in 1914 and by associations for the rest of the groups in the society. These associations agitated for the removal of the social disabilities of their groups, and once this had been accomplished, for legislative representation,[36] and access to government positions.[37] The Ezhavas continued to spearhead reform protests, and their efforts enmeshed with the national movements sweeping the country. The mobilization of the lower castes provided fertile ground for an incipient Communist movement which gradually gained momentum in the state. The Ezhavas were the largest supporters of the movement.[38]

The new state of Kerala was formed in 1956, when the Indian states were reorganized based on the linguistic principle. The state comprised the Malayalam speaking areas of Malabar, Cochin, and parts of Travancore in the south. The first general elections of 1957 brought a Communist government to power. The Kerala government initiated a program of land reforms that further impoverished many Brahmins and Nayars who were the big landlords in the state (Varghese 1970). The Communists also abolished the last vestiges of the traditional caste system like distance pollution and the differential privileges accorded to castes. The freedom and mobility that the Ezhavas obtained spurred a large migration to Singapore and Malaysia from around the 1940s where they worked in a range of semiskilled occupations.

Colonialism and Ethnic Formation

In the previous section, I described the sequence of events that led to the dismantling of the stratification system that existed in the precolonial period. Under colonial rule, religious and caste identities which had been defined in terms of the position of each group within the larger social order were reified and made immutable, and the subgroups and subcultures developed into autonomous and distinct units. In Susan Bayly's words, "The long-standing pattern of 'integration' gave way to rapid and irreversible disintegration" (1989, 276). David Laitin's discussion of British strategies that gave rise to Hindu-Muslim divisions is relevant here. He quotes Francis Robinson who argues that "the British insisted on discussing Indian politics and society in terms of Muslims and Hindus . . . They had done so from the beginning of their contact with Indian society" (Robinson 1974, 99, quoted in Laitin 1985, 310). However, unlike in the Western situation, in the precolonial context in India, there had been no well-developed "Hindu" or "Muslim" identity and no clear social or political separation between the two groups. Thus the salience of religious identities and the subsequent cleavage that developed between the religious groups was fostered through colonial policies. The general conclusion Laitin draws from his case studies is that "a colonial hegemon . . . , can instill in certain cleavage patterns a sense of reality and objectivity that is not fully supported by the social structure" (Laitin 1985, 310).

In the following section, I will use the sketchy historical material available to develop a tentative description of the ethnicization of the three groups over the period of colonialism.

The Ethnicization of the Mappilas

In the precolonial period the Mappilas were treated almost as honorary Nayars. The development of the Mappilas as a separate ethnic group (in contrast to being a subgroup within Hindu society) with a distinct identity and culture began with their migration to the interior. The departure of their Arab mentors, the loss of their income and occupation, their exodus to the interior, and the struggle to reestablish themselves were experiences that served to weld the group together. The meaning of their religious identity took on a special significance with the invasion of the Muslims from Mysore state. For the first time since the Arabs left, the Mappilas again had the support of powerful religious allies, but this time ones who used their power to emphasize and deepen the cleavages—religious and economic—between them and the Hindus. They blossomed in the brief period of Mysorean occupation with the land and special privileges conferred on them. The group began to organize itself into a community with the Tangals (believed to be direct descendants of the Arabs and accorded a high status) as their leaders.

The conflicts the Mappilas had with the Portuguese and later the British so alienated them that they withdrew into their own community and also led to their developing a culture that rejected and opposed Western practices. Their experience also created a deep suspicion of such Western institutions as secular education, medicine, and bureaucracy. The Tangals, apprehensive about the attempts at "cultural and ideological hegemonization by the colonial state and the activities of the Christian missionaries" (Panikkar 1989, 60) sought to propagate Islamic ideology and theology, to systematize its practices, and to provide its believers with an institutional framework through the building of mosques and madrasas. All this was done with a view to create and nurture an Islamic identity and solidarity. The Tangals also sought to purify Islam of the Hindu practices which its converts tended to carry along with them (such as the honorific mode of address of the upper castes, the eating of leftover food from the latter and the nonobservance of the Mohammedan Sabbath) (Panikkar 1989, 62). It was in this period that the Mappilas adopted distinct types of clothing and hairstyles, food prescriptions, and rituals to demonstrate their separation from the Hindus.[39] Ronald Miller (1976, 251) notes that in the pre-British period, Mappilas wore similar clothing to that of the Hindus. However, from the time British records were maintained, both Muslim men and women had adopted clothing that distinguished them from the other groups in society (see Innes 1951).

The development of the norm and practice of sequestering women was probably gradually institutionalized as a way of symbolizing and protecting the exclusivity and purity of the community. This in turn led to the formations of conceptions of gender different from those in the other communities. It is likely that this sequence of events accounts for the features of their ethnic structure—their separatist stance, greater solidarity, low education, their proclivity toward participation in the informal economy, their practice of sequestering women, early marriage, and their high fertility rates.

The Ethnicization of the Ezhavas

The position and identity of the Ezhavas changed dramatically during the colonial period. From an out-caste group, only a little above the slave castes, they escaped from many of their caste restrictions and gained access to the institutions and occupations which until then had been reserved for the higher castes. This was possible because of the relative economic prosperity and freedom from caste control that they obtained as a result of commercialization. Under the guidance of leaders like Narayana Guru, they brought about a concomitant change in their sociocultural structure. According to Jeffrey (1976, 146–147), "the growing Irava [Ezhava] aim, unstated but perceptible from the 1880s was to achieve the status of Nairs (Nayars) . . . and they took over several of the customs of the Nairs." Narayana Guru launched a crusade against untouchability and casteism with the slogan "One caste, one religion, one God for mankind." He rebelled against the domination of the Brahmins and the avarna (impure) status of the Ezhavas by installing *savarna* (pure or higher-status) deities in the low-caste temples, performing the worship rites himself and getting the other Ezhavas to do the same. He tried to *Sanskritize*[40] their practices and rituals and encouraged the aggressive pursuit of educational and occupational opportunities. Thus, the Ezhavas forged a new identity by the end of the colonial period. Due to their late access to educational and occupational opportunities, their educational levels were lower than that of the Syrian Christians, but unlike the Mappilas, they eagerly embraced these opportunities and were able to make rapid progress in a relatively short period of time. Some of the matrilocal and matrilineal practices were retained, but as a consequence of the reform movements, the Ezhavas gradually shifted toward a bilateral system of inheritance. Since women had long worked outside the home in this community, they also had some degree of autonomy and freedom.

The Ethnicization of the Syrian Christians

In the precolonial period, the Nazranis, like the Mappilas, were treated as quasi-Nayars and their culture and identity derived from the larger Hindu society. However, their ethnic identity as a distinct group began to develop under the Portuguese. Though the Portuguese did extirpate some of their Hindu practices, the rationale for the identity formation of the native Christians during this period was that they were a different type of Christians—Syrian or St. Thomas Christians. They considered themselves to be "Hindu in culture, Christian in religion and Oriental in worship" (Podipara 1973, 107). They took pride in continuing many of their traditional practices and in being different from the Portuguese. According to Susan Bayly, under early British colonialism (when the Syrians lost their role as warriors), they abandoned their martial tradition and adopted Brahminical rituals and vegetarianism. This, together with the patronage of the colonial state, drove a wedge between them and the Nayar population (Bayly 1989, 286). Their ceremonies and traditions gradually became Christianized versions of the Brahminical ones.[41]

The Brahminization of Syrian Christians manifested itself in the realm of gender by the strict separation between the male and female domains and the practice of such customs as prepubertal marriages. According to the 1901 census, the Syrian Christian community in southern Kerala had earlier and more universal marriage, higher fertility, and a shorter life span than the Hindus and Muslims in the area. Podipara (1973, 107) describes gender relationships among the Syrian Christians in the pre-twentieth century in this way: "In the house, women had separate quarters. Men and women would not eat together; husbands and wives were not an exception to this. Wives would not speak of their husbands mentioning them by their names . . . Grownup boys and girls would never go out together nor would talk together." At this time, the Syrian Christians were patrilineal and patrilocal and had an extended family system where all the family members lived on the ancestral property (though often in different households). Generational differences were also pronounced.[42] Several of these characteristics changed, but only in the late colonial period, after the turn of the twentieth century.[43]

The identification and alliance of Syrian Christians with the British led to their increasing participation in modern institutions. The higher levels of education necessitated by their large-scale participation in schools, colleges, and hospitals, the greater mobility brought about as a result of having to move for college education and jobs, and the opportunities for women's professional employment were probably responsible for the development of nuclear families, a higher age at marriage, greater egalitarianism in gender relationships, and the emphasis on education and professional training. A survey of male Syrian Christians in rural Kerala in the late 1950s found that the overwhelming majority of men (72 percent) preferred to live in nuclear households. The reason given by most of the men was "the freedom from interference by members of the family" (Kurian 1961, 55). A smaller majority of men (58 percent) surveyed agreed that women should take up careers if they had the time (p. 94). It is unlikely that any other Malayalee group would have given such high responses favoring nuclear families and women's employment in the 1950s.

Conclusion

The identities of the three groups which are the focus of the book—the Mappilas, the Syrian Christians, and the Ezhavas—were completely recast at critical junctures over the four-hundred-odd years of Western domination. Although the three groups identified themselves religiously as Muslim, Christian, and Hindu throughout this period, the meaning and content of that identity were completely different at different points of time. The redefined identities of these groups in turn were articulated through changed ideas regarding what was prestigious and honorable and were visibly manifested by new rituals, patterns of behavior, and clothing styles. These practices were gendered, and frequently the activities and physical appearance of women were modified to embody and symbolize these changes in group identity.

In the period preceding that of Western control, the Mappilas were wealthy and politically powerful Arab-Malayalee coastal traders practicing Islam, who were considered (and apparently considered themselves) honorary Nayars. By the late Portuguese period they had become a group of impoverished Malayalee peasants who practiced some aspects of Islam but still continued several of their earlier Hindu customs. The Mysorean Muslim rule initiated the process of group reconstruction, and resulted in the creation of a Malayalee Islamic identity by which the Mappilas sharply distinguished themselves from Malayalee Hindus. New types of rituals, clothing, and practices symbolized this change. This process was intensified during the British rule due to the discrimination they faced in this period. Thus, the oppositional orientation was emphasized even more, against Western Christian colonists and local Hindus. The Syrian Christian identity was similarly reconstructed from one where they were classified as a high-status Nayar subcaste with several special privileges, to an identification with Brahminism and the formulation of a "Hindu Christian" identity under the Portuguese, to a greater Westernization of their religion and social customs and a partial identification with the British in the late colonial period. And finally, the Ezhavas moved from being an "untouchable" group to developing some degree of social and political power, a far better economic position and a Sanskritized identity in the late colonial period.

In both the precolonial and colonial periods, economic and political compulsions were crucial in shaping the sequence and pattern of events. In the first part of the chapter, I briefly referred to the role of the politico-economic nexus in giving rise to the precolonial caste order. The Brahmins conferred legitimacy on the Kshatriyas (Kings) and thus increased their power and control over the society. In turn, the Kshatriyas bestowed economic favors and political protection on the Brahmins. The coalition between the Brahmins and the Kshatriyas was responsible for the gradual institutionalization of the oppressive social system characteristic of this area. I have also pointed out that kings frequently "created" castes, particularly those of warriors and traders. The position of the

Mappila Muslims and the Syrian Christians within the social order was also at least partly shaped by state action. Thus, in both the precolonial and colonial periods, it was the state that was the crucial determinant of the formation and transformation of societal stratification patterns. The material presented here also throws into doubt the distinction between the old or "natural" ethnicity and the new or "manufactured" type, since it has shown that the social formations of both the precolonial and colonial period were created and then naturalized over time.

From the evidence we also see that once cleavages have been developed, there is a tendency for the fault lines to persist even after the causal factors disappear, though the content of the ethnicity inevitably changes, generally in response to new economic or political factors. As Barth (1969) emphasized, boundary maintenance is the key factor in the division of society into ethnic groups. These boundaries are maintained over time (though they may be modified) and provide a certain continuity to the groups, even if the cultural content enclosed by the boundaries is completely transformed. Precolonial social divisions shaped the responses of the groups to the process of colonialism, and colonialism in turn had the effect of reifying and reformulating the larger caste and religious identities of the groups. The ethnic structures that were developed during this time continued to mediate and differentiate the behavior of the three communities in the postcolonial migration period.

CHAPTER 4

The Middle Eastern Migration from Kerala

Kerala is a small state (by Indian standards) occupying a narrow strip of land on the southwest coast of India with a total area of 15,000 square miles and a coast line of 360 miles. Physically, Kerala is one of the most distinctive areas in the country. The territory of the state falls into three natural divisions, running north to south—the highland, the midland, and the lowland. A long, high chain of mountains called the Western Ghats comprise the highland and effectively seal off the state from neighboring states on the east. A consequence has been that the region has been more exposed to foreign influences from overseas than to those from the rest of the subcontinent. There are only two significant passes in the entire range. The Ghats are covered by forests in the upper elevations and by tea and cardamom plantations in the lower regions. The midland is the primary agricultural region of the state, with rice, tapioca, spices, and cashew being the most important crops. In the slightly higher elevations where it meets the highland, pepper, rubber, ginger, and turmeric are grown. The lowland stretches along the coastal plain and the sandy landscape is covered by coconut palms. Kerala is a richly watered state, being intersected by forty-four rivers and having a continuous chain of lagoons and backwaters.

Economically and socially, Kerala has several unique features. According to the 1991 census, its population was twenty-nine million, and it was one of the most densely populated states in the country, with 655 persons per square kilometer, as against the all-India average of 216 persons. Kerala's high population density is particularly remarkable since it is largely agrarian and rural, with cash crop production and processing constituting its major source of income. The state also had the highest unemployment rate in the country,[1] and its per capita income of Rs. 2,371 (1987–1988) was much lower than the national average of Rs. 3,713 (Jeffrey 1993, 5).

On social indicators, however, Kerala has tended to do very well in comparison with the rest of the country. It reached a literacy level of 90.59 percent in 1991, whereas the national average was only 52.11 percent. Its life expectancy in 1991 was sixty-eight years as compared to fifty-seven for India as a whole. Similarly, the infant mortality rate (27 per thousand) and birth rate (22 per thousand) were much lower than the all-India figures (86 and 32 per thousand, respectively). The crude death rate was 7 per thousand, whereas the all-India rate was 12 per thousand.[2] Kerala was also the only state in which women outnumbered men (1040:1000). These unusual social statistics have made the state the subject of many studies aiming to dissect the reasons for the "Kerala model of development" (Jeffrey 1993, 4–9). As mentioned, the religious composition of Kerala is quite different from the rest of the country with a substantial proportion of Muslims (23.45 percent) and Christians (19.31 percent) in addition to Hindus (56.90 percent). Kerala is also the first place in the world where a communist government came to power (in 1957) through democratic elections. Ever since, communists have been an important power in the state, both in and out of elected office.

The rest of this chapter focuses directly on the Middle Eastern migration. In the next section, I discuss some of the many complicated ways in which the Gulf migration took place. This is important to understand, since one of the central differences among Veni, Cherur, and Kembu was that in each area, the dominant migration pattern was distinctive. In the final section I review some of the studies of the Gulf migration from Kerala. These studies give us an indication of the tremendous impact the migration has had on the state as a whole and also hint at some of the ethnic differences that I discuss in the rest of the book.

Routes to the Gulf

There are historical, economic, and social reasons for the large-scale international migration from Kerala. In the previous chapter, I discussed Kerala's long history of trade and foreign contact. As we will see, these trade routes were an important means through which the early migration to the Persian Gulf regions were initiated. Economically, Kerala has been largely agricultural and agro-processing based, with a negligible industrial sector. However, due to the tremendous population density of the state, land has been scarce, resulting in a very high unemployment rate. These two factors, coupled with relatively high educational levels, gave rise to strong "push" factors propelling migration. The large-scale international migration from Kerala began in the early twentieth century with the first migrants going mainly to Sri Lanka and Malaysia (Joseph 1988, 41).

While both historical and economic factors were important preconditions for the Middle Eastern migration, its spread and concentration in a few areas of the state (known locally as "Gulf pockets") was largely due to the functioning of social networks which resulted in chain migration. These networks worked particularly well in Kerala since the migration was mostly from rural communities.

In the early period of migration (1950s and 1960s), Middle Eastern migration was not regulated very much, but as the migration became institutionalized, Gulf countries imposed a variety of restrictions on migrants. Over time, the whole process of getting the necessary papers and clearances to enter the Gulf countries became tremendously complex because of the proliferation of intermediaries and types of visas granted—some legal and others illegal to differing degrees. Although it always had to be an Arab from the Middle East who issued the job contract or the sanction for a visa, after that a host of middle men took over, each pocketing a substantial cut of the "charges." In a highly oversimplified schema, there were three main types of work visas—the group visa, the individual visa, and the general visa.

The group visa was issued when groups of workers were recruited for a particular type of job or for a particular company. (In the latter case, the types of jobs for which visas were issued could run the whole range of the company's requirements—from managers to peons.) Migrants who went on this type of visa generally had less flexibility and were usually bound to the contract period, job, and sponsor. Also, the contract could not be renewed without the worker leaving the country for a specified period of time and then reentering.

Individual visas were for particular jobs, and while in practice, some could turn out to be as restrictive as the group visas, they were usually much more flexible. The length of stay and security of the position depended to a large extent on the nature of the work which could range from domestic help (such workers had special, time-limited visas and could not change their sponsor) to professionals such as doctors, engineers, lawyers, and nurses who had their contracts automatically renewed without having to leave the country and could therefore continue in their job for decades.

The general visa was theoretically not really a distinct type of visa, but turned out to be so in practice, being a visa for a nonexistent job. Typically, a Middle Eastern citizen would set up a fake organization and apply for a license to recruit a certain number of people. He then deputed someone to hire workers (who in turn subcontracted the task to another and so on down the chain). The workers went over on the contract for the fake organization but tried to get a real job once they got to the Gulf.[3] When they managed to get a formal, full-time position (which could sometimes take one or two years), they went to their original sponsor to get released from the contract. The sponsor was usually only happy to do so since he could then bring over other workers in their places.

In addition to these work visas, there were four main types of nonwork visas through which a person could get to a Gulf country. They were the *Haj* or

Umra visa for religious pilgrimages (to Saudi Arabia), the spouse visa, the visitor's visa, and the transit visa. Since these visas did not require most of the formalities connected with the work visas, the expenses connected with them were lower, except that they required the purchase of a round-trip ticket. Many aspiring migrants went to the Middle East on such nonwork visas and then tried to find a job during the permitted period of stay. If the person was unable to find a job during the time allowed, they generally continued to stay on illegally. This was a very common method of "migrating" to the Middle East, and most travel agencies that specialized in Gulf travel would refund a good portion of the unused return ticket.

In the late seventies, many cases in which Indian workers had been exploited in the Middle East came to light, and there was a public outcry. In response, the government of India imposed several restrictions on prospective migrants. Under these regulations, the migrant had to have an official job contract deed which was examined by a government agent. If the deed was found to be in order, a "No-Objection Certificate" (NOC) was issued. Then a surety had to be paid as a deposit (which was used to cover the return journey costs of the migrant if he or she was forcibly repatriated). But these governmental regulations only applied to those who went through the legal channels and also did not apply to professionals. In practice, there were many ways of avoiding these formalities. Often, the clearance certificate was forged. Or the person went on a nonwork visa (which did not require going through the above procedures).

There were two main ways in which Keralite migrants procured their visas—through relatives and friends working in the Gulf who contacted Middle Easterners directly or through recruitment agents.[4] The former was cheaper and less risky since every year thousands of potential migrants were duped by unscrupulous agents and sponsors. There were pitfalls at every step when a recruitment agent was involved. The agent could take the money and then vanish, or the documents of the migrant could be seized at the airport if they were suspected to be fake. Even if the migrant actually got to the Gulf without difficulty, he or she could find that the job that was promised did not exist, or was different from that promised, or paid much less than specified on the contract. Tales of such deception abounded.[5]

This is why having a personal connection with the intermediary was so important. Even if the migrant relied on an agent, going through someone known to be reliable could make the difference between getting a job which would pull the family out of poverty or forfeiting the large sum of money borrowed for the migration. Having people to stay with and to turn to for help in the initial period of job hunting in the host country was also a factor differentiating successful and unsuccessful migrants.

The uncertainties did not end even after a job was obtained. The conditions of work, and the amount and regularity with which the salary was paid, were subject to the pleasure of the Arab sponsor. There were many cases in which workers were ill treated or were not paid at all for months at a time, or were not paid the full amount promised.[6] However, if the Arab sponsor happened to be particularly pleased with the worker, the latter could rise to very high positions, irrespective of education and qualifications. I heard of several cases, where for instance, a peon had eventually worked his way up to becoming the manager of the concern.

Migrants could also set up businesses in the Middle East with the restriction that the business had to be in the name of an Arab partner who had to be given a majority of the profits. Typically, the Arab received 51 percent of the profits. Such Arabs were called "sleeping partners" since they generally let the migrant do all the work. Muslim workers sometimes had an advantage over non-Muslims, particularly in such business partnerships, since many Arab sponsors preferred to employ a fellow Muslim. In short, therefore, initiating the process of Gulf migration was a little like participating in a lottery. However, the odds of success varied greatly and depended on a host of factors, some of which I have discussed in this section (see also Nambiar 1995, 76–110).

Studies of the Gulf Migration from Kerala

Almost all of the studies of the Gulf phenomenon in Kerala have focused primarily on the economic aspects of the migration. I have pointed out that the survey studies which examined the economic impact of Gulf migration on villages, districts, and Kerala as a whole were designed on the assumption that the typical migrant went on a legal contract, for one particular job with a fixed monthly "salary," that the entire amount saved was remitted to the immediate family at regular intervals through banks, and that this amount represented the total monetary benefit gained through the migration.[7] Consumption patterns of migrant households were examined through questions which asked how much of the monthly income was spent on fixed categories such as food, clothing, fuel and light, education, and so forth (see Government of Kerala 1987; Prakash 1978). Again, in trying to determine the manner in which the remittance had been used, some studies (e.g., the Commerce Research Bureau 1978) looked at the physical asset position but excluded the financial.[8] From my research it was clear that few of the migrants or their households fit the generic migrant model on which these questionnaires were based. Thus the studies were inappropriately operationalized due to a lack of understanding of the way in which the Gulf migration took place in a majority of the emigrant communities in Kerala. It is likely that the conclusions based on such assumptions were inaccurate and that the policy directions were correspondingly misdirected. The focus on generalization also meant that crucial variations among groups were missed.

Data from survey studies (Government of Kerala 1987,[9] Gulati and Mody 1983, National Family Health Survey 1992,[10] and the most recent, the Kerala Migration Study 1998[11]) of the Gulf migrants in Kerala indicate that they were overwhelmingly male (92.5 percent), young (half were 25 years or younger), married (81 percent), poorly educated (70 percent had less than ten years of education), and unskilled (73 percent).[12] Thirty-six percent of them were unemployed at the time of their departure, and another 19 percent were self-employed (Goverment of Kerala 1987, 18–19). Almost half of the migrants were Muslim (as compared to 23 percent in the general population), a third were Hindu (compared to 57 percent), and about a fifth were Christian (roughly equal to the general population figures [Banerjee, Jayachandran, and Roy 1997, 5; Government of Kerala 1987, 9]). While most of the migrants hailed from lower-middle-income families, there were very few scheduled castes (former slave castes) and tribes in the group—only 1 percent according to the survey, whereas they comprised 12 percent of the state population (Government of Kerala 1987, 9). Since expatriate workers were allowed to stay in the Gulf only for the period of their contracts, the migration was strictly short term. The contracts could be renewed, or new ones obtained, so several migrants did manage to migrate for ten to twenty years or even longer, but the average length of stay was around seven years (Zachariah, Mathew, and Rajan 1999, 12).

Migration was an expensive venture. According to the Kerala Migration Study of 1998, the average migrant from Kerala spent Rs. 44,000, more than twice the annual income of most white-collar workers. They also estimated that on average, the cost of the ticket was Rs. 13,000, the visa fee was Rs. 32,000 and the agent's commission was Rs. 14,000. The study found that about 27 percent of the migrants raised the funds for meeting emigration costs from family savings, 50 percent borrowed the money from relatives, 60 percent took institutional loans, and 40 percent sold gold ornaments and jewelry. Only a small percentage sold land. As is clear from the figures, most migrants used more than one source of funding (Zachariah, Mathew, and Rajan 1999, 7).

The Government of Kerala survey found that when compared to nonmigrant households, migrant households obtained about 60 percent of their total income from remittances, had larger houses with more amenities, more than twice the income, almost twice the amount of land holdings, and three times the amount of gold and jewelry. Expenditure patterns were also different between the two groups with the biggest difference being the proportion of money spent on marriages and other ceremonies (Government of Kerala 1987).[13] Thus 18.6 percent of the expenditure in Gulf households fell in this category, compared to only 9.3 percent for nonmigrant households (Government of Kerala 1987, 16).[14] The Kerala Migration Study found that migrant households also possessed far more consumer durables than their nonmigrant counterparts (Zachariah, Mathew, and Rajan 1999, 21–22).

Another state-level sample survey on the Gulf migration was conducted by P.R.G. Nair in 1984 (Nair 1987b). The sample consisted of 696 returned migrants selected from eleven localities (eight rural and three urban) located in the five districts of Kerala which had the largest concentration of migrant households. The study has an interesting comparison between "successful" and "unsuccessful" migrants, success being measured mainly by economic criteria. Accordingly, 21 percent of his sample were deemed "highly successful," 45 percent "moderately successful," 26 percent "non-gainers" and 8 percent "failures." Surprisingly, there was no difference in the family backgrounds (in terms of occupation and education, religion was not a variable considered) between the highly successful and the failures, according to the criteria selected. Both groups of migrants came from rural areas and from poor families with little education. This sample of returned migrants consisted of 78 percent Muslims, 12.2 percent Hindus, and 9.8 percent Christians. The dominance of Muslims in the sample (who, as I argue, manifested one type of migration and remittance pattern) could explain why family background differences turned out to be insignificant.

The successful migrants were slightly better educated (high school and above compared with no education or only a primary school education among the unsuccessful group), had work experience before migrating, migrated early (before 1975) through the help of friends or relatives, and stayed longer (over seven years compared to one and a half years for the unsuccessful group), had good relationships with their employers, worked in more than one job (going back again after their first contracts expired), had relatives and friends in the host country to fall back upon, and had their finances efficiently managed at home, and thus were able to work in the Gulf until they reached retirement age.

The consequences were also very different for successful and unsuccessful migrants. Successful migrants were able to remit a large amount home, which in turn enabled them to repay their debts, purchase land and construct a house, acquire consumer durables, and provide the amenities necessary for the house. In addition, they could get their sisters and daughters married and invest in an income-generating activity while still having a substantial cash balance. They were also able to send several of their family members for employment to the Gulf. Unsuccessful migrants were not able to achieve most of these goals.

The socio-psychological consequences were also correspondingly positive for successful migrants—stronger family relationships, greater attention to the needs of children, and an increase in social prestige. Successful migrants were older (44.4 years compared to 34.5 years for the unsuccessful group) and lived in their own houses in nuclear families (average size 5.21 compared to 9.24 of the unsuccessful migrant who continued to live in the parental home).

Community Differences in the Survey Studies

Raju Kurian has made an interesting comparison between the migration patterns from Elakamon village, which was in the same region as Cherur, and Koipram village near Tiruvalla, which was close to Kembu. His study corroborates many of the differences in migration patterns that I found between Cherur and Kembu. Although Kurian does not refer to differences in religio-ethnic background between the two areas, we can infer from the location of the two villages that the migrants from Elakamon were predominantly Hindu and probably largely from the Ezhava caste and that those from Koipram were predominantly Syrian Christian (Kurian, 1978).

According to Kurian, migrants from Koipram had a better premigration economic position and a much higher educational level (87.85 percent of the migrants had at least completed high school and 50 percent were college educated; in Elakamon only 33.86 percent of the migrants had completed high school). He also points out that the villagers from Koipram had a much longer tradition of international migration (beginning from the first part of the twentieth century), and greater exposure to the world outside the village (due to the fact that many had gone to other parts of India for higher education and jobs). As a consequence of these cumulative advantages, most of the Koipram migrants did not have to pay for their visas (77.79 percent) and even those who did pay parted with relatively smaller amounts. Compare this with the situation in Elakamon where 75.47 percent had to pay for their visas and frequently with fairly large amounts. The other expenses connected with the migration were higher for the migrants from Elakamon, and a large proportion had to borrow money for these expenses at high rates of interest.

The following table shows the differences between the two areas with respect to the type of jobs obtained in the Gulf.

Elakamon had almost no professional or semiprofessional migrants (1.60 percent) while almost 23 percent of the migrants from Koipram fell in this category. Again, only about 4 percent of the migrants from Koipram obtained unskilled jobs in the Middle East, compared to 32.26 percent in Elakamon. P.R.G. Nair, who compiled educational data from several case studies, also indicates that 35.10 percent of the migrants from Koipram were "Postgraduate, Engineers, Doctors, etc." (1986a, 72).

TABLE 4.1   *Occupation of Migrants in the Middle East*

Occupation	Elakamon Number	Percentage	Koipram Number	Percentage
Unskilled	20	32.26	3	4.06
Skilled	24	38.71	16	21.62
Professional and semi-professional	1	1.61	17	22.97
Clerical and other white-collar work	13	20.97	23	31.08
Teachers	—	—	7	9.46
Own business	—	—	1	1.35
Unknown	4	6.45	7	9.46
Total	62	100.00	74	100.00

Source: Kurian 1978, 43, table 3.3.

Nair's statewide survey (Nair 1986a) has some data on the differences between Hindu, Christian, and Muslim migrants. Christian migrants were generally older and were much better qualified and educated. Seventy-one percent of Christians had at least a high school education compared to 37 percent of Hindus and 16 percent of Muslims. Again, 26.5 percent of the Christian migrants had a professional or technical degree compared to 6.8 percent of the Hindus and only 3.2 percent of the Muslim migrants. The Christians also had the smallest households and the most amount of land and assets prior to migration, while the Muslims had the largest households and least amount of assets prior to migration. Paradoxically, however, in terms of annual income in the premigration period, the order was reversed with the Muslims having the highest amount and the Christians the least. The author indicates that there was no clear explanation for this pattern. Thus, though this survey sampled migrants from all over the state, we can see that the broad characteristics of the migrants conform to the community-level differences presented in chapter 1 between Veni, Kembu, and Cherur.

A recent survey (the Kerala Migration Study of 1998) also paid some attention to community differences, and the authors conclude, "Among the factors associated with migration, community status is one of the most powerful. If one is a Muslim, one's chance of emigration is 2.2 times (49 percent) the general average (22 percent). . . . Viewed from another angle, more than one-half the number of emigrants were Muslims and 13 percent Ezhavas, 12 percent Syrian Christians, 8 percent Latin Catholics and 8 percent Nairs. The Scheduled Castes constituted only 1.4 percent" (Zachariah, Mathew, and Rajan 1999, 16). They also note that the distribution of migrants by community varied considerably across districts in Kerala and that Muslims were the dominant emigrant group in the north, Syrian Christians in the south-central regions, and Ezhavas and Muslims in the south (Zachariah, Mathew, and Rajan 1999, 16).

The Impact of Gulf Migration

Since economists have studied the Gulf migration, not surprisingly, the focus has been on the economic consequences of the migration. Remittances to the state have been difficult to calculate for many reasons.[15] I have mentioned that the estimates of annual remittances have ranged from Rs. 5 billion (Nair 1987, 20) to Rs. 10.14 billion (Nair 1994, 109) and that it contributed from 22 to 28 percent of the state domestic product. According to some calculations, the percentage was as high as 50 in 1983, which was the peak year for remittances.[16] This is an extremely impressive figure and must have had major impact on the economy of the state, particularly given its small industrial base. However, the problem about actually assessing this is that Kerala is only a state within India. The foreign exchange earned and the bank deposits that accrue in the state are credited to the nation as a whole. Similarly, the remittances may not be utilized within Kerala. Perhaps for these reasons, the remittances seem to have had little effect on the various statewide economic indices of the eighties. Economist P.R.G. Nair summarizes the above issue by stating:

> [T]he available evidence suggests that migration and the resultant receipt of remittances do not seem to have made any significant [positive] impact on the economic growth rate of the state economy. Nor did they have substantial effect on employment rates, labor market conditions, agricultural development and industrialization. It would appear then that the major part of the remittances which flowed into Kerala seeped into other regions of India through the mechanism of trade in consumption goods and construction materials caused by the changes in consumption patterns and the 'boom' in the house construction sector. (Nair 1989, 344)[17]

However, in a more recent article, B. A. Prakash (1998) argues that "since the mid 1970s, the factor which had the greatest impact on [the] regional economy, especially on [the] labour market, consumption, savings, investment, poverty, income distribution and economic growth, has been the Gulf migration and migrant remittances."

Surprisingly, the unemployment rates, which were already high, continued to increase during the Gulf boom period.[18] However, wage rates also rose— very rapidly for the construction workers (the rates of increase between 1978 and 1983 were almost twice as high as in the preceding five years) and slowly for agricultural workers (Nair 1989, 353).[19] During the decade 1975–1976 to 1986–1987, agricultural production in Kerala registered a dramatic decline with a negative growth of –0.60 percent as compared to a growth rate of 3.20 percent in the fifteen years preceding this period (Oommen 1991, 11). This was, at least indirectly, due to the exodus to the Gulf. As a consequence of the migration and the increased demand for housing, land prices skyrocketed, particularly in the migrant areas, so a lot of agricultural land was converted into housing sites.[20] In addition, as mentioned, wage rates also registered a major increase, so many who did continue cultivation converted to perennial, and less labor intensive, crops like rubber and coconut palm.

While the agricultural and industrial sectors stagnated in the migration period, the tertiary sector, especially transport (number of motor vehicles), trade, hotels and restaurants, banking, and real estates, showed a rapid growth rate (Kannan 1990, 1952). K. P. Kannan argues that this had deleterious results since, unlike the normal pattern of growth, the expansion of the tertiary sector was unrelated to the developments in the primary and secondary sectors. The rapid increase in private-sector savings that came about due to the migration ended up being invested in the high-yield/quick-return speculative financial activities[21] rather than in the productive sectors, further distorting the pattern of economic development in the state (Kannan 1990).[22]

With respect to consumption, Nair's report has this to say:

Sample surveys conducted on the consumer expenditure of households suggest that there has taken place substantial reduction in the degree of inequality in the distribution of households according to per capita expenditure of consumption during the period 1977–1978 to 1983. In 1977–78, 21.16 percent of households had a monthly per capita expenditure of less than Rs. 40. In 1983, only 5.42 percent of the households had a monthly per capita expenditure of less than Rs. 60. Such reduction could be attributed mainly to the fact that the remittances have accrued in Kerala largely to the lower income households. (Nair 1989, 356)[23]

The Kerala Migration Study also indicates that international migration "has had a very significant impact on the proportion below the poverty line. The proportion declined by over 3 percentage points as a result of remittances received by the Kerala households from their kith and kin abroad." The authors note that this decline was largest among Muslims (six percentage points) followed by Ezhavas and Latin Catholics (Zachariah, Mathew, and Rajan 2000, 29). Zachariah and his coauthors seem to feel that, on balance, the effect of migration on Kerala was positive and that migration should therefore be seen as "an unconventional path to development." They point out that in the late nineties, migration was Kerala's "most productive 'industry' employing nearly two million persons directly and seven to eight million family members indirectly. Its spin-off effects extend to every facet of life in Kerala, and even outside Kerala to the producers of consumer goods and construction materials all over India. Migrant remittances in 1998 were about 4 billion, about 10 percent of the state's GDP. . . about four times the export earnings from the state's seafood industries and seven times that from export of spices . . . the two most acclaimed export sectors in Kerala." They conclude that the state therefore needed to support the migration at least as much as it supported other industries (Zachariah, Mathew, and Rajan 2000, 46).

During my stay in Kerala, I was able to see some of the many ways in which the Gulf migration had affected the state as a whole. At the time of my fieldwork, the state seemed to be in the grip of a strong consumerist orientation. Foreign goods, once considered exotic and elitist, had become widespread and were deemed a necessity to maintain a basic status in society. There was an explosion in the ownership of consumer durables such as cars, televisions, and music systems, as well as refrigerators, blenders, and electric irons. The proliferation of VCR's had given rise to a tremendous market in illegally copied video movies. Pornographic films also glutted the video rental shops. Even people living in small thatched huts owned some of these gadgets. Many a time I have walked into such a home to find the family preparing or eating a frugal meal to the blare of music from a shiny boombox, replete with dancing LED indicators.

The rising expectations regarding material standards of living made it difficult for the average nonmigrant to keep up and had only increased his or her feeling of deprivation and frustration.[24] Dowry rates had skyrocketed (see also Gulati 1983, 1987) as had the expenses connected with marriage and other life-cycle rituals and festivals. Thus, the female child was beginning to be viewed as a tremendous burden to the family.

Food patterns were also affected with a shift away from many of the traditional home-grown tubers such as cassava and yams, fruits such as mangoes, papayas, and jack fruits, and vegetables such as drumsticks and different kinds of greens (all of which came to be viewed as low prestige foods) to a diet with greater amounts of ghee (clarified butter), sweets,[25] and meat.[26]

The Gulf migration permeated the popular culture of the state. The Gulf theme was portrayed in many of the films made in the past few decades. Even many films that did not deal with the theme as its central focus had at least one character who was a Gulf migrant. The migrant's vanities and pretensions were often the butt of jokes, but the films also portrayed the shattered dreams of the unsuccessful migrant, the stresses his family faced, the break-up of relationships, and his children's waywardness. These issues were the central focus of many of the Malayalam novelists and playwrights and many popular songs. An old genre of "letter songs" had been revived, using the Gulf theme. The songs would generally portray the lonely, love-lorn wife of a migrant pouring out her feelings in a "letter" to her husband, and the poignant reply of the husband.[27] (Some migrants did in fact send cassettes to their families instead of letters.)

As may be expected, the Gulf migration had a tremendous psychological impact on the migrants and their families. The Kerala Migration Study estimates that, in 1998, as many as a million married women (one out of eight) were living apart from their husbands due to the migration of the latter (Zachariah, Mathew, and Rajan 2000, 2). The study found that wives of Gulf migrants rated loneliness as the biggest problem they faced, followed by "added responsibilities," "adverse effect on children's education," "debt incurred to finance emigration," "increased anxiety" and the fact that the financial gains of the migration were not "up to expectations" (Zachariah, Mathew, and Rajan 2000, 40).

During my fieldwork in Kerala, I learned that many "Gulf wives" (particularly the young wives of migrants) exhibited a characteristic set of psychosomatic complaints labeled the "Gulf syndrome" since it manifested itself in the Gulf pockets (both in Kerala and in Pakistan). In Trichur district (which had the highest number of migrants to the Middle East), a psychiatrist was reported to have observed that "almost every second family which has a relative in the Gulf has a history of mental illness" (Gulati 1986, 210). This may be an unsubstantiated claim, but the presence of this syndrome in Kerala and Pakistan has been extensively noted.[28] It was also reported that the children of Gulf families were becoming delinquents and turning to alcohol and drugs (Nair 1986, 102). Again, this is a sweeping charge, but from my own observations, I can verify that this was true in a minority of cases.

Leela Gulati's (1993) in-depth study of ten women whose husbands were in the Middle East documents the profound and often poignant consequences of the migration for women. Of the ten, five were Muslim, four Hindu, and one Christian. Although she indicates that "religious diversity was, frankly speaking, the least important aspect of our selection" and that the aim of the study was to collect "stories of families as different as possible from each other" (Gulati 1993, 22), her own material demonstrates that the religion of the household was an important factor affecting the migration and its impact on women. Almost all the women refer (at least in passing) to the way their religious and caste background shaped aspects of their life such as their age at marriage, educational status, physical mobility outside the home, income-generating activity, relations with their husband and his family, and the likelihood and organization of the migration.

Conclusion

This chapter presented an overview of the Gulf migration from the state as a whole—the variety of ways it took place and some of its consequences. We also saw that even the studies that were not explicitly focused on community differences in migration patterns were still able to document some of these striking variations. It is not surprising that a phenomenon that has affected about 23 percent of households (Banerjee, Jayachandran, and Roy 1997, 3), and contributed up to 50 percent of the income of the state, should have a major impact on the economy, society, and culture of the state. These impacts were even greater in the high migrant areas where 60 to 90 percent of the households had participated in the migration at one time or another. In the following chapters, we will look at three such areas—Veni in the north, Kembu in south-central Kerala, and Cherur in the south.

CHAPTER 5

Ethnicity and Migration in Veni

STRENGTHENING SOLIDARITY AND THE JOINT FAMILY

$\mathcal{T}$he organization of migration and remittance flows in Veni provides a vivid illustration of how ethnicity shapes community behavior. What was distinctive about this region was that the process of migration increased and strengthened social networks and enhanced ethnic solidarity. Male migration also strengthened the extended family since males needed the help of relatives to finance their ventures and to look after their wives and children while they were away. This chapter focuses primarily on describing the complicated migration patterns of the villagers and the impact of the migration on the women left behind.

Like most of the other Gulf pockets in Kerala, Veni experienced dramatic changes as a consequence of the Middle Eastern migration. Every older person I met talked about how different life had been in the premigration period. After a brief overview of the historical background of the region, I present a profile of Veni, before the large-scale migration to the Middle East, to set the stage for the subsequent developments.

Veni is in the Mappila heartland of Malappuram district in northern Kerala. At the time of my fieldwork, the administrative village was very large—over eighteen square kilometers according to the 1981 census—but my study was confined to three subsections of Veni, each of which could be described as a social community. Part of these areas fell within the administrative boundary of adjoining villages. The population consisted mainly of Muslims (around 85 percent),[1] most of whom belonged to the orthodox Sunni sect.

In the colonial period, Veni was part of the Ernad taluk of the province of Malabar. Malabar, as I have explained, came under the direct control of the British and suffered from their land policies. Ernad was the only taluk where

Mappilas outnumbered the Hindus. Despite this, only two Mappilas (1.8 percent) were numbered among the principal landowners, most of whom were Brahmins (54.9 percent) and Nayars (38 percent) (Radhakrishnan 1989, 39, table 2.3). Most Mappila peasants were impoverished and near-famine conditions prevailed frequently. Thus, Ernad had long been a center for the Mappila uprisings. The rebellion of 1921 broke out in a town which was only a few kilometers from Veni, and peasants from Veni and the neighboring villages marched there to fight against the British forces. The rebellion was brutally crushed and the area around Veni bore the brunt of the aftermath. Thousands of Mappilas (estimates indicate figures of three thousand to ten thousand) were killed, and thousands more were sent to prison (estimated at between fourteen thousand to twenty thousand). Fines were collected from at least five thousand others suspected of involvement in the rebellion. Mappila women suffered at the hands of soldiers, and the countryside was ravaged (Miller 1992, 148–150).

The economic impoverishment and political harassment that the Mappilas experienced during the colonial period caused them to turn inward, rejecting Western culture and institutions, such as secular education (which was deemed to be Satanic), modern medicine, and the bureaucracy, which were identified with the British (see also Miller 1992, 157). Thus, in the late nineteenth century, Ernad taluk had "the unenviable distinction of being the most illiterate taluk in the district" with a literacy rate of 15 percent among males and 3.3 percent among females (Innes 1951, 296). Although the Mappilas comprised about half of the population of Malabar,[2] in 1911, only 486 Mappilas were literate in English, compared to 5,895 Nayars and 2,897 Ezhavas (Panikkar 1989, 54). Most Mappilas were given only religious education. K. N. Panikkar (1989) points out that this had significant ideological and social implications: "First, the early socialization of the Mappilas was dominantly within a religious framework and, secondly, a professional middle class hardly emerged among them. Consequently, they tended to remain within the parameters of religious ideology and to submit to the guidance and leadership of traditional intellectuals" (1989, 54–55).[3] It is also likely that the Mappilas did not have the skills or the desire to participate in the formal sector. All of these factors led to the development of a tightly knit community with a strong corporate identity, a high degree of group solidarity, and relative social egalitarianism. According to Ronald Miller (1992, 221), the Mappila "resistance" to modern education was gradually overcome from the 1950s. By the early seventies, the educational levels in Veni had picked up a little, and boys were sent to school for around five years and girls for around three to four.

Socioeconomic Profile, 1950–1975

This was an area of dire poverty, particularly in the early decades of the century as one disaster followed another. After the 1921 rebellion and its aftermath came the Great Depression of the thirties and then the Second World War.

The situation improved a little after India became independent in 1947. The land reforms of the Kerala government (in the 1960s) also alleviated the situation to some extent. Mohammed Ali Haaji, an elderly villager in Veni, put this very eloquently: "Before 1940, smoke rose only from about ten out of fifty houses. From 1940 to 1960 most houses had at least one meal of rice (if they had anything else during the day, it was *kanji* [rice gruel]). From 1970, there was rice two times. And now, there is hardly any real poverty here anymore."[4]

Until around the early 1970s, much of Veni was covered by scrub jungle and inhabited by wolves. There were only a few *pucca* houses (with concrete walls and tiled roofs). Most people lived in *katcha* huts (with mud walls and thatched roofs). Many slept in the open or under shop awnings. Veni was comprised mainly of petty business people and agricultural laborers, with a few wealthier businessmen and middle-range landlords. The village was an important regional node in the wholesale trade of agricultural produce. Thus, agriculture and the trade of agricultural products formed the main source of income for the villagers. Most households cultivated the land around the house, rotating ginger, a variety of rice, and cassava in a three-year cycle. Coconut and arecanut were grown, and there was some paddy cultivation. There was no school in the area and just one ayurvedic dispensary. Buses to and from Veni were very infrequent, and there were just a few shops in the market.

Dr. Narayan, a Hindu and the first medical doctor in the area, described the situation in the fifties: "When we first came here in 1954, the people were so poor. There were only little huts around. And we would often see people walking around in wet clothes since they had only one set and they wore it again immediately after washing. And the kind of illnesses I saw! Of course, then people would come to me only as a last resort, after everything else failed. My wife was miserable here in the first few years and cried a lot."

The poverty and political oppression that the region experienced forced many of the young men in the village to migrate to other parts of the Indian subcontinent in search of employment right from the turn of the century.[5] According to Abu Bekr, another elderly resident: "The Mappila is a born migrant. We have long had the habit of jumping into a train when things here got difficult." Their low education and social marginality meant that Mappila migrants could only obtain work in unskilled or semiskilled jobs. The ethnic networks that were built up over time facilitated the continuing migration of villagers into such occupations. People from Veni specialized largely in hotel and bakery work. A few managed to work their way up, to become the managers or owners of these concerns. The typical pattern was that the men would leave their families behind in the care of their parents or relatives. Thus a tradition of migration was established from the first few decades of the century.

Since religion had become the fulcrum of group identity for the Mappilas in the colonial and immediate postcolonial period, the social structure and culture of Veni was shaped by its own brand of Islam, which mixed elements from the Arabic tradition and the local folk culture. According to Miller, "Devotion to Islam may be isolated as the key element" of the Mappila community. He continues, "Before anything else, the Mappila is a Muslim" (1992, 226–227).[6] However, he points out that the idea of what "Muslim" meant had been changing (1992, 224). The main tenets of Islam—the daily prayers, the Friday worship service at the mosque, the Ramadan fasting, and the festivals—were observed.[7] All children were sent to the madrasa for at least a few years. The Mappilas held saints—both living and dead—in high regard and periodically visited the shrines of important saints to make an offering, utter a prayer, or make a vow (Miller 1992, 243). Members of certain Tangal families were also believed to have special powers for physical and mental healing. In addition to the traditional Muslim festivals, the Mappilas celebrated *nercha(s)*—special festivals connected with particular localities and mosques.[8]

Although relationships with individual Hindus were harmonious, even cordial, there was still a strong feeling of community exclusivity and of communal solidarity. A "minority" consciousness was deeply rooted, characterized by hostility and suspicion of non-Muslim "outsiders," particularly government representatives (see Miller 1992, 309).[9] The local Mappila dialect, which was often blended with Arabic, was rather different from the standard Malayalam, though many could speak the latter with ease.[10] Mappilas in Veni followed the Islamic calendar.

Like the other subgroups in Kerala, the Mappila social identity was visibly manifested by their distinctive clothing and adornment style. Mappila men wore a *mundu* (sarong) like their Hindu counterparts. However, they wore it from left to right instead of right to left like the Hindus. Their hair was cut very close to the scalp. Mappila women traditionally wore a dark blue *mundu* and a long blouse, with a black scarf covering their hair. Another distinctive characteristic was that they wore five to eight gold earrings in the helix of their ears, in addition to the earrings worn in the ear lobe.

Scholars have described Mappilas as having a five-fold caste structure (D'Souza 1978, 41–56). At the apex were the *Tangals,* a small group that traced its ancestry to the Prophet. The *Arabis* were also a small group concentrated mainly in a particular area. They claimed to be descendants of Arabs and had retained their Arab lineage. The main body of the Mappilas were called *Malabaris* (people of Malabar). Below them were the *Pusalars* or "new Muslims," also known as *Mukkuvar* (fisherfolk). They were the converts from among Hindu fisherfolk. The *Ossans* were the barbers and were ranked the lowest in the caste hierarchy. Their women folk acted as midwives and as singers for occasions like weddings. I had read about these caste structures but when I asked the villagers whether there were any caste groups in Veni, they told me that except for some barbers in the area, all the Mappilas were of the same caste. It took me some time to verify this, but I learnt that Veni was comprised entirely of Malabaris and a few Ossans.

Since I wanted to study the impact of the Gulf migration on the caste system, I also went to Pullad, a high migrant coastal area where caste distinctions were very clear. In such areas, there was a distinct separation between the fisherfolk (the Pusalars) who were considered "low caste" and the others, the "good caste" (Malabaris). The two groups lived in different areas though very close to each other—the fisherfolk on the seashore and the higher-status group a little more to the interior. In the particular area that I studied, the two groups were known as "Ten" and "Eleven," with the fisherfolk being "Ten." "Eleven" consisted of several proprietors of fishing equipment and owners of coir (coconut fiber) industries. Males of the "Ten" group fished in the fishing season and took up other "coolie" (unskilled labor) jobs during the lean period. The women worked in the coir industry. Thus there was frequently a patron-client relationship between the "Eleven" and the "Ten." However, in the premigration period, there was little social intermingling and no intermarriages between the two groups.

At the household level, Veni was characterized by the presence of joint families (usually comprising of an older couple and at least one or two of their married sons and their families, besides unmarried children and divorced or widowed daughters), and a large number of children per couple (around seven to eight on average). The older generation was held in great reverence and respect. Due to the joint family system, parents maintained economic and social control over their children and their families. The family system was male dominated, and women had a markedly subordinate position. The Koranic injunction of female seclusion was held as the ideal but was practiced mainly by the upper classes. Education (except Islamic studies) was not deemed necessary for women since, in the words of Fatima, a woman in her fifties, "What use is education for someone whose sole task is kitchen work?" Normatively, young women were not permitted to go out—except perhaps to the neighboring house—and certainly never alone. Many villagers, however, were very poor, and in such families the women were forced out of necessity to go out seeking work (transplanting agricultural crops, gathering grass for cows, dehusking arecanuts, and so forth).

Marriages were arranged (a general feature in the Indian society at large) and, particularly among the wealthy, took place very early—sometimes even before the girl attained puberty. Among poorer families, girls were married later, since their income contributed to the upkeep of the household and because it also took longer for the family to save enough to conduct the wedding. Dowries were given, but this seems to have been more of a token gift in the early period, perhaps because most of the villagers were poor. The young couple lived with the man's family until the house became overcrowded (which did not take too long since fertility levels were high), at which point they set up another household, usually in an adjacent plot of land. As is common in the case of joint families, the personal relationship between spouses was normatively weak, especially during the early years of marriage.[11] Their lives were lived in two completely separate domains with neither being much aware of the activities of the other. They were not supposed to speak to each other in public, and it was considered shameful to "go out under the same umbrella," in other words, to be seen outside together. While polygamy was not very widespread, divorces (usually initiated by the husband) were easy and fairly frequent. The man was often advised by his parents to dissolve his marriage if they did not approve of his wife. The villagers explained, "The girl, being barely more than a child, often did not know how to behave 'decorously,' and the boy was also very young with no financial or social autonomy at that stage." Most divorced men remarried quickly. A smaller proportion of the women (mostly the wealthy) remarried.

Middle- and upper-class women spent their days doing (or supervising) the housework and taking care of children. They generally did not even have the autonomy to select the food to be cooked. Khadija, a middle-aged woman, reminisced, "If and when the men brought provisions back to the house, we would cook them." Even women's clothes were bought by the men of the household. The position of women gradually improved as they grew older, and by middle age, the mother was a formidable moral presence in the household. Her sons, and even her husband to some extent, generally deferred to her advice on familial matters. A Koranic injunction, "Heaven lies at the feet of the mother" reinforced her authority and was cited to me as justification for the power of the matriarch.

In contrast to the relationships between men and women, relationships between individuals of the same sex were very close, particularly for men. In general, men never stayed at home even if they were not working. They would instead go to the marketplace and "hang out" with their male friends, returning home only late at night. Women did not have the opportunity to develop many friendships with other women since they could not leave the house as freely. However, there was often a strong bond of solidarity and affection between sisters-in-law.

The Gulf Migration Pattern

Early Migrants

The ethnic structure of Veni, described above, fundamentally shaped the migration patterns from this region. There had long been trade between this region and the Middle East.[12] The common heritage and Islamic identity that the Arab traders and local Muslims shared resulted in a special relationship between the two groups. News of work opportunities in the Gulf spread through this connection, and most of the early migration occurred with the Muslims taking illegal passage on the merchant launches of the Arabs. Possibly the Islamic bond and the venturesome migratory tradition of the Mappilas led the men of Veni to take the risk of going to an unknown country. The first migrants from Veni to the Gulf (around five in all) went as early as the mid–1950s through this route.

Kunjukutty *Haaji* (honorific name taken by men who completed the Haj pilgrimage), one of the earliest migrants from the area recounted,

> I migrated in 1955 after several unsuccessful attempts at setting up businesses, here in Veni and then in Bombay. I left without telling anyone at home, using the money I had earned in Bombay for the passage (which cost Rs. 500 then). The launch was crowded with people and we had a long and uncomfortable journey with very little food and water. The launch dropped us off in the shallow sea at Abu Dhabi and we then had to swim to shore. I got to the market place and found some Malayalees there. They come running when they see a Malayalee looking person appearing and offer food and a place to stay to the newcomer.

These migrants in turn sponsored others from the village once their position was legalized, or at least provided indirect impetus for further migration through their economic success. The early migrants faced difficult conditions in the Middle East and had to work hard for very little pay. Kunjukutty Haaji continued: "In the first few years, my shops would keep getting pulled down by the local municipality for town improvement schemes. What did I do then? Why, I would rent another place and start again."

Many of the migrants first worked as "houseboys" (domestic workers) and over time managed to set up their own businesses (with an Arab "sleeping partner"). Several did well for themselves. Most of the rags to riches stories were from migrants in this pioneer group. The large-scale migration started from the mid–1970s. In late 1989, when I conducted my fieldwork, there were Gulf migrants in around 50 percent of the households in the areas of Veni that I studied.

The lack of education and the illegal nature of the entry of many of the Mappila migrants into Middle Eastern society (see also Nambiar 1995, 76) meant that most of them obtained jobs in the informal sector. According to the travel agents that I interviewed, most of the migrants from Veni performed unskilled work (around 60 percent), about 15 percent were in domestic work, and around the same number were in "business," which ranged from petty pavement trade to the management or ownership of big supermarkets and stores. The 1980 Kerala government survey of Unemployment and Housing noted that of the 2,340 migrants from Veni at that time (1,367 going to the Gulf countries) 11 percent were skilled workers, 86 percent were unskilled, 2.6 percent were technical workers, and a mere 0.3 percent were professionals (Government of Kerala 1982). Many worked "underground," without formal contracts. "I lived in constant fear of being caught by the police. And the work itself—it was so hard. I had to work outside in the frigid cold and the blazing heat. It is as though one is in chains, from the minute one disembarks there to the time of departure," said Nawaz, who had been a construction worker in the Middle East. He finally decided he could take no more and returned home to a modest little business in Veni. Some migrants did odd jobs (loading and unloading things from trucks, painting, cleaning houses) or filled in temporarily for other workers. Most had more than one job at a time.

Later Migrants

A distinction should be made between two time periods in the Gulf migration—the period before 1983–1984, the peak period of Gulf migration (before the oil price crash) and the subsequent years. There are many differences between these two time periods. There was a change in the countries to which the migrants went in the two periods (see table 5.1).

Job opportunities and salaries decreased after 1984. Many of the migrants complained about the increasing competition from migrants from other countries like Sri Lanka, Bangladesh, Thailand, and the Philippines who were "undercutting" Malayalees since they would agree to work for less. The bitterest complaints were about Filipinas. "Earlier we used to get jobs as cooks or drivers and could earn about 1,000 dinars per month. But now [in the post–1984 period] there are these Philippine women who are willing to be cook, driver, baby sitter, and English teacher, all for 400 dinars." Veni migrants also criticized the Indian government "which tries to do everything to put obstacles in the way of migrants," comparing it to the governments of the other countries like Sri Lanka and the Philippines who they said were doing a lot to facilitate the migration.

An important consequence of the decrease in the wages and work opportunities in the Middle East was that many more villagers were trying to migrate on Haj or Umra pilgrimage visas. An estimate by the local travel agents was that around 40 percent of the migrants from Veni were doing so in 1989. I was told that each migrant usually "bought" themselves several passports since a person was not officially allowed to go for the pilgrimage for at least two years upon return. Also, having multiple passports was convenient. If one of the passports was impounded or invalidated in the Gulf due to the migrant being caught in illegal activity or repatriated, he could always use another the next time. Again,

TABLE 5.1   *Percentage Distribution of Gulf Migrants from Veni
in the Middle Eastern Countries*

Country	Period	
	1975–1984	*1984–1989*
United Arab Emirates	70	20
Saudi	20	50
Kuwait, Oman, Bahrain	10	30
Total	100	100

Source: Information obtained from the two oldest travel agencies in Veni.

a passport fetched an enormous amount in the black market. There were intricate networks that provided the know-how and the contacts necessary for such dealings. During my visits to the travel agencies, I observed the bewildering array of means that were used to get to the Gulf illegally. Despite the high risks, people were so desperate to migrate that they were willing to try almost anything to "grab a foot-hold" (the local term for migrating illegally, particularly on a nonwork visa) in the Middle East. There were also several villagers who made it a business to go on one of the transit visas, buy things, return, and sell them. According to the people in Veni, there were many Mappilas in jail in the Middle East due to violations of the work permit or because of public intoxication.

The dominant characteristic of the migration from this region was the basic instability of the job situation of many of the migrants. Thus, a person could go for months with just occasional part-time jobs. Knowledgeable villagers estimated that around 10 percent of the Gulfites from Veni incurred a net loss in their venture. That only made them more eager to go again and make good their loss. Another special characteristic of Veni was that persons from the entire socioeconomic spectrum participated in the migration. Thus, there were many migrants even from the poorest manual-laboring class. This was not immediately obvious to me when I visited the "coolie" enclaves since the households there seemed to be poor with very few migrants. However, as I came to realize, any household from the area that was economically successful (whether or not it was as a consequence of migration) moved out from the enclave. Thus, those who remained were a residual group of individuals who, for whatever reason, could not migrate or were unsuccessful migrants. There was also a fairly large proportion of lower-caste migrants in the Mappila fishing community that I studied.

Gender and Migration

Not surprisingly, given the restrictions on women, almost all the migrants from Veni were males. Both in the case of the earlier internal migration and the more recent Gulf migration, most men would go alone, leaving their families behind. The nature of the jobs undertaken made it difficult for many to afford the high rent and expenses necessary to have their wives with them. In addition, Middle Eastern governments imposed restrictions preventing lower income migrants from having their dependants with them.

The lower priority given to the relationship between spouses as compared to that between kin (and even between male friends) also contributed to this phenomenon. In the case of the Gulf migration, for instance, even wealthy businessmen and those migrants who had government jobs, such as those in the defense sector (where accommodation was provided together with an allowance for dependants), left their wives behind. The older generation took this for granted, and my question about why wealthier migrants had not taken their wives with them was met with incredulity. Both men and women told me that "it was not done." When I probed further, men said brusquely that the Middle East was no place for women. Women told me that they would have been terrified to leave their parents and the security of the village to go to a strange country. "That is for men," they said.

For the younger generation of migrants and wives, going abroad together was conceivable and often desirable. However, they told me that even if the men themselves wanted to have their wives and children in the Middle East, there was social pressure to prevent them. A man was expected to put his duty to his parents above his obligation to his wife and thus the first thing an obedient son had to do when he had saved up money was to send his parents on the Haj pilgrimage. Even after this duty was accomplished, most parents would tend to be against their son's taking his family to the Middle East, fearing that he might subsequently neglect them. Again, a younger brother would not be allowed to take his wife to the Gulf if his older brother had been unable to do so. In the case of the first man in the area who had flouted convention and gone off with his wife, apparently a rumor campaign had been launched (which was sustained for years) that he had allegedly been "forced" to do so due to her "misbehavior" with local men when she had been left behind.

The relatively strong relationship that men shared with male friends and the relatively weaker relationship with their wife and children facilitated male migration. The strong kinship ties of the Mappilas of Veni also meant that the migrant could leave his wife and children behind, knowing that they would be well looked after. The close relationship that men had with their mothers came in especially handy here since the migrant entrusted his family primarily to her care.

The Lure of the Gulf

To understand the lure of the Middle East for the people of Veni (and to some extent for the other two communities as well) certain of its characteristics must be sketched. In the Veni region, literacy levels were low, and even those who could read generally did so only with great effort. Consequently, hardly anyone subscribed to newspapers or magazines. Thus information about the Gulf countries was disseminated mainly through word of mouth. The tight-knit character of the community helped greatly. Although few nonmigrants knew exactly where the Middle Eastern region was, everyone had heard about its wonders. Information about life there, the type of work available, and how to go about getting across was all gained through the ethnic grapevine. The Gulf had developed a mystical character of the promised land, filled with Muslims and money.

All the young men grew up dreaming about finally being able to go there— to see and experience its marvels and to make a lot of money.[13] Young girls dreamed of having Gulf husbands who would come back with suitcases full of lovely, shiny clothes and jewelry, who would provide them with a television, VCR, and kitchen gadgets, and who would take them out in a car. Mothers envisioned sending their sons to "Persia" (as it was popularly known) so that they could redeem all the family debts, accumulate the gold and dowry to get their daughters married, and afford good medical care. Fathers hoped that their sons would support them in their old age so that they could rest their weary bodies after decades of labor, renovate the leaky, crumbling house, and provide a dowry that was ample enough to get a good husband for their daughters. "At least now our family can be saved" [from the crushing burden of poverty] was a frequently heard expression when a young man was able to obtain a work visa. Relatives were also eager to have someone in the family in "Dubai" (another popular name for the Middle East as a whole) since they knew that they could expect gifts from the migrant (including large sums of money for occasions like weddings) and could get him to take men from their immediate family over (in such cases the migrant often bore the expense of the visa). The poor people in the area expected money and clothes on the migrant's return. In addition, they would write to him requesting help with wedding expenses and expenses concerned with building or renovation of their houses. I was told that the migrant was treated as the "milch cow" of the family and the community at large.

From discussions with travel agents and vacationing and former migrants, I was able to get some idea about the salaries migrants obtained in the Middle East. To provide a baseline to understand the impact that remittances had on migrant households, I estimated that in 1989, a family of four in Veni would have needed about Rs. 750 a month to take care of their routine expenses and live fairly comfortably.[14] I gathered that during the peak period of Gulf migration (1978–1984), the average Gulfite who went for an unskilled job made a minimum of Rs. 5,000 per month. (At best, he would have earned around Rs. 500 to 600 a month locally, if he had been lucky enough to obtain a job.) In 1989, after salaries had fallen, laborers were able to earn only between Rs. 2,500–3,000, of which they were able to save between Rs. 1,000 and Rs. 1,500.[15] Some migrants sold sandwiches or peanuts in the parks in the evenings and earned an extra Rs. 1,000, which increased their savings to Rs. 2,000 to Rs. 2,500 a month. Of that amount, about Rs. 1,000 was sent home for routine expenses, which left just a little over Rs. 1,000. The migrant kept this money with him to finance his return trip home which would cost around Rs. 30,000. The expenses involved in a visit home were high since the migrant typically brought back a lot of gifts for family, friends, and neighbors. In addition, there was usually a lot of travel, home renovation, marriages, or other ceremonies that had to be financed during such a trip. Although the migrant usually brought back some things from the Gulf to sell, he could not hope to earn much that way—not even enough to pay the money for the passage. So, generally, there was little or nothing left over as savings among this group of migrants. Businessmen who were successful were able to earn an average of around Rs. 10,000–15,000 a month and thus were able to have fairly substantial savings. Of course there were some very wealthy business people who were probably earning at least Rs. 50,000 a month.

Ethnic Networks

Social networks were even more crucial in the Middle East than in the internal migration. Such networks created community enclaves within the foreign country which helped support temporarily unemployed migrants and made it possible for newcomers to take the risk of migrating even without having prearranged jobs. As an elderly villager pointed out, "People go from here to the Gulf without fear since there are so many local people there. I myself stayed there for three years without a proper job (I did some odd jobs in between). My relatives took care of me. Besides food and accommodation, they even gave me 'pocket money' regularly without my asking for it."

Most of the migration from this area took place as a result of relatives or friends using their contacts with Arabs to arrange for jobs and visas for the prospective migrant. The money for the passage and the visa was raised through relatives and friends who would pool their resources together to send a migrant to the Gulf.[16] Often, this amount was obtained by selling gold or using gold as collateral. Some banks in the area provided "gold loans" at 18.6 percent interest, paying Rs. 150 per gram of gold (for one year). If the gold was not redeemed within that period, it was sold by the bank. Bank managers estimated that this happened in around one-third of the cases.

Ethnic networks were also crucial in organizing the process of sending back money. Villagers from Veni generally joined a chitty group (comprised usually of other Mappilas) soon after getting a job in the Gulf. Every month, the members would contribute a certain amount into the chit fund, and each month, one person in the group received the whole contribution. Thus the chitty was a means of pooling money so that the person who was going back home for a visit could mobilize the large sum of money he needed.[17] It depended almost entirely on the trust between the members of the chitty group since there was no security and the whole system would have collapsed if even a few members defaulted.

Many of the villagers who went for unskilled jobs and those who went on illegal visas supplemented their meager earnings by engaging in petty smuggling (the larger-scale smuggling was done by established, "professional" smugglers). Smuggling of gold and electronic items from the Middle East to Veni was common. In fact, the village was a known center for such illegal activities. "When the customs agents in Bombay see 'Veni' on the passport, they make an extra-careful check since they know the reputation of this area," claimed one young migrant, while his friends laughed in agreement. A large part of the money earned by the villagers was sent back through the "tube." This was money that was sent through illegal channels and converted at the higher black market rate of exchange (at rates between 1.3 to 1.5 times the official exchange rates). Both smuggling and "tubing" money depended on having a good, safe, and widespread network and having the know-how and contacts to conduct the transactions. Even if money was not sent through the "tube," migrants from Veni preferred to send the money directly through relatives and friends returning to the area so that they did not have to pay the remittance charges (i.e., of the bank draft). Bank managers in the area estimated that only around 20 percent of the Gulf money came through banks. Such money was also generally withdrawn immediately.

Each migrant came back home only around once in two or three years, but because of the ethnic network both at home and in the Gulf, he could send and receive most of his letters through friends who were visiting home (thus saving both sides the high postage charges). Besides money, the migrant could also send gifts to his family members (and could ask, for instance, that a certain article be given to his wife without his parents' knowledge). Due to the affection and trust that existed among relatives and friends, the migrant had the assurance that the money and gifts he sent would reach the intended persons. The average migrant carried between ten to twenty-five letters or packages to and from Veni. The friend who came to deliver the letter and gifts also conveyed to the family the news of the migrant and in turn was entrusted with the local news to take back. Because of this, the migrant who returned for a visit was rarely found at home. He was always busy doing the rounds of visits to his relatives and friends—soon after he arrived, to deliver messages and presents, and again just before leaving, to pick up the same. Thus, such networks greatly reduced the social distance between Veni and the Gulf.

There were several reasons for the remittance patterns adopted by Veni migrants. The relatively low income earned by many villagers, and the fact that the wives of migrants generally were not in the labor force, meant that migrants could support their families only by using the black market rates of exchange or by smuggling in a little gold (or some other item) each time. Again, the nonformal and nonlegal types of occupations that they worked in made it impossible for them to use the official channels for remittances since these were recorded and scrutinized by tax officials. In addition to these economic reasons, it is likely that social factors such as the cohesiveness, solidarity, and trust between the members of the community were also important in the choice of these channels of transmission.

The Fieldwork

As I will describe below, the ethnic structure of Veni and its distinct migration pattern had a profound impact on my research in the area. Through the help of some of my relatives in Calicut city, around thirty-five miles north of Veni, I was able to make a preliminary visit to the region and also arrange for housing. During the five months that I was at Veni, I rented a one-bedroom unit in one of the newly built "line quarters" within walking distance of the central shopping area. "Line quarters" were rows of single-story, one- or two-bedroom units. Most of these had been built fairly recently, mainly to provide accommodation for the many nonlocals who had moved into the area to staff the hospitals, schools, and banks that had mushroomed as a consequence of the Gulf boom. The families of some of the younger migrants also lived in line quarters until they could save up enough money to build a house of their own. Line quarters were considered great investments for Gulf migrant families since "they could just sit at home and scoop up the money."

I have referred to the fact that Muslims in this part of Kerala have had a long history of being subject to official harassment. As a consequence, they were very suspicious of outsiders, who were usually believed to be government agents. Most of the villagers also had extremely low levels of education, so the concept of research was totally alien. To them it sounded extremely far-fetched that a stranger would want to know all the details about the households and the community for purely educational purposes. I discovered some months after living in Veni that government fieldworkers from the agricultural department and the rural development offices (who conducted studies throughout the state) had designated the area as being one where it was almost impossible to conduct field studies. They told me that they had never been able to do a successful survey in Veni and the surrounding villages and that they had subsequently started using "guesstimates" for the region.

There were many obstacles to field research in Veni. On a house visit, only the women were liable to be at home (even unemployed men and migrants who had returned for a holiday did not stay at home during the day). Since it had been constantly instilled into them that the outside world was evil, the women were frightened if a stranger appeared on their doorstep and often would not even come out, particularly if the visitor was a man.

The large-scale Gulf migration from the area had only exacerbated the suspiciousness of the villagers. Many unscrupulous people had tried to exploit the gullibility of migrant families by tricking them into parting with their wealth. I heard several such stories including some about men who came disguised as women and of women who were sent first as decoys. I am not sure how much truth there was in those accounts, but the informal transmission of these rumors served the function of making the villagers extremely cautious. After I got to know some of the women, they confided: "We noticed that you always carried around a blue bag with you. Someone told us that in it you had drugs or a smoke releasing medicine to make us unconscious."

Since the area also specialized in illegal activity of various kinds connected with the Gulf migration, there had been frequent income tax and customs raids on the houses in the area. So, when I went around asking questions, particularly about the migration, the villagers were convinced that I was a "CID" (Central Intelligence Detective). Those working in the local hospital (who had a greater awareness of the world and knew that I was from the United States) were afraid that I was a CIA agent. For all these reasons, the villagers would often not even disclose to me that there were members of the house in the Middle East.

In addition to these general obstacles were some personal factors that made things difficult for me. My hairstyle proved to be among the biggest problems. Many people in the area had never seen a woman with short hair before, and I was therefore perceived with amazement, but more often with downright hostility (probably since I posed a threat to the clearly defined gender system of the area). Consequently, I had to face constant harassment and jeering comments such as, "Here comes the man-woman" and "There goes the woman with no hair, the egg-head" (these were among the milder of the remarks made) whenever I walked on the road.[18] While most of the harassment came from young boys and men, it was far from confined to them. Once a young girl came up to me when I was walking in the marketplace, hissed, and said, "look at your hair," then spat in my face. Another time a woman commented, loudly enough so that I could hear, "It is these women with short hair who are out to trick us." Even the littlest children (sometimes they were the worst) streaming to and from school would participate in the jeering with gusto. It was only the older men (above thirty-five years of age or so) who would leave me alone. This could be because it was considered disrespectful for men to address women. Also, since most of them were migrants, they had probably seen other women with short hair in the airplane and in the Middle East. During this trying period, I would come home and try to intellectualize these encounters by pondering about the construction and maintenance of the gender system of the area.

Also, there I was, in an area where women were married when they were between thirteen and fifteen years of age (and then ideally secluded and chaperoned until middle age), a young, unmarried woman living alone, walking all over the village, traveling around to "distant" places by myself (such as Madras [Chennai], where my family lived, which was an eighteen-hour journey by train), and talking to a range of men. I was clearly violating all the local norms regarding appropriate feminine behavior, and it was, therefore, not surprising that the villagers regarded me with curiosity and alarm.

When I started my work in Veni, I focused on getting the village-level picture first, visiting all the likely sources of information such as the village, panchayat, block and district offices, banks, travel agencies, schools, hospitals, and the police station. Some of the acquaintances I made during these visits gave me the names and addresses of "knowledgeable" people to talk to. They in turn gave me the names of others, and I "snowballed" for two weeks in this manner. But soon this method stopped working, the main problem being that the men were reluctant to accompany me from house to house and the women could not do so. It did not help to carry a letter of introduction since many villagers could not read.

I tried to get a research assistant from the village to help me with my work, but here again I was not successful. I did not want a male assistant, since that would have created problems in the village, and most of the women were unwilling. After some effort, I finally located a female college student from a Hindu family who was very enthusiastic about the project and who agreed to help me, but the next day she came to me tearfully to say that her (younger) brother had forbidden her to do the work. I gathered that most of the men in the area did not want their women to associate closely with me, fearing that I would "fill their heads with dangerous notions."

Fortunately for me, a doctor in Veni came to my rescue at this juncture. Dr. Jebbar suggested that I go for house visits with the health workers (nurses) and *balawadi* (preschool) teachers in the area and introduced me to several of them. Due to the welfare commitment of the state, there were government health workers and preschools in many of the poorer villages of Kerala, but the Veni region was the focus of a particularly intense health program. As an area with high levels of infant mortality, early marriage, and high fertility, Veni had been brought under an Integrated Child Development Scheme (ICDS) starting from 1975. Dr. Jebbar's help proved to be the turning point since I discovered that these government fieldworkers (most of whom were Hindu women) were invaluable contacts. Although they had also faced tremendous hostility and suspicion when they first started working in the area, over time, the women had become trusted and highly esteemed.[19] Since they went from house to house on regular health checkups, they were in close contact with the villagers and were veritable mines of information. These workers also maintained detailed records on each household—such as the number of people in the house, their ages, sex and relationship, educational levels, the type of house structure they lived in, the type of toilet facilities they had, in addition to the health records relating to immunization, sterilization (the most common form of birth control in Kerala), pregnancy, and contraceptive use. I made extensive use of the records. Since the women knew "their families" (the families in the areas assigned to them) so well, I only had to open the record book to a page and then ask them to tell me about the family. I would later corroborate their accounts with the household members themselves (if possible) and the other fieldworkers (each house was visited by the balawadi teacher and the government nurse who maintained separate records). I was very favorably impressed by the commitment and efficiency of these women who put in much time and effort for very small salaries.

As I started going with the government workers for the house visits, I gained some measure of access to the community. I would later go back alone to houses where I had been well received and talk to the family members. I was able to have long discussions with cooperative persons in the community in this way. I would generally not take notes during the interviews (tape recording the conversations was out of the question) but would come home and write down all the details, including as much of the wording of the conversation as I could remember. In all, I made longer visits to seventy-nine households in Veni. This included houses of migrants and nonmigrants of different economic levels and occupations. I also made tabulations from the records of the fieldworkers, which gave me the basic household information for the area.

As I discovered after I was finally able to make the house visits, I did not learn too much about the migration as such from the members of the household since, by and large, the women were quite ignorant about the details. It was clear that neither men nor women knew very much about the lives of the other. Many women did not even know which country their husbands were in. A group of young women explained: "We don't ask and they don't tell. We have our lives and they have theirs. We are not interested in the boring details of their jobs. And they know we won't understand. As for the men who are in the Middle East, they live in a different world altogether. How can we understand about that when we have never been there? That's why many women don't even know what [jobs] their husbands do in the Gulf." And as a young woman living in that society, I could not go to the houses in the evening or night, when the men were at home. I therefore obtained most of the information about the migration at an aggregate level—from knowledgeable men in the community, such as returned or holidaying Gulf migrants, panchayat members, and the local travel agents.

Getting even a basic idea of the income of the households was a totally impossible task. The women were either not aware of it or would not divulge such information. The family ration cards and the statistics of the health service workers had ridiculous amounts for income such as Rs. 100 per month for a family of nine or ten.[20] (This would be roughly worth an equivalent of the purchasing power of fifty dollars in the American context.) One of the preschool teachers told me that when she had asked the wife of a Gulf migrant why she was giving them such a low figure for the income, the woman had replied: "Yes, he sends us Rs. 1,500 per month now. But who knows how long this job will last? Gulf jobs are temporary but your records are permanent, so please enter only Rs. 100." I therefore relied on the more general estimates I obtained about migrant workers in different types of jobs. I also learned to pick up cues that would give me an approximate indication of the economic status of the family.

Consumption, Investment, and Exchange Patterns

In the two decades between 1970 and 1990, Veni had changed beyond recognition. Brick and concrete houses had sprung up everywhere, with concrete or tiled roofs (during my stay in the area, I only saw about five katcha or thatched houses). Dr. Narayan told me the story of his neighbors to illustrate the tremendous changes that some families in Veni had experienced due to the Gulf migration: "They were firewood sellers and used to live in a tiny thatched shack. They had to walk for miles with firewood on their heads to earn a little money. Most of the time, they barely had enough to eat and would come and ask us to help. But now, look at them. They have a huge two-story house and they are very rich."

The price of land went up dramatically. Between 1970 and 1985, it had increased over a hundred-fold in some areas as most of the traditional agriculture was abandoned and the land was used to build houses. Wage rates also went up tremendously. Despite the high wage rates, there was a shortage of local labor, and migrant laborers from Tamil Nadu (the neighboring state) were being hired to work at around 75 percent of what local labor was paid. Since this rate was still much higher than the wage rate in Tamil Nadu, I was repeatedly told, "For them (Tamil laborers), this is the Gulf."

The central market area (around half a mile long, with shops on either side) had developed rapidly as a consequence of the migration, and in 1989, Veni had the look of a small town rather than a village. Besides shops of all kinds, the market area had twelve travel agencies (there were others scattered around in the village), thirty-six gold jewelry shops, four video libraries, and dozens of small department stores. There were also over a hundred commercial vehicles of different kinds—jeeps, taxis, vans, and three-wheelers. The villagers accounted for the large numbers of vehicles and shops in the area by saying, "When one person from Veni is seen as successful in some type of business, everyone else immediately wants to go in for the same thing."

There were also six banks, five or six tax consultants, around thirty doctors with private clinics, four small private hospitals (in addition to the government-run primary health center), three high schools, and ten primary schools in Veni. Buses came and left Veni every two or three minutes. The rapid pace of change in the area can be seen by the fact that in the five months that I was at Veni, the following new businesses were established in the central market: one new audio-video store, two or three new gold jewelry shops, one travel agency, one department store, three new fruit stalls, one clothing shop, one cement shop, and one shoe store. Also, in that period, four new doctors moved into the area, and two medical laboratories and one private hospital were established. Several shops and line quarters were also under construction.

Ethnicity and Economic Behavior

I have argued that economic behavior is not autonomous and that economic choices are an important way in which personal and group identities are expressed. Thus, the patterns of consumption, investment, and exchange undertaken by the three groups as a consequence of migration manifested, as well as shaped, their ethnic structures and identities. A strong business orientation was a distinguishing characteristic of Veni and one of the main targets of Gulf investment in Veni was business. This was demonstrated by the rapid development of the market area. There were several reasons that this investment pattern was chosen. The main factor was probably the prior involvement of the community in trade, and the fact that the village had been a trading center in the past. Investing money in business was also the easiest means of laundering black money, an important consideration in an area which specialized in such activities. In such cases, the business owner underreported the money invested in his business.

As a consequence of the Gulf migration, there was a brisk gold business in the area. Gold was the most convenient form of investment for poorer migrants since it was the most liquid. It was also easy to smuggle in small bits of gold from the Middle East. Most of the gold was converted into jewelry and given as gifts for various occasions or as dowry when a girl was given in marriage. The status of a family partly depended on the amount of gold jewelry worn by the women. Since an untrustworthy goldsmith could easily keep some of the gold for himself, it was also important for the people of Veni to conduct their gold business with fellow villagers whom they could trust. All of these factors could account for the big increase in the numbers of jewelry shops in the area.

The value placed on the purity and seclusion of women manifested itself in several ways in the expenditure patterns of this area. Because women were not allowed to go out, most of the daily shopping in the Gulf households was done by the children of the house, and it was necessary to have the basic provision shops nearby. This last factor was probably the reason for the tremendous number and spread of vegetable and provision shops (shops selling rice, sugar, lentils, oil, spices, etc.) all over the village. A good deal of money was also spent on transportation, particularly on taxis, since it was considered a more decorous and prestigious way for women to travel (as compared to walking or taking the bus). This partly explains the tremendous spurt in the number of commercial vehicles in the area. The number and scale of "feasts" (organized when relatives and friends visited one another) had increased a great deal after the Gulf migration, which also provided business for the taxis.

Due to the mass education programs launched in the state and the exposure to other communities gained by the Gulf migration, there was a greater emphasis on education in the community, particularly at the primary and secondary levels (this explains the rise of schools in the area), but compared to the other two areas, Veni villagers spent very little on the process. All the schools in the area were public (government) schools, which charged very nominal fees. By enriching relatively uneducated people, the Gulf migration only acted to reinforce the low priority given to higher education.

Medical care had become a major item of expenditure in the area, a remarkable change given that this was a community which, until the recent period, had been deeply suspicious of Western medicine. A dutiful migrant was expected to send his family for regular checkups and medical treatment. In Veni, this had come to represent an index of love and concern. Those who could afford it also had their wives and other female family members admitted to hospitals for childbirth.[21] To understand the reasons for the sudden popularity of allopathic medicine in the area, we must view the role of doctors and of medical treatment within the cultural context of Veni. Doctors in the area, particularly the more popular ones (who, not surprisingly, were mostly the Muslim doctors), had a multifaceted role. To some extent they were still treated like the charismatic faith healers to whom the community had turned to for help earlier, for a variety of problems. Such doctors were held in reverential respect and were frequently called on to arbitrate in conflicts. Again, for the young women of the community who were confined to the house, a trip to the doctor was one of the few permissible reasons to make a trip outside. Saying that she was ill was also one of the few ways a woman could get the attention of her in-laws.

Health workers in the area told me that "injectionism" was very common and that patients were satisfied only if they got the *sooji* (needle). According to Geetha, a nurse, one of the doctors that she was working for was giving a lot of vitamin B complex injections to his patients, just to keep them happy. Veni villagers also insisted that the doctor examine them with a stethoscope, whatever the ailment. I saw this myself once when I was at a doctor's office. A family had brought in a young boy with a leg injury, and the doctor, on the request of the parents, solemnly listened to the injured leg with his stethoscope.

Due to the solidarity and tight-knit character of the community, together with the fact that the villagers of Veni felt that their identity as Mappila Muslims meant that they had a strong obligation to share their wealth, a lot of the Gulf money was spent on gifts to relatives, friends, and community members. In Veni, a major source of status was being in the position of a donor and thus many migrants helped the poor in a variety of ways. As a wealthy migrant put it: "I, my father and his father before him have until recently had to depend on the 'big' people in the area—for a job, for medical emergencies, for weddings and funerals. With Allah's blessings I have been fortunate enough to become a person that other people can depend on." I was told (both by the poor and the rich) that a poor person could write to a Gulfite from his area if he had any major or unexpected expenses to meet and that it was a matter of honor for the Gulfite to respond to such a request. The local community also felt a sense of responsibility for widows and orphans without any relatives to help them. There were committees for each area (usually organized by the local mosque) to collect and disburse the money to the needy. I gathered that there were three main ways in which help was rendered through the committees. Money was given to help poor families build a "pucca" house, to provide a dowry to get a girl married, and to support the local orphanage.[22] In addition, migrant households provided food to poor families nearby in return for household help and for clothes when the migrant returned from the Gulf. Wealthier Mappila migrants, particularly those in business, provided loans and arranged visas to take over poorer Mappilas to work as their employees in the Middle East.

Besides the fact that many more Mappilas could now practice the Islamic tenets of charitable giving, Gulf migration also led to the establishment and strengthening of Islamic institutions like mosques, madrasas, Arabic colleges, and Muslim orphanages since many of the migrants contributed generously to their support. Several new mosques had sprung up in the area, prominent because of their distinctive architecture. The traditional Mappila mosque was a Kerala-style, two-story building with a tiled roof. The new mosques that were built following the Gulf boom, however, used domes and minarets, reflecting a Middle Eastern influence. Some were actually funded by Middle Eastern Arabs. Gulf affluence also permitted many of the villagers to perform the Haj pilgrimage.

Migration and Gender

Many migrants from Veni went to the Middle East when they were between eighteen and twenty years of age and still unmarried. They would marry later when they came home for a holiday. The average Veni migrant returned to the village once in two or three years and spent around three to four months before leaving again. The marriage of a migrant was usually hurriedly arranged during a holiday visit, and generally the new bridegroom had to return to the Middle East a few days or weeks later. Since the period immediately following the wedding was spent visiting relatives, the two strangers united in marriage barely got to know each other before they were separated for another two to three years. The girl bride (girls were usually married when they were between thirteen to fifteen years) was then left in the care of the husband's parents. She was expected to be quiet, modest, and obedient and to do a good deal of the household work. If the in-laws (particularly the mother-in-law) were not pleased with her, they would write to their son asking him to divorce her. He frequently complied, often without even consulting his bride.

Kumari, one of the preschool teachers (almost all the working women in the area were either Hindu or Christian), told me about one such case: "The parents wrote to their son asking him to divorce his wife since she had gone home [to her own house] and refused to come back. He did it, without even bothering to write to her and get her side of the story. What had happened was that her mother fell ill when Fatima [the wife] was at home. So Fatima stayed on to look after her siblings, who were very young. But her mother-in-law did not like this, saying, 'When there is so much work in this house, why should she go and stay there for so long?'" In another case, the mother-in-law was trying to get her son to divorce his wife because she was not doing her share of the work in the house. However, the girl (she was hardly more than that) told me that her baby had been premature and so needed a lot of attention, which took up her time and also made her very tired. I came across several similar cases during my stay in Veni. On the basis of the household visits I did with the health workers and their family records, I noted that there were one or more divorced women in approximately 5–8 percent of the households. This figure did not include women who had been remarried, and so the actual divorce rates must have been higher.

The migrant sent his remittances to his father and generally addressed his letters to his parents—it was rare that newly married spouses wrote directly to each other. "If a man writes personal letters to his wife, particularly in the early years of marriage, it could lead to problems with his parents. Why? Well, they would feel that it was improper and an indication that she was gaining an undue influence over him," said Pushpa, one of the health workers in the area. When the migrant sent gifts home, he had to make sure that everyone in his immediate natal family got something before his wife did and that their presents were of superior or at least equivalent value. When he came home, he was supposed to open his suitcases first in front of his mother (and not his wife). A young wife who was living in her own parents' house in Veni because she did not get along with her in-laws told me: "My sister is lucky. Her husband is a real exception. He sends her clothes and even perfume and pays no heed to the grumbling of his parents and sisters. [With a sigh] Yes, he is affectionate and likes to indulge her. My husband? Oh, he is like all the rest."

Even when the migrant did return for a holiday, he barely spent time with his wife. He had the round of visits to make—to the houses of relatives and comigrants for whom he delivered gifts, letters, and messages. It was considered "unseemly" for a man (unless he was elderly) to spend his days at home with his wife, so even after the visits were over, most young men would spend their days in the bazaar with their male friends, returning home only at night.

During the years that the woman lived with her in-laws, they were very strict with her, wanting to maintain the ideal of seclusion and to guard against any rumor of improper behavior on her part. So she could not go out alone, and, even when escorted, could leave the house only for important reasons like visiting her family or going to the doctor. Even after her children were fairly grown up and she and they had moved to their own independent house, she had to be very careful not to give the slightest grounds for the rise of rumors. Ayisha was a woman with a fourteen-year-old son and an eight-year-old daughter. She had moved out of her in-laws' house and had been living with her two children in an independent house for two years. She narrated the following incident to me: "One day, I had gone to the bus stop to see the Sister [one of the nurses who worked in the area] off—she was going away for a month and had a lot of luggage, so I went to help. I was away only for a short while but during that time my mother-in-law came to my house. Seeing that I was not there she left in great anger. My neighbors told her that I had gone 'gallivanting'—they are always trying to cause trouble for me. My mother-in-law then wrote to my husband complaining about my behavior. It is only after I wrote to him explaining the situation and he wrote back to his mother, that this was patched up."

The whole community kept a watchful eye on women like Ayisha, and there were always illwishers eager to write to the husband about the misconduct of his wife. Wives of Gulf migrants were far less likely to go out of the house even to do the marketing, sending their children to do this instead. Once the woman moved out of her in-laws' house she had more control over household decisions, but financial responsibilities were still entrusted (by her husband) to a male relative who received the remittances and gave the wife a portion of it for household expenses. Khadija was a woman in her forties living in an independent house with her two sons and a daughter. "How much do I spend every month? Well, I don't really know. I don't keep track. His [her husband's] cousin is in charge of the finances. When I need money I ask him for it. But he buys me the basic provisions for the month, so I ask him for money only when someone has to see a doctor or something like that."

There was a tendency toward earlier marriages for girls in the community following the Gulf migration.[23] Early marriage had been another longstanding ideal in the community (due to the emphasis on the purity of women), but since marriages were very expensive for the bride's side as they had to pay a dowry and to incur most of the wedding costs, less wealthy families had to wait a few years before they could accumulate the necessary amount. With their newfound wealth many families no longer had to wait as long (this despite the fact that dowry rates had increased dramatically during the same period). I often heard it said that "once a girl starts menstruating, the parents are in a hurry to get her married. It is considered shameful if she stays unmarried."

Earlier, girls had not been educated (or had been educated only for three or four years), but since the 1980s the number of years of schooling had increased dramatically. Gulf migration had a mixed effect in this regard. At the time of my fieldwork, the necessity of basic literacy for girls was highly stressed. Parents said, "We want her to have enough education so that she will be able to read and write letters." However, the number of women being sent to college (which had been picking up) had declined. This was due to the greater emphasis on women's seclusion, early marriage, and the fall in the educational aspirations and qualifications of the young men who, with the large-scale Gulf migration, realized that they could get lucrative jobs without much education (it was considered undesirable for a woman to be more educated than her husband). Thus, the Gulf migration from Veni led to an increase in the social restrictions on younger women, when compared both to nonmigrant households within the community and to nonmigrant communities which were similar to Veni before migration. A brief discussion of nonmigrant households will make this clear.

As a result of the "change in times" as the villagers put it, in the past two decades, relationships between spouses had become generally closer than those typical in the premigration period. Due to the factors mentioned above, however, the gender relationships in migrant households remained more or less as they were in an earlier period, or became even more distant in some respects.

When the husband had a local job, there was time and opportunity for a personal relationship to develop between the spouses. Once a relationship was established, the position of the woman was more secure and the man might be willing to take his wife's side in the case of conflicts with other family members. In the case of migrants, even if the husband knew that the wife was right, he would be less willing to support her case and run the risk of antagonizing his parents and siblings since he knew that he was dependent on them to look after his family while he was away. So he was more likely to tell his wife to "be patient" and to "bear with it" than to take any decisive steps.

Due to the notion that a woman could not live in a separate household until her son was at least eight or ten years old (and even after that only under the constant supervision of male relatives and neighbors), the separation and independence of migrant households came relatively later than that of non-migrants. Wives of nonmigrant husbands were not under such community scrutiny since it was assumed that they left the house with the permission of their husbands. Because a wife only had to get the permission of her husband (who was generally likely to be much less strict than his parents), the wife of a nonmigrant generally had greater freedom. There was also a greater likelihood of her being consulted (by her husband) on household decisions.

We can also compare the lives of the wives of migrants in the contemporary period with that of the women in the older generation. Earlier, as mentioned, women had to go out by necessity to work and to the market. Kemal Pasha, a returned migrant who had started an X-ray and lab service in Veni, describing the difference between the two periods, told me: "My father cultivates betel nut palms on a large scale and has them processed at home. Between around 1950 and 1970 this work was done largely by women who used to come in droves, seeking employment (he always had to turn many of them away). Now, after the Gulf boom the women are not willing to come. In fact, there is no local labor available in Aliya [a subdivision of Veni which had the largest outmigration] and people come from non-Gulf pockets or from Tamil Nadu." Thus, Gulf affluence permitted women to conform to the demand for stricter seclusion (which was seen as more honorable and therefore a privileged option).

I must stress that the impact of migration discussed above was not confined to the migrant households alone. While there obviously was a difference between migrant and nonmigrant households, the broader changes mentioned were common to the community as a whole. I could see this particularly when I compared Veni with other nonmigrant villages in the area. While Veni was more developed economically and technologically and the villagers generally had a higher standard of living, women in Veni (in both migrant and nonmigrant households) were more secluded and had far less freedom in comparison with their counterparts in the nonmigrant areas that I studied.[24]

How did the women in Veni feel about these changes and how did they deal with them? The responses of individual women varied considerably depending largely on their particular situation. What I presented above was an ideal typical description of the impact of migration on women. However, there were several variations within this broad pattern. Economically, there is no doubt that a *successful* migrant considerably eased the financial situation at home (but several migrants were not successful). As several women pointed out, if their husbands had not migrated, they would probably have had to go out to do backbreaking agricultural work. Many considered it a privilege to stay at home and have all their needs taken care of.

Socially and psychologically, the situation of women varied. On the one hand, I discovered (through local doctors, villagers, and my own household visits) that a considerable number of women in the area had psychological and psychosomatic problems (which I did not find in either of the other areas). These ranged from sleeplessness, chronic headaches, stomach ailments and menstrual disturbances, to fainting fits and possession. According to the doctors, some of these were "not real" and were merely attention-getting devices. They told me that, occasionally, the women themselves would ask the doctors to tell their in-laws that their illness was due to being overworked or neglected.

Several women mentioned the many problems that they had to deal with as a consequence of the migration—constant worry about the husband's welfare (particularly since many of them were illegal immigrants), also a concern that he might divorce them or marry a second wife, demanding and unkind in-laws, jealous neighbors, disobedient children, and, in the case of women living independently with their children, the general stress of managing a household by themselves. In some cases where a migrant's wife was not being treated well by her husband or her in-laws, the woman's family had insisted on a divorce and had taken her (and her children if she had any) back. These were generally the wealthier households since they had to then bear the costs of supporting her. They also had to give a larger dowry to arrange her remarriage.

However, on the positive side, there were a significant number of women who seemed content and well adjusted. In these situations, one or more of the following usually applied: they had considerate in-laws; they had developed strong bonds with their sisters-in-law and close friendships with women in neighboring households; they were permitted by their husband and in-laws to continue to live in their own parental homes (though in many cases, this living arrangement was a consequence of tension with in-laws) or were allowed to spend considerable amounts of time there. Several of the women who had moved to an independent house stated that they enjoyed the freedom and leisure they had while their husbands were away.

Many women seemed to see the hardships caused by marriage and by their husband's migration as something inevitable, to be endured for a few years until they had borne children and had established a stronger bond with their spouses. "When you left home for the first time and went so far away, didn't you find it difficult?" a group of women asked me. "Yes," I replied. "Particularly at first. Then I got used to it." "That is exactly how it is with us also," one of them said triumphantly.

There were also indications that younger migrants and their spouses had a closer personal relationship. Many of these men wrote directly to their wives (sometimes up to three letters a week). Young married couples went out together occasionally, and even publicly there was a more informal and affectionate relationship between them. More and more younger migrants were also trying to take their wives to the Gulf for at least a short period of time.

There are several possible reasons for this change. As a consequence of migration, there was a weakening of the structural authority of parents over their adult children since local agriculture had largely been abandoned and parents had become financially dependent on their migrant sons. This reversed the earlier situation and strengthened the relative power of the sons over their parents.[25] This development could have the eventual consequence of undermining the basis of the extended family, one of the cornerstones of the community.

Further, young men, and to some extent young women, in Veni had a greater exposure to the outside world in the 1980s compared to the relative cultural isolation they had earlier. The large-scale migration from Kerala had begun in the mid–1970s, and the second generation of migrants from Veni had a much greater opportunity to meet and make friends with comigrants from other communities in Kerala. There was some overlap in the occupations of Muslim and Hindu migrants (many Hindus from Kerala were skilled workers and technicians in the Gulf) and thus members of the two groups often interacted closely.[26] Isolation from the family, the common linguistic background, and the similar treatment accorded to the workers created bonds that often superseded that of religion. Increasingly, it seemed to be the Hindus (as the dominant community in Kerala) who were becoming the reference group for the migrants from Veni. Although women were secluded and remained within the house, they, too, had become more aware of the world outside Veni due to the increase in the numbers of televisions and VCRs as a consequence of the migration. Since Indian movies and serials featured several romantic stories and themes, both migrants in the Middle East (who also spent a lot of time watching TV) and the families at home were becoming influenced by such ideas.

In the early period of my fieldwork in Veni, I would frequently go back to my rented apartment feeling privileged and grateful that, unlike the local women, I had the "freedom" to study, travel, and work. Over time, however, I began to realize that many of the women in Veni had a very different point of view regarding our respective situations. I discovered, in fact, that they felt very sorry for me. As one of them remarked to a friend, "Poor thing, she has to exert herself so much, going out in the heat, the dust, and the rain, and meeting all kinds of strange men. And she has to travel and live alone, so far away from her family."

The women believed that I had to do all this because it was expected of women in my subculture. My stock answer to the question of why I was not married was to say that I wanted to finish my education and get a job first. There were some single Hindu and Christian women from south-central Kerala (my ancestral home) working in the Veni area. When they got married, these women generally left the village and went back to southern Kerala (where their husbands worked). Thus the villagers inferred that getting educated and working for a few years (sometimes far away from home) was something that non-Mappila women had to do to qualify for marriage. When I thought about it, I realized that they were not too far off the mark. Mappila women considered themselves very privileged in comparison. This was one of the many times during my fieldwork when I was forced to pause and reexamine the role of agency and constraint in my own life, as well as my assumptions about gender.

Migration and Caste

Although most migrants from Pullad, the coastal village, were from the Malabari Mappila "Eleven" group, a fairly large proportion of the lower-caste Pusalars, locally called the "Ten" group, had managed to migrate as well. Many of the early migrants from the Pullad region (who also went on illegal launches like the migrants from Veni) had been from this group. Migration had spread among the Ten group to a certain extent. A significant number were even able to become relatively wealthy. However, since such individuals had moved out of the Ten area, it was difficult to estimate how many had "escaped" through this route.

The primary reason for the success of the Pusalars seemed to be that they were able to take advantage of many of the ethnic resources of the higher caste, Malabari Mappila Muslims. Thus, the Pusalars were able to use the Mappila networks to migrate on the less expensive pilgrimage visas and were able to obtain employment as domestics in Arab households. The fishermen migrants, like the poorer migrants from Veni, also sent their money through the "tube" and engaged in petty smuggling, which increased the financial benefits of the migration. Again, since the women of this group had a moderately well-paying, steady source of income (coir work), the family was not entirely dependent on migrant remittances.

However, members of the Ten group still had many disadvantages when compared to the Eleven and thus were far less successful when compared to the latter. The Tens went illegally at first and later mainly through agents, whereas the Elevens were taken over by relatives and friends. Since the Ten group was poorer, members had to borrow money at very high rates of interest. In the case of the Elevens, not only were expenses lower since they were taken over by relatives, but being wealthier, they often had enough personal or family savings to finance the expenses. The Tens went for low-level, unskilled ("coolie") jobs, whereas the Elevens took up business or skilled positions in sectors, such as defense, which paid very highly. The occupational differences between the two groups also meant that members of the Ten group were only able to stay in the Gulf for a short term, three to four years on average, when compared to the members of the Eleven group, who were able to work there for well over a decade. Thus many more from the Eleven group were able to become significantly wealthy when compared to the Ten group.

Despite these disadvantages, I heard of several cases where Pusalar migrants had been successful enough to move near the main road (where the higher-caste Malabaris lived) or out of Pullad to a semiurban area in the interior. There they built a nice house, and a few were even able to procure alliances with Malabari families by giving large dowries. Thus, they were able to overcome the stigma of being from a lower-status group. "Now, except for the very aristocratic families, most people here do not look at the family background [when it comes to marriage]. It is only the economic standing of the man and his personal qualities that are important," several people from Pullad told me. Although only a few individuals from the Ten group had managed to marry into the Malabari, Eleven caste, the improvement in the economic and cultural standing of the fisherfolk brought about by the presence of large numbers of Gulf migrants, helped to raise the status of the community as a whole. Thus, the barriers between the Pusalars and the Malabaris were gradually being eroded as a consequence of the migration.

Reformulating Identity and Status

I have mentioned that the migrant wealth resulted in the strengthening of many Islamic institutions in Veni. Several professors at the local university mentioned that there was a "new Muslim consciousness" among the Mappilas due to the migration, as they encountered Arab Muslims in the Middle East. However, most Veni villagers seemed to feel that, as a consequence of Gulf affluence, religious faith had actually declined. According to them, the earlier practices of keeping to the five daily prayer times, strictly observing the Ramadan fast, and following the other daily prescriptions and proscriptions of Islam had been largely abandoned. Being a "good" Muslim still continued to be important for Mappilas, but as a perceptive young man pointed out, it had become redefined in terms of "external show." Attending the Friday mosque (for men), sending children for private religious education coaching (instead of the local madrasa), having a gold embossed copy of the Koran on the coffee table, secluding women, "driving them about in cars with darkened windows," going for the Haj pilgrimage, and the ostentatious giving of charity had become the prestigious ways to assert a Muslim identity. "The same people that act so pious at the mosque go home and drink [alcohol] and eat pork," one of the older villagers said disparagingly.

Gulf wealth had also eroded many of the other traditional manifestations of a "Mappila Muslim" identity. The most visible changes were in the attire of the Mappilas. Mappila men had adopted the clothing and hairstyles prevalent in the wider society, and Mappila women had discarded their dark blue sarongs and black head cloths for brightly colored synthetic mundus, blouses, and headscarves.[27] Many of the younger women, particularly the wives of Gulf migrants, sported colorful polyester sarees (brought back from the Gulf) with matching headscarves. Again, the Mappila practice of women wearing many sets of earrings on the helix of the ear was being abandoned. Some of the older women of the area who had been on the Haj pilgrimage had started wearing a black or brown Middle Eastern style *burkha* (which covered their full body and face) with gloves on their hands and socks on their feet when they traveled outside the home, probably as a visible sign of their "Haj-returned" status.

In the ceremonial realm, too, several Mappila practices were being relinquished, such as the holding of frequent *mauluds* (occasions when there were antiphonal readings from the Koran), the performance of the *oppana* (the dance of the Mappila women), and the customary singing during wedding ceremonies. In their place, new betrothal, marriage, and post-marriage rituals were introduced and existing ceremonies were celebrated more lavishly. In the traditional system, the marriage was arranged by the elders, and the couple met for the first time only on the day of the wedding. Perhaps as a consequence of the shift in the power balance from the older generation to the younger (men) as a consequence of the migration, the bridegroom-to-be had begun to have a much greater say in the choice of the bride. To symbolize this change, a new "watch tying ceremony" had been institutionalized. After the initial negotiations (when the man's wishes were consulted), the prospective bridegroom went to visit the young woman with a few of his brothers or friends. He talked to her for a short time and, if he approved of her, he gave her a gift (often a watch) as a betrothal present. It was only after this that his parents visited to fix the details of the wedding.

Some Mappila marriage ceremonies were also being replaced by Hindu practices. Thus, though the traditional wedding ritual was the *nikkah* (the contract made by the bridegroom and the father of the bride in the presence of a mosque functionary and attended only by a few selected witnesses), in many cases, this function had been supplemented or substituted by a public *tali-tying* ceremony. (The *tali* is the marriage pendant th
at the bridegroom puts on the neck of the bride, and tali-tying is a traditional Hindu custom which has long been practiced by several other groups, such as the Syrian Christians.) After the wedding, many Mappilas even had a "kitchen-viewing ceremony," adapted from the Hindu practice where the bride's family visited the young couple (in the bridegroom's house) with gifts of furniture and kitchen equipment.

These changes in the ceremonial practices could broadly be described as attempts to adopt the status models of the wider society. As such, it should probably be taken as an indication of the community's becoming more outward oriented. The foreign exposure brought about by the migration and the interaction of the Mappila migrants with Hindu migrants from Kerala in the Gulf (in general, close social relationships were confined to other Keralites due to language barriers), as subregional boundaries crumbled in a foreign country, could be some of the factors responsible for this change.

Conclusion

The case of Veni provides a good example of everyday ethnicity at work
starts to corporealize the theoretical concepts discussed in chapter 2. I be-
by a discussion of the "habitus" of Veni before the large-scale migration.
i was a poor agrarian community with a strong Islamic identity and minor-
consciousness, a high degree of group solidarity, and relative social egali-
anism. The community as a whole had low levels of education. They had a
t family structure which was patrilineal, patrilocal, and strongly patriarchal.
nder differentials were marked, women married early, and fertility levels were
h. These factors, together with their tradition of trade and participation in
informal economy, resulted in male migration to other regions of the sub-
ntinent where the Mappilas worked in hotels and bakeries.

I also discussed the way this ethnic matrix was shaped by the colonial ex-
riences of the Mappilas and the dialectical relationship between structural po-
tion and ethnic culture. The relatively low social and economic position of
Mappilas within northern Kerala society was responsible for their "inward turn"
nd greater solidarity, as well as their suspiciousness of the government and of
ion-Muslim outsiders. However, these very characteristics also led them to es-
chew modern education and professional occupations and resulted in their participation in the informal economy and petty businesses, thus reinforcing their
social and economic marginality.

However, when it came to the Gulf migration, the experience of surviv-
ing on the margins proved to be an advantage for the villagers of Veni. The background of the Mappilas helped them initiate and sustain the migration of a
multitude of villagers through nonformal channels, for unskilled and semiskilled
jobs, without formal contracts. The ethnic solidarity of the Mappilas was crucial to fostering the migration and in augmenting its material benefits.

We have also seen how the ethnic matrix of Veni was the "unifying principle" or the guiding logic underlying such seemingly unrelated practices as the
formation of chitty groups, the sending of money back through the "tube" and
through fellow migrants, the emphasis on charity, the investment of money in
local businesses, the explosion in the numbers of gold shops and taxis, and the
seclusion of women.

The interpenetration and interrelationship between religion, status, and
gender is clear. The manner in which Islamic identity was defined in Veni shaped
their conceptions of status and of appropriate gendered behavior. Thus, the seclusion of women was regarded as indicating high status and devotion to Islamic
tenets. As mentioned in chapter 2, this was not a view that was even shared by
many other Mappila villages in the same region.

In this chapter, I have also demonstrated the relationship between ethnicity
and migration. As an oppressed minority and a marginalized group, Mappila
Muslims emphasized the maintenance of the solidarity of the community. Both

(213) 740-8361
Fax (213) 740-3535
e-mail: kurien@mizar.usc.edu

the migration process, with its heavy dependence on community members for information, visas, and sustenance in the Middle East, and the remittance process, which created and strengthened widespread networks, had the effect of fostering ethnic unity. Gulf money also contributed to the solidarity of the community by increasing the number and range of people who were involved in exchange and dependency relationships, and by creating new religious institutions in the community. While the tension Bloch and Parry (1989) identified between individual acquisitive activity and larger community demands existed, it was fairly well contained in this community. Their identity as fellow Mappila Muslims was constantly used to stress the necessity for charity, brotherhood, and equality. The emphasis on purity, seclusion, and the subordination of women was another important ethnic value. Here again, the newly earned affluence permitted its implementation by making possible the withdrawal of women from the labor force, earlier marriages, and the rise of a wide network of provision shops.

The patterns and effects of Gulf migration were shaped by the ethnicity of the area but also recreated it. Thus, at the time of the study, Mappilas were moving from being an inward oriented and anti-modern community to one which increasingly participated in the larger society. The formulation of a modernized Mappila identity involved the adoption of some of the customs and symbols of success of this wider society. Thus, they were taking pride in adopting some of the rituals of Hindus (particularly during the marriage ceremony). Having the latest consumer durables and modern building styles for their houses had become a matter of prestige. Religiosity had also become redefined in terms of "externals." The redefinition of group identity that was being brought about manifested itself in the realm of gender relations through the modification of some of the distinctive features of earlier Mappila culture, such as the public formality between spouses, as well as the seclusion and the clothing of women. Some of the younger Mappila women had adopted the sari and the jewelry patterns of Hindu women. It is important to emphasize, however, that by adopting the sari, they were not attempting to look just like Hindu women, since the kind of saris worn by Mappila women were usually distinctive (in terms of color, design, and fabric). They also wore a headscarf that set them apart from women of other groups. In fact, I would argue that the appearance of women symbolized the refashioned identity the younger Mappilas were trying to create—one that was closer to that of the wider society but still distinct.

CHAPTER 6

Ethnicity and Migration in Cherur

THE DECASTIFICATION OF STATUS

*C*herur is a village in southern Kerala, about thirty miles north of Trivandrum, the capital city of the state. The areas that I studied were entirely Hindu—I did not come across even one family from another religious group during my fieldwork there. The caste system that existed in Cherur was fairly typical but for the fact that there were very few Brahmins in the village. The three main groups were the Ezhavas (the largest group in the area), the Nayars, and the Harijans. Since the Gulf migrants in Cherur were largely from the Ezhava community, my research focused primarily on this group. However, I also studied the other two communities to examine the impact of the migration on caste relationships in the area. Like Veni, the Cherur administrative village was very large, over seventeen square kilometers, but I concentrated on three main localities in Cherur village—Muttam, which was predominantly Ezhava; Palam, inhabited almost entirely by Nayars; and Sripuram, where there was a large Harijan colony. Of the eighty-nine households in Muttam that I visited to conduct my household survey, sixty-four were Ezhava, ten Nayar, five Harijan, two Brahmin, and eight, other castes. In Palam, the Nayar area, I went to thirty-six houses, and except for one house owned by Ezhavas, they were all owned and occupied by Nayars. There were around eight hundred houses in the Sripuram Harijan colony, but since there were very few migrants from among the Harijans, I only visited nine houses in this locality.

As we will see, Cherur presents a distinct contrast from Veni, both in its sociocultural organization and in the impact of migration. Social networks were much less important in initiating and sustaining migration in this region, when compared to Veni, and migration had only increased the competitiveness between

105

members. Matrilocality and to some extent matrilineality were strengthened since wives often stayed in their natal villages when their husbands migrated. However, the most important outcome of the migration in Cherur was that it resulted in the reformulation of caste identities and relationships. Thus, this process will be the focus of attention in the ensuing pages.

Of historical significance is the fact that Cherur is only two or three miles away from Sivagiri, where Sri Narayana Guru, the Ezhava spiritual leader, established his ashram. Therefore, the Guru had a very important influence on the area. The Ezhava organization that he established—the Sri Narayana Dharma Paripalana (SNDP) Yogam[1]—was active in the region in the early decades of the century and mobilized Ezhavas to fight against the injustices of the caste system and to improve their social and economic position in society. The Ezhavas of Cherur were strong supporters of the movement.

According to the information I obtained from the older villagers, Cherur (particularly the areas occupied by the Harijans and the Ezhavas), like Veni, was covered with scrub jungle in the early decades of the century. It was gradually cleared by settlers, and the availability of land encouraged the further inmigration of relatives. This factor, in addition to the custom of cross-cousin marriages, meant that there were kin relationships between many of the members of the Ezhava community in Cherur.

Before 1950, Nayars in the area owned most of the wetland. A few were moderately large landowners owning over fifteen acres of land, but most had between three to eight acres. The Ezhava caste formed the largest section of the population in Cherur. The traditional occupation of the caste was the tending of the coconut palm, but in Cherur, most of the Ezhavas were petty agriculturists—sharecroppers, tenants, and hired workers of the lands held by Nayars. Some even owned a few acres of land. The Harijans did the hard manual work, such as the transplanting and the harvesting.

As among the Nayars, the family structure of the Ezhavas in this region was matrilocal and matrilineal. However, Ezhavas did not have the large taravads of the Nayars, and, in fact, their families were closer to the nuclear pattern (Jeffrey 1976). Ezhava women married within their caste. Unlike the Nayars, many of the women, even from the wealthier Ezhava families, used to work outside the home. They worked in the fields, their own as well as those of others, and would then sell the share of grain they received as payment. The women had control over such money and often used it to supplement the household money given by their husbands. Many women also bought land and gold. Thus, with the combination of matrilineal inheritance, matrilocality, and a certain degree of economic independence, Ezhava women in Cherur had some autonomy and freedom of movement. Radha's and Vijaya's mothers were good examples of such middle-class Ezhava women. At the time of my fieldwork, they were both close to seventy years of age. Radha's mother lived in a tiny unplastered cottage next to her daughter's large two-story house. According to Radha, her mother had insisted on living independently and had built the cottage by using the money she got from selling the coconuts and fruit from the property and from *olah* work (weaving coconut fronds which were used to thatch the roofs of katcha huts). Despite her age, she still walked several miles a day (she would not take the bus) to do the shopping and sell her produce and, except for emergencies, refused to take money from her daughter and family. Vijaya's mother was also very independent and active. She lived with her daughter and looked after the cows and hens that they owned and also grew some vegetables. I would see her going about her chores briskly from morning to evening. Since Vijaya was not in very good health, it was her mother who took care of most of the shopping and the household tasks.

Until around the middle of this century, neither the Ezhavas nor Nayars followed the practice of giving dowries, common among many of the other groups (such as the Brahmins, the Mappilas, and the Syrian Christians), presumably due to the matrilineal inheritance pattern. Dowries were introduced only from around the middle of the century and at that time the amount given was relatively small. The practice probably began as the matrilineal system started to disintegrate.[2] The disintegration of the matrilineal system eventually gave rise to a system in which theoretically both sons and daughters received equal shares of the property. However, in practice, daughters continued to be favored for inheritance. Matrilineal practices continued in the social, symbolic, and religious realms. Matrilocal residence was slowly being abandoned.

A consequence of the Ezhava movement that had its base in this region was that members of this caste in Cherur had a strong sense of group identity and history (which was reinforced through the Ezhava organization, SNDP, which was active at a formal level in this area).[3] However, in practice, this ethnic awareness did not translate into a fulcrum of solidarity. In fact, as many of the villagers themselves told me, the Ezhavas of this region had long been characterized by a low degree of group cohesiveness as well as a great deal of intragroup competition and conflict. The lack of solidarity of the Ezhavas could probably have stemmed from their position as the majority group in the region.

Singapore Migration, 1930–1965

Like other parts of Kerala, Cherur experienced great hardship between 1930 and 1945, during the Great Depression and the Second World War. The first international migration from this area started during this period, with several villagers setting off for Singapore and Malaysia. Due to a combination of social and economic reasons, the migrants were mainly Ezhavas. In thirty-one of the sixty-five Ezhava households that I visited, one or more of the immediate family had gone to Singapore between 1930 and the mid-sixties. However, there were only three such households among the forty-five Nayar households (in Muttam and Palam) that I surveyed.

The Brahmins and the Nayars had their land to turn to, and their family structure and narrowly defined occupational roles did not give them the independence (or the desire) to undertake such a risky venture. "They preferred to enjoy an easy life," according to Sarasa, a Nayar woman from Palam, who became my good friend. At the other extreme, the Harijans were too poor and were also ignorant of such opportunities. Since most Ezhavas worked on leased land or as hired labor, they had only rather tenuous links with the land. They also had a more flexible family structure than the Brahmins and Nayars. As a group, they were also more innovative and adventurous since they had been used to engaging in a range of occupations during the late colonial period. The social awakening experienced by the caste as a result of Sri Narayana Guru's movement created a desire for status improvement. All these factors resulted in Ezhavas taking the lead in the migration.

Like the villagers from Veni, all the migrants were male and most of them went alone, leaving their families behind. The matrilocal tradition was resuscitated and many wives stayed in their own villages and were looked after by their parents and siblings. The husbands would send money to them to cover the basic household expenses of his wife and children (his wife's parents would look after the rest). The migrants obtained skilled and technician jobs in Singapore and Malaysia. Most of the migrants from Cherur were drivers of heavy vehicles or car mechanics. Because of the time and cost involved (it was a long journey by ship), the men would return home very infrequently, usually only once every five to six years.

Both Radha's and Vijaya's fathers were early Singapore migrants from the area. Radha narrated their family's story to me: "My father had been coming back every five years or so and writing periodically but then there was no news from him for a long time. Everyone thought he was dead, and his family wanted my mother to move out of the house he had built for her. But all of a sudden he showed up. He had made a lot of money by then but most of it was in Singapore. A few years later, the currency was changed and the old currency lost its value so he lost a lot that way." Vijaya's father had been in Singapore for thirty years: "I was the only child. My father came once or twice during the first eight years. Then he didn't come for twenty-two years because he quarreled with my mother. It was over a very small thing—he had told my mother not to go for a wedding but she had still gone. Finally, my cousin—his sister's son—went and brought him back from Singapore."

Some of the Ezhavas from Muttam who were in Singapore in the seventies went over to England with their families because they were given British citizenship. According to Radha, "Now they are all facing the problem of their children's marriages." Several of the girls had returned to Muttam, married men selected by their parents, and had then taken them back to England. The boys were apparently less obedient, and two of them had married non-Indians, despite opposition from their families.

Gulf Migration, 1970–1990

The Gulf migration from Cherur started only in the seventies, after job opportunities in Singapore and Malaysia had been exhausted. The first migrants from the larger region were Muslims from the coast (around ten miles away) who went on merchant launches, like the Muslims of Veni. This took place during the 1960s, but the pattern did not immediately spread to the Hindu belt (of which Cherur formed a part), except for a few from the Harijan groups. By the time the villagers from Cherur started going to the Middle East, the Gulf migration from the coastal regions had become institutionalized and had also spread to the surrounding regions. A network of agents had sprung up and the exodus from Cherur was largely through this route, except for those who were taken over by close relatives. Here again, most migrants from the area were Ezhavas. Of the sixty-five Ezhava households that I surveyed, fifty-nine had from one to four migrants in the Middle East at some time—either a household member or a close relative. However, only nine Nayar households out of the forty-five studied had a member or a close relative in the Middle East.

It was partly because of the lower degree of solidarity among the Ezhavas of Cherur that the migration took place primarily through agents, who of course charged a hefty fee. At the time of my fieldwork, "agent visas" cost around Rs. 30,000. However, ethnic networks still played an important role in the migration. Since there were thousands of agents of varying degrees of reliability, ethnic networks helped to disseminate information about which agents were most trustworthy. Some members of the community also used their position in the Middle East to act as agents for their community members. While such agents were generally more reliable, using an agent within the community did not reduce the cost of the visa. In general, if the migrant was not an immediate relative, the community member had to pay as much as he would have paid a professional agent.

Community resources were used to facilitate the migration in yet another way. The community members specialized in lending money to one another for interest. The interest charged was generally from Rs. 3 to 5 per month for every Rs. 100 (or 36 percent to 60 percent per annum), depending on the relationship between the families. If the borrower was a relative or close friend, interest was still charged, but at the lower rate. Charging community members the agent rate and high rates of interest would have been completely against the ethos of Veni and is a good indicator of the difference between the two areas.

Migrants from Cherur found jobs in the Gulf which ranged from unskilled wage labor (but this was not too common) to semiskilled (masons, welders, workers in companies), to technical work (electricians, auto mechanics, air-conditioning repairers). There were also a few drivers. I came across only one clerical worker in the area. The largest category, by far, was technicians. Most of the villagers went on group visas which again restricted their options. Within the occupational categories mentioned, the hierarchical level at which the person worked determined the salary and benefits received (supervisory workers like foremen were well paid). Thus the average income range was from Rs. 4,000 to Rs. 15,000 a month (this is in comparison to a range of Rs. 500 to Rs. 2,000 for equivalent local jobs). Most of the migrants went to the United Arab Emirates, but a few of the more recent migrants were in Saudi Arabia. There were no female migrants from the village although a few women had been taken over to the Gulf for a short period by their husbands. The type of jobs that the men obtained made it difficult and uneconomical for them to support a family in the Middle East. Furthermore, like the Mappilas, the Ezhavas also felt that having women stay in the village while their husbands migrated was more suitable than having the whole family in the Gulf (see also Osella and Osella 2000a, 43).

Kumar, a middle-aged man who had been in the Middle East for many years, described his situation to me: "I worked as a mason in Muscat. The work was hard, in the scorching sun. But I did it so that I could get my children into a good situation. Every time I came home I would be tempted to stay but then, seeing the hardships, I would go again. The only good thing about life there was the food. We had a mess there and the food was excellent—wonderful *basmati* rice, all kinds of fruits, vegetables, meat, cold drinks and all in unlimited quantities!" Kumar told me that he was a little disappointed that, despite his hard work, his children were still not in a financially sound position. Though he had got them educated, the education had not helped his sons obtain good jobs. While he was glad to be home for good, Kumar told me that the negative side was that now he had no income of his own and had to depend on his children.

The typical migrant from this area hailed from a relatively poor family of tenant cultivators. The money for the migration was generally raised through the dowry of the wife (part of the land and gold thus obtained would be sold for cash), and the rest on loan for high rates of interest. So, the migrant had to first clear this loan. He was expected to send money for household expenses and the support of parents and siblings. He also had to build a house for his family and to take care of the dowry and wedding expenses of his sisters.

On their return visits (which took place, on average, around once in two years), the migrants had to bring back gifts for members of their families. With all these expenses to meet, it generally took several years before the household of a migrant could accumulate any significant savings. Some money was sent through the tube, but this was not common. In general, the migrant would keep a portion of his salary for personal expenses and for the next trip home and would send back the rest of the money at regular intervals in the form of a postal or bank draft. In the early period of migration, some migrants had started chitties, but, due to defaulting by members, this had collapsed. There seemed to be a few cases of small-scale smuggling, too, but only a few people were involved and even they did so only occasionally.

There was a big change in expenditure patterns after 1983, as wages were cut and workers retrenched. According to Narayanan, an older migrant, "Now the Gulf boom is over and the Arabs are taking over many of the jobs. Earlier, they were totally uncivilized. Why, I have seen an Arab swallowing a tube of toothpaste, thinking it was something to eat! But they sent their children abroad to be educated and so there are now people to work the upper-level jobs. There are even people for the lower levels and I think that process will be completed in a few years and then there will be no jobs left for Malayalees." Many people who had thought their jobs secure and had therefore been spending money very lavishly had either lost their jobs or had suffered drastic cuts in their salaries. The mid-eighties was a period of great hardship for many families and most went back to a simpler lifestyle.

The most dramatic case was that of Jyothi, the wife of a foreman in a company in the Middle East. Jyothi's husband was one of the earliest and most successful migrants in the area, and he had used his money to build a local hospital, which had done very well for a time. Many of the women in Cherur told me about Jyothi's arrogance and extravagances during this period. This account is from Jaya, Jyothi's immediate neighbor:

> When the hospital was doing well, she would throw around her money— chicken, lamb and fish for every meal, glittering silks for herself and her children. She would even take the car all the way to Trivandrum and Quilon [cities that were over an hour away] just to do her grocery shopping. During this time, she was so arrogant, she would not even acknowledge us. But then the hospital ran into problems and a little later, her husband lost his job. In the worst period, they did not have the money to pay their house tax and Jyothi has even had to walk to Varkala [the nearest town which was around eight miles away]. Then she came to plead with all of us to lend her money. She has borrowed large amounts which she has so far refused to return. It is only in the past few years that their situation has improved after her husband was able to get another job in the Gulf. He has also made money by charging high rates and taking over some people from here.

The Fieldwork

Since I had originally planned to study an urban Muslim community, I had tried to find a place to rent in Kuttur, along the main interstate highway where the Muslim community lived. As a single woman, however, I had a difficult time because people would not rent to me, suspicious of my motives. It was only through the help of a coworker of my uncle that I was finally able to rent a one-bedroom cottage in Kuttur. When I decided to do my study in Cherur, I tried to find a place in the village to move into but there was no equivalent of the Veni line quarters in Cherur and, in fact, no houses for rent. As Kuttur was an easy bus ride from Cherur, I stayed on there and took the bus everyday to Cherur. Unlike Veni, there were no health workers in the Cherur area, but there was a government-aided balawadi in the heart of Muttam, taught by Sarasa, a Nayar woman from Palam. Sarasa was a very intelligent, outgoing, and open-minded woman, well liked by all the villagers. Although she was a Nayar, she told me that she found the other Nayars in Palam very narrow minded and that her closest friends were Ezhavas in Muttam. Sarasa's help was invaluable for my fieldwork in Cherur. It was through her that I made friends and contacts in Muttam. Sarasa also accompanied me on the household visits to Palam, the Nayar area, over a couple of weekends and organized my initial visit to the Harijan colony. Unlike in Veni, however, balawadi teachers did not have to conduct house visits or maintain records about the households, so I was not able to obtain the types of basic demographic information that I had in Veni. I had discussions with several knowledgeable people such as elderly residents, schoolteachers, doctors, and politicians for details about the community as a whole and its history. (Most often I would be directed to such people by the villagers themselves.) In the Cherur area, I would arrive at the balawadi in the morning, leave my things there, and go for my visits. I generally returned to eat my packed lunch and also spent time in between visits at the balawadi, helping Sarasa. I caught the bus back to Kuttur whenever I finished my work for the day.

The differences in the social atmosphere between Cherur and Veni, the personalities of the women, and my own reception were tangible and struck me very forcefully when I started my research in Cherur. Since a lot of the local men were in the Middle East, Cherur was a female-dominated village and being a female researcher was an advantage in this area. I was immediately and warmly received by Sarasa and all the families I visited in Muttam. Several of the women took me under their wing and helped me considerably with my research, patiently answering my questions, telling me about all the goings-on in the village, and organizing various visits for me—both to see officials and to visit households. When I did the initial household visits, they would accompany me themselves or send their children with me. Many of the local women read newspapers and magazines. They also had some exposure to television programs (they would congregate in the houses of those who had televisions when special programs were on the air) so they were much more knowledgeable about the world outside Cherur than the women in Veni. My hairstyle did not occasion much comment except for a few times in the beginning when one or two women I met would urge me to grow my hair, saying that I would look "so much nicer" with long tresses.

While I was still somewhat of an anomaly in this area, the villagers accepted that my study of the *jeevitha reethi* (lifestyle) of the people of the area and the rapid changes that had taken place due to migration was something that I had to do to finish my higher education. Since education was highly respected, and generally both men and women married only after completing their education, my being unmarried did not give rise to much comment or discussion. The issue came up only once in the house of one of the families that I was close to. They were telling me that they hoped I would come back "after my studies" and live in their village. In that context, the father of the household smiled and remarked, "Don't worry, we can find a nice man for you." It was my being in the United States that was the biggest novelty for the people in Cherur. To my discomfiture, Sarasa would insist on introducing me proudly to everyone we met as her friend from "Ameeerica." The women in this area were substantially better informed about other countries than the women of Veni, so everyone had heard about the United States. Many of them wanted to know about the white people and the *jeevitha reethi* in "Ameeerica," so unlike in Veni, there was a much greater give and take between the villagers and myself in Cherur.

I was invited to join household meals several times (which happened only one or two times in the other two areas) and to stay overnight at some of their houses. I was also invited to the wedding of one of the local men which was taking place during the time of my fieldwork, again something which did not happen in the other two areas. I had, by far, the easiest and most enjoyable fieldwork experience in Cherur. I was treated with affection and concern and incorporated into the community as a sister. The women confided in me and talked fairly openly about problems within the family and between families. In November, when I took up residence in Trivandrum city to conclude my work by doing some archival research, I returned to Cherur for a three-week period (taking the "Super-Express" bus) to supplement my earlier fieldwork but also to spend some time with my friends there before I left Kerala in December.

Consumption, Investment, and Exchange Patterns

Because of the earlier Singapore migration, the economic changes brought about in Cherur as a consequence of the Gulf migration were not as dramatic as in Veni. However, the Gulf migration was much more widespread, the return visits of migrants far more frequent, and the income earned was much greater, and thus the changes that were slowly beginning to be introduced during the Singapore migration were tremendously accelerated with the second exodus to the Middle East.

At the time of my fieldwork, most of the migrant houses in Muttam were built on either side of a tarred road and were in the new, fashionable terraced style (houses built completely of concrete with flat concrete roofs). Most were medium to large in size. Many had modern gadgets—electric pumps for running water, gas stoves, refrigerators, televisions, even an occasional VCR. The people were well dressed, usually in synthetic material from abroad. Young women wore the fashionable maxis (nightgowns) when at home. The children were also dressed according to the latest Kerala fashion. Most households ate well with fish or meat for both lunch and dinner and plenty of fruit, vegetables, and milk. "Earlier, my neighbor was quite poor and would come back from the market with her basket loaded with cassava, because that is all she could afford. But now, her basket is loaded with plantains and other fruit. And right on top, she places a video cassette, to let everyone know that she owns a VCR!" said Radha's sister, Valsa.

There seemed to be a lot of competitive spending as a consequence of the Gulf migration. Pramod was complaining about how expensive it had become to live in Muttam. "In today's world," he said, "it is the 'make up' that matters. Even if a person does not have money, he has to act and dress as though he does if he wants to be treated well. Otherwise, the rich will crush him under their foot. It is like a tiny sparrow versus a kite. If the sparrow sits quietly and sadly, the kite will come and pounce on it. So the sparrow must fly with the kite to make sure it is not eaten."

Unlike Veni, there was very little investment of Gulf money in local business. This was despite the fact that there were very few shops in the area. Most villagers took the bus to the nearest town (around six miles away) to do their shopping. The few people who had tried to start new shops wound up with big losses. According to the villagers, this was due to the lack of a business tradition and the competitive nature of the community, which did not support local entrepreneurial activity. Apparently, many people preferred to go to the town for their purchases rather than give their business to a fellow villager. They also felt that goods sold locally were inferior to and more expensive than what they could get in the town.

The major items of expenditure in this area were the life-cycle rituals and festivals that constituted an important part of the social and religious life of a Hindu community. Life-cycle ceremonies had been elaborated, and several new rites of gift giving (largely of gold) had been introduced. The ceremonies were also conducted on a far more lavish scale than earlier "with lots more guests, lots of different food items, and several more meals." Marriages were the biggest of such celebrations, and thus migrants spent a good proportion of their Gulf money on the weddings of their sisters, daughters, and close relatives. "Now weddings have become so expensive to conduct. You have to book the wedding hall and have to serve several meals to all the invitees. Then you have to buy clothes for the relatives and pay the travel costs of the important guests. There are several trips back and forth between the bride's and groom's place before and after the wedding where you have to rent taxis for everyone. You also have to provide accommodation for the guests. So all of this together comes to Rs. 50,000 easily," said Chaaru, a woman in her fifties. Dowry rates had risen sharply due to the new affluence.[4] According to Sarasa, the balawadi teacher, "When a Gulfite whose family used to work for the old rich celebrates the marriage of his daughter, he will give one hundred and one *pavan* [the local unit of gold, about eight grams] knowing that his former employer gave fifty pavan when his daughter got married, to establish himself as the new elite."

Life-cycle ceremonies and festivals were also occasions when the members of the community were expected to give fairly substantial gifts. Vidya, the wife of a man who had returned from the Middle East after only a few years and who was now supporting the family on a modest income, was telling me about how there was always some ritual or the other among families in the area—such as weddings and births, where they were expected to give gifts. "It is demeaning if we don't give a certain amount. Since we are not wealthy, my brother and brother-in-law [who were both in the Middle East] meet these expenses, so we don't have to suffer a loss of face." These gifts were in cash or gold and the amount to be given was informally specified and depended on the closeness of the relationship and the relative economic position of the two parties. Thus a close and wealthy relative would be obliged to give a large gift. I gathered that in Muttam, the minimum amount one could give as a wedding gift was Rs. 25 unless one was very poor, in which case, Rs. 15 or 20 was acceptable. However, if the wedding was in the house of a neighbor or a distant relative, people were expected to give at least Rs. 51 to Rs. 101. A close relative had to give at least Rs. 1,001 or gold of equivalent value. If the household had a member in the Gulf, they had to give Rs. 5,001 for the wedding of a close relative. Thus, as in Veni, Gulf money had created a circle of reciprocity and redistribution within the community in Cherur. The difference between Veni and Cherur in this respect was that in Veni, it was redistribution that was emphasized and it often took place between migrants and poorer nonmigrant community members. In Cherur, redistribution was mainly among close relatives, and it was reciprocity that was stressed. Unlike in Veni, there was no mechanism by which poor people were helped in the area, even for emergencies.

Temple festivals were cited as another major source of expenditure. Several villagers told me how "people from the temple committees just descend on us during *ulsavam* [festival] time. They leave a receipt for an amount which they determine by looking at the house. You have to give them the money when they come next." Gulf migrants often sponsored various activities at the temple during the ulsavams such as the lighting for a particular day, the dance drama, or the fireworks.

Education was another major item of expenditure. As low castes, the Ezhavas had not been allowed to attend government schools and colleges in the earlier period (although the state as a whole had traditionally placed a lot of emphasis on education). Thus, investing in education was yet another means that the Ezhavas used to achieve a change in status (see also Osella and Osella 2000a). Many of the children were sent to the relatively expensive English medium schools, and money was also spent on various coaching classes to make sure the children obtained good results. Some Gulf migrants also paid the large "donations" or "entrance fees" demanded by private colleges so that their children could get a college degree.

Expenditure on medical care was another item that received a big boost after the Gulf migration. Gulf migrants avoided the public, government-run hospitals and went instead to expensive private clinics, even for relatively routine matters. Several large private hospitals had sprung up in the towns and cities around Cherur. There was one such hospital in Kuttur, very close to where I lived, and a doctor who worked there told me that the hospital was "flooded with Gulfans." She continued, "For instance, for a delivery the woman comes early and then lies here for weeks. It is 'fashionable' to spend between thirty to forty thousand rupees on the whole process."[5]

Earlier, many Gulf houses had invested money in land but the prices had dropped a great deal from the mid-eighties. At the time that I did my fieldwork, the primary source of investment in Cherur was usurious lending to other community members. I have mentioned that interest rates were from 36 to 60 percent per year. Thus this was a very lucrative source of income. Here again, a few members had defaulted in the last few years, and so some of the Gulf money was also being deposited in banks.

Migration and Caste

In chapter 1, I argued that the desire for status was the main driving force behind the patterns of economic behavior manifested by Gulf migrants. Besides legitimizing and buttressing economic standing, status plays a central role in creating communities and in binding members of a collectivity together. The Indian caste structure has long been seen as the quintessential embodiment of such a status system, organizing societal membership, community formation, and identity. In this section, I examine the ways in which the relationships between members of different castes, the meaning of caste and community identity, and the caste structure itself was affected by the Gulf migration. While caste-like structures were present in both the Christian and Muslim communities, the Hindu community had the most elaborate and well-defined caste structure and ideology. As such, the greatest amount of "status work" was needed in this group as the Ezhavas staked a claim to community recognition and standing.

The Indian caste system has generally been viewed as being a rigid and unchanging hierarchy. In practice, however, change and mobility have always been a part of the system. Over the centuries, there have been many castes that have risen or fallen within the caste hierarchy. Conventionally, when a lower caste became affluent or powerful, a process of caste mobility called Sanskritization (Srinivas 1968) was initiated, whereby the style of life and the customs and rituals of a higher caste were adopted. Typically, the low caste gave up its former low-status occupation, adopted vegetarianism and teetotalism, maintained stricter control over the "purity" of its women, and took over some of the Vedic rites confined to the upper castes, including the wearing of the sacred thread. Generally, these changes were "followed by a claim to a higher position in the caste hierarchy than that traditionally conceded to the claimant caste by the local community" (Srinivas 1968, 6). Social mobility took the form of Sanskritization or collective mobility since individual or family mobility was traditionally more difficult within the caste system. The achievement of a higher status was usually a slow process, taking several generations, and was generally undertaken by castes who were able to advance economically *and* acquire political power. Some of the well-known historical cases are the *Kayasthas,* traditionally assigned the status of a Sudra caste, who were able to become influential members of the Mughal court and who subsequently fought legal battles to have their caste position changed, and the *Noniyas,* who were considered "almost untouchable" but whose economic mobility has since gained them a position among the top few castes of the area (Pandey 1986, 77–78). The *Nadars* of Tamil Nadu are another example. Originally an untouchable caste called *Shanars,* they succeeded in developing a mercantile upper stratum and then claimed Kshatriya status and the new caste name in the 1901 census.

In Cherur, the Ezhava migrants had changed their occupation and lifestyle and, as in the case of Sanskritization, adopted new rituals and ceremonies. What was different about this case and distinguished it from the conventional processes of Sanskritization was that the rituals that the Ezhavas introduced were not those practiced by the higher castes of the area. On the contrary, it was the Nayars and even the Brahmins in the village who were subsequently forced to modify some of their existing practices and to adopt ones more in consonance with those of the Ezhavas.

The new rituals can be studied as a cultural text—a symbolic expression of the emerging social order. My argument is that, unlike Sanskritization which resulted in *positional* changes of castes within the existing structure, what was taking place in Cherur and the high-migrant Hindu areas nearby was a *reformulation of the structure* itself. This was not merely a consequence of the migration but was the end product of a long sequence of changes initiated by colonialism and commercialization. The migration of the past two decades precipitated the transformation of the system by bringing about a reversal of the economic position of the major castes.

While Hinduism has its philosophical doctrines, the main way in which the ordinary Hindu traditionally demonstrated his or her religiosity was by punctiliously performing all the religious observances. In Kerala, these included observing the rules of pollution and purity of the caste system, the performance of the various rites of passage, the celebration of the major festivals, and the regular visit to temples as well as the observance of fasts and other religious austerities. In general, the degree to which the various prescribed practices were observed varied directly with caste (and subcaste) status. Thus it was the Brahmins who were strictest in these observances. However, prior to the seventies, it was the Nayars of Cherur who were known for the lavishness with which ceremonies and festivals were celebrated. I was told over and over again about Nayar families that had lost their landholdings over time by "selling and eating" (selling land in order to throw lavish feasts for such occasions).[6] During this period, the Ezhavas continued to follow most of the ceremonial practices of the Nayars.

The Nayars maintained their tradition of living off the land even in the post–1970 period, when the Middle Eastern migration was spreading rapidly in the Ezhava sections of the village, but their landholdings grew progressively smaller due to partitioning. The wages of agricultural labor also increased tremendously during the same period, primarily due to unionization and the scarcity of labor created by the large-scale Gulf migration. As a consequence, the Nayars gradually became impoverished. Their decrease in economic standing was all the more glaring because of the steady enrichment of the Ezhavas during the same period. At the time of my fieldwork, the differences between the two groups were great and very visible. I have indicated that the pattern of settlement in Cherur was such that the Ezhavas were clustered together in one area, the Nayars in another, and the Harijans in a third. This made the differences between the areas even starker.

In contrast to the large "terraced" houses of the Ezhavas, on either side of the tarred road, Nayar houses were mainly set on the two slopes on either side of a long strip of paddy fields. There were only dirt roads or tracks leading to the houses, and the houses themselves were on the older model with thatched or tiled sloping roofs. They were also far smaller than those in the Ezhava area and for the most part without the gadgets in the latter. In the matter of clothes, too, the two areas presented a sharp contrast, with Nayars dressed in rather drab, old cotton clothes. Again, almost no Nayar child was sent to the English medium school, and few parents could afford to have their children take coaching classes.

New Ceremonies and Rituals

Besides making changes in their lifestyle due to their Gulf affluence, the Ezhavas had also introduced changes in the ceremonial and ritual sphere. In general, rites of gift giving had been inserted in several parts of the older rituals, all ceremonies were conducted on a grander scale, and several new ceremonies had been instituted by Gulf families.

Most of the changes related to the ceremonies connected with marriage. Thus, at the time of my fieldwork, there was often a lavish "engagement" ceremony at the woman's house and a "tea party" on the evening before the wedding. Guests at the wedding eve ceremony (relatives and friends of the bride's family) brought gifts of cash which the bride's family used to defray the expenses of the wedding. This function had been introduced around the late sixties, and from the early eighties, a similar ceremony was often arranged at the man's house for the relatives and friends of the bridegroom's family, who would also bring gifts of cash.[7] The actual wedding was conducted on a far grander scale than in the past and, where it once used to take place in the home of the bride, it was now arranged at the wedding hall in Sivagiri (the Ezhava religious center) with expensive catered meals. Large amounts of gold were given as part of the dowry or the trousseau of the bride (in addition to the bride's property share).[8]

However, the most interesting innovations were the new gold and gift-giving rituals interspersed during the course of the marriage and post-marriage ceremonies. Some examples of these are given below. The new rituals are in italics:

1. When the groom's sister presented the wedding saree to the bride, *she reciprocated with a gold bangle or a watch* (earlier she would only give a brass vessel).
2. When the groom put on the wedding chain (of gold) on the bride, *she gave him a gold chain in return.*
3. On the bride's crossing the threshold of her new home (the house of her husband's parents), her mother-in-law welcomed her by giving her a lamp. *The bride gave her a gold bangle in return.*
4. When the bride's family went to the groom's house for the first time after the wedding, *her father had to give pocket money [English words used] to the bridegroom.* (Earlier this used to be more of a symbolic gift. At the time of my fieldwork, a fairly large sum of money was given.)
5. On that visit or later, when the woman's family came to the man's house "to see the kitchen," *they had to take gifts of furniture and kitchen equipment with them* (earlier they only had to give a few cooking pots and some sweets).
6. After staying at the man's house for a few days, the couple went to stay with the woman's family. At this time, *the woman's side was expected to give some gold to the man's sister and had to give an equal amount to the bride.* The man's side would bring clothes for the woman's family and *the woman's side also reciprocated.*

When we examine these new prestations, we see that all of them are from the woman's side to the man's. This pattern of gift giving was introduced by the newly rich families of the bride and the gifts were usually given in reciprocation for ritual services performed by the bridegroom (or someone from his side) during the course of the marriage or post-marriage ceremonies.

Wealthy Gulf grooms on their part had started a trend of their own. They generally turned down (as demeaning) the monetary inducements offered by the families of prospective brides and looked instead for such attributes as education and family status. In such marriages, unlike the above cases, the flow of benefits was more equal or the direction was actually reversed. The groom often bore most of the expenses for the marriage (conventionally, it was the bride's family that did this); the wedding chain he gave the bride was far more expensive (in one case that I witnessed, he gave her two chains instead of one); he gifted his in-laws expensive consumer items (a color television was common) in the first few years of marriage; he built a luxurious house in a few years time (or sometimes even before getting married) with labor-saving gadgets and entirely with his money (here again the conventional pattern was that the woman's dowry went toward part of this expense and her father would have been expected to come forward with more if the couple had financial difficulty).

In one such case, Rajan, a young migrant in Cherur who worked as a mason in the Middle East, had built himself a house even before getting married. Neighbors told me with awe that the house was "equipped with everything: television, VCR, mixer, grinder, and even a device to lie down and bathe" (a bathtub, which until then had not been seen in that region). He subsequently returned from the Gulf during the period that I was doing my fieldwork, and married a woman with a bachelor's degree (he himself had only had five or six years of schooling) at a lavish wedding ceremony that he paid for. After the wedding he took her on a tour of some of the scenic areas in the neighboring states (such honeymoon trips were also a recent introduction in the area).

The Social Meaning of the New Rituals

While the new rituals and prestation patterns had to do with changed wife-giver/wife-taker relations, they could also be seen as symbolic of the transforming structure of social relations in the area. Marriage was a crucial sphere in which such changes were manifested. In India, marriage is the most important and the most public (with the largest number of invitees) life-cycle ritual. Thus, it is the best occasion to demonstrate a change in social standing. Perhaps even more important, a marriage in the typical Indian context is arranged by the elders of the two sides and is seen as the formation of an alliance between the two corporate groups. The forging of important and prestigious alliances are fundamental to social and political status and marriage is socially significant for this reason as well.

The villagers (particularly the nonmigrants) felt that the lavishness and all the new gold-giving rituals were introduced by the migrants to "show off" and to "assert their position as the new elite." And why did Gulf grooms begin to turn down offers of large dowries? I was told: "They have money, what they need now is status, so they try to get girls from 'good' families or who are well educated. It is demeaning for them to be seen to be marrying for money." In short, the seeming contradiction between these developments in the patterns of marriage exchanges can be explained by the desire of Gulf families (both of the bride and groom) to obtain higher-status matches as one of the ways by which they could rise in status themselves (see Osella 2000a, 81–116). Thus, Gulf migration had given rise both to hypergamous marriages (where the man's side is of a higher status than the woman's side) and hypogamous marriages (where the reverse is the case). This, however, was a significant change from the earlier pattern where there was "a positive preference for isogamous unions, i.e., for unions in which both spouses' families are of equal status" (Fuller 1976, 74–75). Hypogamous marriage in particular was "anathema" in the traditional Indian system (Fuller 1976, 77). As cross-cousin marriages used to be the pattern among the Ezhavas (and Nayars), conventionally the "lawful spouse" was a relative and there was an overlap between kin and affinal relationships.[9] Cross-cousin marriages also meant that wives were *exchanged* between two (or more) intermarrying groups. Both these factors account for the traditional isogamous pattern of marriages and probably accounts for prestation patterns being more or less equal (going by the descriptions given by the respondents).[10] However, by the late eighties, cross-cousin marriages had fallen out of favor.

Typically, it was the formation of a marriage alliance between two families of unequal status (generally hypergamous marriages) that resulted in the large and continuing flow of prestations from the lower- to the higher-status family. In such cases, there was no prior kin relationship between the two groups and only a one-way affinal relationship, not a reciprocity. In other words, it was clearly the introduction of hypergamous marriages that was responsible for the new gift giving from the bride's side, and vice versa, hypogamous marriages had brought about the reversal of the prestation patterns in the case of Gulf grooms.

The Decastification of Status

The introduction of hypergamy and hypogamy illustrate that the traditional principles underlying marriage patterns were being eroded. What is of even greater significance than the change in the *pattern* of marriage (from equal to unequal status matches) is the change in the *content* of status. Hypergamous marriages in Kerala and elsewhere in India are typically between members of a higher and lower *caste* (or subcaste) or at least of higher and lower family status or ancestry. However, an examination of the new marriage patterns, and my conversations with the villagers, seemed to indicate that it was education (and the income that accrues through having educational qualifications) that was most highly regarded. I was told, "If a boy has education, that's what counts nowadays. Then no one looks at family [background] or wealth." (Family status was still quite important, but the two criteria were overlapping since increasingly, family status or ancestry referred to the type of jobs that were held by family members in the past or at the present.)

Thus a good match for a girl was usually considered to be "a doctor, an engineer, a lawyer with a good practice, or a holder of a government job" (in that order). Many wealthy Gulf families were able to get such grooms for their high-school-educated daughters. One coir merchant of high standing in the village recounted: "My relatives and friends tell me: 'Look for education, not more wealth [in the bridegroom] for your daughter. Education begets education so even your daughter's children will be able to get good positions. Wealth, especially

Gulf wealth is ephemeral and can pass away.'" A woman with a master's or a bachelor's degree was considered to be a prize catch for a man and again several migrants with just a few years of education, but with well-paying jobs in the Middle East, were able to marry such women from relatively less affluent families.[11]

The following excerpt from a long conversation I had with women in Muttam regarding marriage practices and ceremonies provides further evidence of the new norms underlying the practice of dowry.

> Generally, men don't *ask* for a dowry when they contract a marriage. It is considered to be in bad taste and most families will not give daughters in marriage to a man who has any financial demands. But of course, it is impossible to get a girl married without giving anything. The men don't ask because they can generally assess how much gold the family will give the girl and how much her property share is worth. Dowries in the form of cash are generally considered vulgar and are avoided.
>
> Men from the lower classes, however, do make financial demands. Poor people have to give [relatively] large sums of cash in addition to gold and property to get their daughters married since this is what the couple uses to start off in life. A huge dowry [including cash and expensive consumer goods] has also to be given to get a man with a professional or salaried job. One has to give a car to get a doctor or engineer and around Rs. 100,000 for a lawyer with a good practice [in addition to a large amount of gold and the promised property share]. *It is only in such cases, where the man is highly educated that the groom's side can make demands and the bride's side has to give what is demanded.*[12]

In other words, it was shameful for an average middle-class person to demand a dowry, but poor men did this because they needed the money. Paradoxically, however, it was perfectly justified (even appropriate) for a highly educated person to make extravagant dowry demands. This seeming contradiction makes sense if the cash dowry in the latter case is viewed as a tribute to the high educational and professional status of the groom.[13] Such payments have been described as being "groom-price" (Caplan 1993, 359ff; Osella and Osella 2000a, 97).

Although it was theoretically possible for a person from a poor family to obtain a professional education and a salaried government job, in general, wealthy families had a distinct advantage. Coaching classes and private schools were expensive and, even if the child was successful at that stage, admission into many of the professional and technical courses conducted by private colleges could only be obtained through "donations" (which ran up to Rs. 300,000 for a seat in a medical college in the late eighties). Getting a job after earning such a degree was still not easy. Most salaried jobs in Kerala could only be obtained by paying another huge donation (often an amount equal to more than the five year income earned on the job).

Thus Gulfites could use their money to purchase a comfortable lifestyle and also to buy education as a means of legitimizing and refining their (new) money. In short, over the second half of the twentieth century, the traditional system had changed to such an extent that not only had the monopoly of the upper castes over the control of income-generating resources been whittled away, but in many ways, status itself had become commoditized.

I have mentioned that it was the Ezhavas who had introduced the pattern of status spending for weddings. The Nayars resisted this pattern at first, justifying it by saying: "We are careful with money and know better than to throw it around unnecessarily. The Ezhavas are just wasteful spendthrifts." As their own social position deteriorated, however, and that of the Ezhavas rose, the wealthier Nayar started following the Ezhava model. As a savvy Ezhava woman put it: "If an Ezhava gave Rs. 25 as a wedding present, a Nayar would only give Rs. 10: if an Ezhava gave a dowry of fifty-one pavan, a Nayar would only give thirty-one pavan. The Nayars have been trying to catch up only in the last few years." The Nambudiris of the area had fairly simple wedding ceremonies. However, even they admitted to having been forced to modify their practices a little in the recent period, particularly in the case of dowries and wedding gifts. Even so, they still continued to give far less than an Ezhava of equal economic standing.

Interpreting the New Patterns

In the previous section, I have described and tried to "decode" the modifications in the patterns of marriage alliances and in the rituals and ceremonies of marriage introduced by the Ezhavas as a consequence of their newfound affluence. Turning now to the interpretation of these new patterns, I would argue that the modifications symbolized a challenge to the cultural hegemony of the upper castes and are indicative of a fundamental change in the traditional system. If colonialism resulted in a *reformation* of the system, the large-scale migration seems to have brought about its *transformation*. Recall that in chapter 3, I indicated that the caste system at the end of the colonial period had become a structure of hierarchical, endogamous status groups. Although it is still too early to say anything definitive about the long-term implications of the recent changes, my impression was that the caste system, particularly in the migrant areas, was moving toward an arrangement that created and maintained community, and that regulated the marriage universe of its members. Thus, my argument is that the new marriage patterns and rituals symbolized a process of the *decastification of status*. This can be seen from the fact that marriages between partners of unequal social status (typically hypergamous marriages) which were earlier based on caste or *ritual purity* were increasingly based on *achieved* qualities such as education, class position, and occupational status. Marriages were still arranged within the caste group but the universe of marriage alliances had become larger since subcaste distinctions had become less relevant. The personal qualifications of the individual and the family generally superseded subcaste considerations.

The changes were not in' the direction of Sanskritization. While the new gold-giving rituals were structured to fit into the broader Hindu cultural context, they were not in imitation of Nayar (or Brahmin) practices, particularly of the groups in the area. In fact, it was the Nayars and even the Brahmins who later followed the lead of the Ezhavas. Again, classic Sanskritization strategies such as vegetarianism (the Nayars avoided beef and many did not eat lamb either, but Ezhavas ate lamb and many even ate beef) and teetotalism were not introduced, and ceremonies such as the puberty festival, which many Nayars still continued to perform, were no longer celebrated by the Ezhavas. Furthermore, while the Ezhavas could have had their weddings conducted at the traditionally high-caste temple by Brahmins, most preferred to go to Sivagiri and to use Ezhava priests. All the evidence seemed to indicate that the Ezhavas were not aiming to "pass" as Nayars, to be like them, or even to have Nayar friends. Instead, they were secure and self-possessed, with a strong sense of caste identity and pride.

This, of course, was not a change that came about only due to the migration. Other developments in the twentieth century such as the social reform movements and the communist movement were also responsible for the rise in the status of the Ezhavas. Furthermore, Ezhava organization and pride were particularly strong in the Cherur region since it was the center of the caste movements initiated by Sri Narayana Guru and had also become a fairly strong communist base. While many of the traditional features of the caste system existed in other parts of Kerala that I visited or knew about (even just a hundred or so miles to the north of Cherur), in spirit if not in form, this was not the case in Cherur. In this area, the numerical preponderance of the Ezhavas, their political power, and the current economic ascendancy gained by the decades of migration had turned the traditional system on its head and class and education were superseding caste as an indicator of status.

There were other developments that could be taken as indications of this change. For instance, interdining between castes had become fairly common. While there were still some Nayars (mainly older people) who did not dine with Ezhavas, this was not behavior that was condoned even by most Nayars. I was told that most people, particularly those who were educated (considered to be the social elite of the community), would have been ashamed to show that they still held on to such old-fashioned rules. Earlier, upper castes invited to an Ezhava wedding would generally only attend the function the day before the wedding when snack items were served (accepting such food from lower castes was permitted even in the traditional caste system). If it was a Nayar wedding, the Ezhavas would be called in to eat after the Nayars had finished and left the hall. The Harijans would be served last and would only be permitted to sit outside the hall. All those practices had been abandoned, and I was told that "now, all those who are decently dressed are served food together." I saw this at the wedding I attended.

Again, while the majority of the Harijans lived in separate colonies and were still treated as a low-status group, I came to realize that this was as much due to class as caste. A few educated, salaried Harijans lived in the Ezhava area and seemed to be treated as equals. During the initial period of my fieldwork in the area, the local preschool was staffed by two Nayar women: Sarasa and a cook. But by the end of June, the Nayar cook had been fired and a Harijan installed in her place. In November, Sarasa went on leave for a few months, and a Harijan teacher was hired for the period. When I asked some of the villagers whether anyone had minded having their child taught and fed by Harijans (something that would have been totally unheard of earlier and would not have been well received in many parts of the state even in the late eighties) I was told that no one had objected. "It is not caste that matters but hygiene."

Transformation of the Caste System

The metamorphosis of the caste system went hand in hand with substantial changes in the economic, political, and social standing of the main castes in the Cherur region. The Nambudiris, once considered to be the semidivine local rulers, had become ordinary landlords and salaried workers (though they were still treated with some awe and respect by the villagers). The Nayars had become a largely impoverished group, in psychological and social retreat from the community that they once dominated, and the Ezhavas, formerly considered noncaste Hindus with few rights and only a little above the slave castes, had become an increasingly affluent section of society, rapidly becoming educated and politically powerful. With their numerical preponderance and economic, political, and social power, they seemed to be taking over as the local dominant caste.

As a group, the Harijans were still economically and socially marginal in society. Although they no longer faced any legal restrictions, in practice, most of them led their lives in colonies that were separated from the rest of the society. Even in the case of the Harijans, however, those who were able to move out of the colonies and obtain salaried occupations were accorded a far better status.

These changes were effected with amazing rapidity. I have argued that this transformation took place due to two principal processes—colonialism and large-scale labor migration. Both processes resulted in the creation of a new structure of economic opportunities in the society at large, one that reversed the preexisting structure and allowed the lower castes and classes to be the prime beneficiaries.

Until the middle of this century, upward mobility took place through the process of Sanskritization. Both the Nayars and Ezhavas had been actively engaged in this process as a means to secure status in the society. But the breakdown of the caste system and the social structure linked with it, together with the large-scale Ezhava migration which brought about an economic reversal in the position between the Ezhavas and the Nayars, resulted in caste mobility taking a new form based on fundamentally different principles. I must again emphasize that while some of these changes seemed to be taking place in Kerala as a whole, this analysis is confined to the high-migrant areas around Cherur.

Migration and the Position of the Harijans

The Harijan colony that I visited in Cherur had around eight hundred houses, but only around twenty-five migrants had ever gone to the Gulf from the whole colony. The initial pattern of migration of the Harijans was similar to that of the Muslim fisherfolk of Pullad since, in both cases, four to five men had gone to the Middle East on merchant launches in the late sixties, had become wealthy, and had moved out of the lower-caste area. But the migration did not spread among the Harijans as it did among the Ten Muslims. Apparently no more Harijans ventured to take this route. These first migrants only took their brothers over to the Gulf but no one else, and thus there was no multiplier effect among the Harijans, unlike in the Muslim case. Later, around seven or eight migrants went to the Middle East after selling some land, and a few from this group managed to do reasonably well. A third group had borrowed money and migrated around 1984. Since the salaries had dropped a great deal by then, most had suffered a net loss. Thus, unlike the Muslim fisherfolk, they could not take advantage of the migration success of the higher-caste migrants in the area.

In chapter 3, I described the abysmal position of the slave castes (the Harijans of today) in the traditional caste hierarchy. The legislation and commercialization introduced during the colonial period brought some relief to their position. Slavery was outlawed, as were many other caste restrictions, such as those limiting the movement, clothing, and possessions of the lower castes. In practice, however, the situation of the Harijans did not improve to any great extent, particularly in the rural areas where they still continued to be economically bound to the upper castes. It was the reforms initiated by the communist leadership that brought about the first significant gains in their economic (and, therefore, their social) position. The land-reform legislation conferred ownership rights to a small piece of land ("hut sites") on a significant proportion of the Harijans; the expansion of welfare state provisions such as minimum wages, pensions for laborers, and low-cost government housing also benefited this section of the population. As a result of affirmative action, a few Harijans were able to rise to very high positions, but these families generally lived in the urban areas.

After 1970, the overall position of the Harijans improved as an indirect consequence of the Gulf migration. The increase in wage levels, the greater demand for casual labor such as masonry workers (as more houses were built after the Gulf boom), together with the movement of Ezhavas out of wage work, all benefited this group. In relative terms, however, a consequence of the pre-dominantly Ezhava migration was a polarization of society between the Harijans and the rest of the castes.[14] This was a change from the earlier pattern, where the society was organized on the basis of a hierarchical continuum, with the Ezhavas being only a little above the Harijans.

Migration and Gender

Since the wives of migrants often stayed in their own parental homes in Muttam, the Ezhava locality, they had a considerable degree of freedom when compared to the women in Veni. This household arrangement was also to the financial advantage of migrants since the husband did not have to send as much money as he would have had to do otherwise. The villagers explained, "Her parents will take care of a lot of the expenses as it is considered shameful to ask for money to support their daughter." As the stories of Radha's and Vijaya's mothers show, sometimes, particularly during the Singapore migration when even letters took a long time, the families of the migrants went for long periods without hearing from or receiving remittances from the men of the household. The long tradition of male absence from the village could explain the financial independence and freedom of movement of the women of this area. The wives of migrants generally supplemented their husband's remittances through the cultivation of the land around the house, olah work, or by keeping livestock. Thus they were not completely financially dependent on their husbands. Some women also did seasonal work in the nearby cashew factory. Only five or six women were employed in salaried jobs.

There were more migrant households in Muttam than in Veni, and this was probably because of two reasons.[15] In Muttam, unlike Veni, the new afflu-ence did not support the development of shops and businesses and thus, there were fewer income-earning opportunities in the area. However, a more impor-tant factor was probably the differences in the gender ideology between the two areas. Since women in Veni were not allowed to go out or to take care of finan-cial matters, a male household member or relative was always necessary to take care of the families of migrants in that area. This was not as necessary in Muttam, which meant that more householders could turn to the migration option.

Perhaps because of the absence of a lot of the men, women from migrant and nonmigrant households were very active in the community in local affairs and in politics. When I was doing my fieldwork, several of the village repre-sentatives in the panchayat council were women. There were official quotas for women in panchayat councils, and so there had been a few women on the coun-cil even in Veni. However, in that region, the husbands went around canvassing votes and doing much of the other public work on their wives' behalf. In Cherur, there were far more women on the council than required by law, and the women took care of official business themselves. At the time of my fieldwork, both the panchayat council member of the area (who belonged to the ruling Marxist party) and the opposing Congress party representative were women. Another woman who was active in community affairs was in charge of the *Mahila Sabha* (women's council). I was regaled with many accounts of the arrogance of the three women and their attempts to siphon off the government money and provisions sent for the preschool. The panchayat member had been a music teacher at a local school, and her relatives owned several provision shops in the area. Such shops often allowed regular customers to buy on credit when they were in financial difficulties. According to the neighbors, the "member" had absolutely no "personality," stage presence, or charm, was rather ignorant, and had turned even her own party members against her. They claimed that she had won the local elections through bribes (using the lump sum pension of Rs. 30,000 she received on retirement) and threats to Harijans (that they would not be allowed to buy provisions on credit if they did not support her) and because most people around were her relatives.

I have mentioned that many migrants raised the money to pay for the visa and the airfare by selling the gold jewelry of their wives (or sometimes their sisters). In this region, the gold jewelry given to the bride by her parents at the time of her wedding was not technically considered to be part of the dowry, but was instead seen as part of the bride's trousseau. Thus men were expected to return the gold if they borrowed it to finance some venture. Similarly, the property share given to the woman at the time of marriage was to be used for the benefit of the couple. The family of the bride could raise questions if they felt that the gold or property had been misused (but in the interest of the marriage could not do more). *Sridhanam,* or dowry, literally referred to the cash and gifts given by the bride's side to the man or his family which could be used in any way they wanted. This was a fine distinction and one that was often not made in practice. However, it did mean that men were aware that they needed the support and cooperation of their spouses and their families (or their sisters and their in-laws) to be a successful migrant. This strengthened the position of women and the relationship between spouses.

In almost all cases, married migrants from Muttam sent remittances directly to their wives. If the couple was newly married, the man only sent money for her expenses and kept the rest with him in the Middle East. But after a few years when they had developed a closer relationship and the wife had shown herself capable of managing finances, the man would generally send all of the money he was able to save to her. The women invested the remittances primarily in high-interest loans to other villagers. Thus women had considerable control over the finances and household decisions. Unlike in Veni, the women of Cherur could provide me with the details about their husband's migration, how much money it had cost, how they had raised the money, what kind of job he had, how much he made, how much he sent back, and how they had spent and invested the remittances.

Women were also closely involved in the construction or renovation of the family home and frequently supervised the process. If the couple was newly married and the wife was young, husbands would often send their money to their fathers-in-law, who in turn would look after the financial dealings on behalf of their daughters. Even though the inheritance system had become formally bilateral in that both sons and daughters were to get an equal share, in practice, daughters still continued to be favored, particularly among poorer families with too little property to divide among all the children. As I was told several times: "Because of this father-daughter flow, men are afraid to entrust their own fathers with the money for a house, fearing that it would go to their sisters instead." This is why they preferred to send the money to their fathers-in-law. If the couple had been married for several years and the woman was older and had no close male family members nearby, the man would send the money to her and she would take charge of this task. Radha and a few other women in Muttam told me that their husbands had sent them the money for a house and that they had themselves supervised every step of the construction.

Sometimes, of course, wives who were entrusted with such tasks were duped by contractors and masons. Others spent the money lavishly or mismanaged business affairs. Neighbors told me that the reason for the downfall of the hospital built by Jyothi's husband was that she was put in charge. On top of her extravagant lifestyle, she apparently had absolutely no management or people skills. She treated the doctors badly and expected them to be at her beck and call. Radha told me that she also used to abuse the patients and insist that people address her as "Doctor." Finally, the hospital had to be shut down because several of the doctors left, and Jyothi had to sell some of the equipment to pay off the mounting debts.

The existence of hypogamous marriages could also indicate a fundamental change in the traditional role and position of women. Conventionally, through a set of cumulative criteria, families tried to ensure that the husband had a higher status than the wife since it was believed that this promoted a harmonious marriage. Thus, husbands were older, had more education and a higher-paying job (if the woman was also working outside the home), and came from a higher or at least equal-status family. It was for this reason that hypogamous marriages were strongly discouraged. In a hypogamous marriage, the structural inequality between the wife and husband is disturbed. From my observations, it did appear that this worked to the advantage of women since women who married hypogamously were accorded more respect by their husbands and in-laws.

As in Veni, successful migrants were able to improve the financial situation of their households considerably. They were able to build or renovate their houses and furnish them with labor-saving modern gadgets such as electric water pumps, gas stoves, blenders, and refrigerators. All of these gadgets considerably eased the workload of their wives. A few of the successful migrants in Cherur were able to take their wives and children over to the Middle East for a few years. While some women complained about disobedient children and spend-thrift husbands, wives of successful migrants were unanimous that the migration had been beneficial for them overall. A few of the younger women talked wistfully about the good times they had during their husbands' visits. "He takes me out to movies, to the beach and to the city [Trivandrum] and we visit all our relatives. Those three months are so full and exciting," sighed Shanthi. Although she would have preferred that her husband got a good local job, she also knew that in the absence of such opportunities, migration was about the only viable option.

While clearly the situation of women in Muttam was far different from that of the women in Veni and migration had strengthened their position in a variety of ways, gendered differences in treatment and status were still pronounced. For instance, I was surprised to note that even in this female-dominated village with its matrilineal tradition, girls were discriminated against when it came to food, with boys being given more delicacies like meat and chocolates. My good friend Vijaya (who only had daughters and could therefore not be accused of this practice) admitted that such discrimination was fairly widespread. "It is only in the matter of inheritance that daughters are preferred," she added. Girls were usually not educated as much as boys and were generally only allowed to complete high school (tenth grade) before they were married (at about seventeen or eighteen). Boys were often sent for at least a one-year PDC (predegree course) and some training at a technical institute. Some of the wealthier migrant families were able to pay donations and get their sons into bachelor's degree courses. One of the sons of "hospital Jyothi" (as she was known in the area) was even able to get into medical school because of the huge donation that his father had paid for him.

A few women (all in the younger generation) in the village had some college education (one of whom was Rajan's newly married wife) but except for one of them (whose family had moved in recently from the nearby town), a teacher in the local English medium school, none of the other women were encouraged to work (many did not want to but in at least two cases I know that their husbands had not permitted it). Unless it was in a salaried government job (which was considered prestigious but was also very difficult to obtain), or due to financial necessity, the community did not view working women favorably (see Osella and Osella 2000a, 44).

Conclusion

With this discussion of Cherur, we gain a better understanding of the power and impact of ethnicity. Although the villagers of Veni and Cherur faced many of the same objective circumstances such as social marginality, an agrarian context, and economic hardship that provided the impetus for large-scale migration in both areas, the organization of migration and its consequences for the social, economic, and cultural life of the two areas were very different. I have referred to the stark contrast between the "common sense world" of both villages with respect to gender practice and ideology, corporate spirit, and conceptions of status. These differences were at the core of the divergent patterns manifested by Veni and Cherur.

Due to the prior Singapore migration, the Middle Eastern movement began relatively late, with the first migrants leaving only in the early 1970s. From the beginning, migration took place largely through agents. The relatively low solidarity of this group resulted in ethnic networks playing a much smaller role here, helping mainly to identify reliable agents. The low-caste position of the Ezhavas prevented their access to education until the first quarter of the twentieth century and meant that education levels in the migration period were still rather low. Thus most of the villagers went for skilled or technical work. Here again the migrants were male, and most of the families stayed behind. The matrilineal and matrilocal tradition, which was a distinguishing feature of this community, reemerged as a consequence of migration.

The ethnicity of Cherur shaped the consumption, investment, and exchange patterns chosen by migrants. In Cherur, the most encompassing value of the social order appeared to be the need to improve the status of the Ezhava community. But in this village, there was greater tension between individual and community needs since the route to status was to distinguish oneself as "successful" by a competitive display of wealth and a stress on education, both of which emphasized achieved qualities over the ascribed status of community membership. Again the practice of community members acting as agents and the use of Gulf money for usury had the effect of individual villagers enriching themselves at the expense of others in the community. However, even here, the focus on the reproduction of the community was demonstrated by the emphasis given to gift exchanges within the circle of relatives and neighbors. Unlike the case of the Mappilas where this was generally a one-way relationship between migrants and poorer nonmigrants, reciprocity was stressed in Cherur. In addition, the exchange relationships were limited to the particular caste members.

The new resources provided by international migration brought about a transformation in the ethnicity of the Ezhava community as the Ezhavas attempted to use their affluence to obtain status and recognition. In the caste-dominated society of Cherur, the status struggle between the "distinguished" possessors and the "pretentious" challengers that Bourdieu describes took on a distinctive form as the newly rich Ezhavas marshaled their forces to reformulate the edifice of caste and be recognized as the new elite on the basis of their economic affluence and educational achievements. I have argued that, at least in this area, they seem to have succeeded, since a gradual decastification of status appeared to be taking place.

As indicated in chapter 2, the nexus between religion, status, and gender was manifested in Cherur by the increased prominence given to the celebration of the Hindu life-cycle rituals, in particular, the marriage ceremony. The new gold-gifting rites introduced during the course of the marriage ceremony were highly gendered, with most of them being from the bride (or her family) to the bridegroom. Gulf rich bridegrooms tried to gain status by reversing the flow of benefits. The rise of hypergamous and hypogamous marriages as central strategies to gain status also demonstrates the interrelationship between status and gender.

CHAPTER 7

Ethnicity and Migration in Kembu

STRENGTHENING THE NUCLEAR FAMILY AND WOMEN

*K*embu presents us with a third pattern of migration, which again shows the distinct stamp of its ethnicity. Unlike in Veni and Cherur, most migrants from Kembu went to the Middle East with their families. Also, a substantial proportion of women were either primary migrants or were able to find jobs in the Middle East after arriving there with their spouses. Family migration weakened community and kinship bonds. The opportunity to be the primary income earners of the family strengthened the position of women. We will examine these issues in the following pages. Since the Kembu region had one of the largest numbers of Kuwaiti migrants in the whole of Kerala, this chapter also discusses how the Kuwait crisis affected the migrant households and the community.

Located in the Christian heartland of south-central Kerala, Kembu was almost exclusively Christian: not more than around 5 percent of the houses were Hindu. Although it was a small village (only around one and a half square miles, consisting of about a thousand houses), Kembu was well known in the region as a base for many Christian denominations and as a center of the Gulf migration. The two factors—the strongly Christian character of the area and the large outmigration were interrelated, as I will demonstrate.

Despite the bewildering array of denominations in Kembu (I counted twelve denominations and nineteen subdenominations), the majority of the villagers were Syrian Christian *Marthomites,* the reformed Syrian Christian denomination that was formed in 1889. Except for a small group of *Jacobites* (the original group of Syrian Christians who were affiliated to the church in Antioch from which the Marthoma denomination had broken away), the other denominations were mainly formed of "converts" from the Marthoma church. According to the historical records of the Marthoma *Valiyapalli* (big church) in Kembu, the area had first been inhabited by forty-one "eminent" high-caste Hindu families and their servants (Marthoma Valiyapalli 1987, 1). For some reason, this group of Hindu families moved out en masse sometime in the eighteenth century.[1] Around the turn of the nineteenth century, the area was forested and uninhabited when a Christian sage, Yohannan, chose the area to live in. This sage adopted a local Christian boy to be his helper, and together they established the first church in Kembu. The Valiyapalli church was rebuilt several times but still stands in the same location. Although the church was built before the formation of the Marthoma denomination, the Valiyapalli is referred to as a Marthoma church right from its inception, since the sage Yohannan called for the abolition of several of the traditional rites and practices of the Syrian Christian church, something that would become central to the Marthoma movement decades later.

Yohannan later arranged for his disciple's marriage with a god-fearing Christian woman from a neighboring village. This couple and their children are considered to be the first Kembu family. Syrian Christians follow the patrilineal system, so the original inhabitants of the village trace their ancestry to one of the three sons of the couple (most villagers were aware of their family tree). At the time of my fieldwork, I was told that the people of Kembu were generally fifth- to eighth-generation descendants. These two features—the strongly religious (Christian) character of the settlement and their kinship ties with each other—contributed a great deal to the subsequent course of events.

Some background to the history of Christianity in the region is necessary here, to understand the socioeconomic character of Kembu in the premigration period. Colonel Munro, the British Resident in Travancore and Cochin, appointed in 1810, was very eager to have the Syriac Bible that the Syrian Christians had been using, translated into Malayalam. He designated the missionary, Reverend Bailey (of the Church Missionary Society [CMS]), to be in charge of this task. Bailey also set up a printing press and by the middle of the nineteenth century, vernacular copies of the Bible were available. According to a college professor in Kembu, this meant that the Bible became accessible and intelligible to the masses. The increased interest and awareness in understanding the Bible, together with the influence of the CMS members, resulted in the development of a religious revival and a reform movement within the Syrian church. Large numbers of lower castes were converted to Christianity during the period. The reformists within the Syrian church adopted some elements of the Protestant theology of the Anglican CMS and also attempted to purge the church of many of the practices that Christians had taken over from Hindus, ultimately breaking away to form the Marthoma denomination. The region around Kembu was the center of the reformation movement and subsequently of the Marthoma denomination.

Noel, an English missionary of the Plymouth Brethren church, arrived in Kembu at the turn of the twentieth century. Later, American missionaries from the Church of God and the Pentecost churches followed. Cynical Marthomites told me that these missionaries were able to garner converts because the latter believed that they would obtain "soap [material goods], soup [food] and salvation" if they converted. Since Kembu gained the reputation of being an area that was hospitable to Christian missionaries, more and more followed and Kembu became the base for their missionary activities.

Kembu villagers give the missionaries credit for establishing many of the basic infrastructural facilities in the area. Noel petitioned the government to set up a post office in Kembu so that he could send and receive international mail. His wife started a dispensary and a Sunday school. The missionaries encouraged the spread of education among the villagers. The first college in the region (in Kottayam, around thirty miles away) was started by CMS members.

The educational and occupational opportunities of Kembu villagers were linked to the development of Christian institutions—most of which were mission owned or affiliated. Syrian Christians from Kembu and neighboring areas obtained their education largely from Christian schools and subsequently went on to colleges and medical schools established by Christian missionaries, to obtain the specialized training and qualifications that would help them obtain positions within mission organizations. As Christians, they were given preference in all of these institutions. Thus, contact with missionaries provided Syrian Christians in the Kembu region with opportunities for English education, which in turn enabled them to obtain good, salaried jobs. Hence there were large numbers of teachers, nurses, clerks, and doctors in the community.

Socioeconomic Profile, 1930–1950

Like other rural parts of Kerala, Kembu was an agricultural area. Early settlers cleared the forest and brought it under cultivation. Between 1930 and 1950, Kembu consisted mainly of peasant cultivators, their tenants, and laborers. Mary Mathews, a social worker and the wife of a well-known doctor, told me that she had been horrified at how rural and backward Kembu was (she had been raised in Trivandrum city) when she came to the area in 1949 soon after her marriage. "All one could see around were vast stretches of land, some cultivated, but a lot of it just wild shrub. My house is two miles from the main junction but at that time, the only means of transport was a bullock cart which functioned as the sole 'taxi' in Kembu. So, of course, even that was not usually available."

At the top of the economic ladder were those six or seven families who had between seventy-five to a hundred acres of land. But often much of it was not cultivated. Mrs. Mathews told me of a relative who had between a hundred and a hundred and fifty buffaloes and so much land that he just let them roam free. (The buffaloes were not maintained for their milk—this would be distributed free to all the neighbors since it had no market value—but for their dung which would fertilize the land.) While around 50 percent of the population had some land, most had only very little—between half to one acre each. The rest of the villagers lived through their labor on other people's land—either as tenants and sharecroppers or as bonded laborers. Some of the large landowners also had other occupations (some were schoolteachers, lawyers, and doctors) and were thus largely absentee farmers, but for the most part, even those who had large landholdings at least actively supervised the cultivation (mainly paddy). This was because Christians were less bound by the Hindu ideology proscribing physical labor for the higher castes. Several of the elderly villagers described the amount of physical work that even men and women from fairly wealthy families had to do in the "old days." "The men would be out in the field for a good part of the day. We women had to get up early and cook huge meals for them and all the laborers. In those days of course we did not have the spice powders and mixes and the numerous gadgets that are available nowadays. Everything had to be done the long and tedious way," said Sarah Varghese, a retired school headmistress.

Internal and international migration from Kembu and surrounding regions had begun as early as the 1900s. Many villagers moved to other parts of India to study and obtain work in mission-run institutions. Others went to countries like Malaysia and Singapore to work as supervisors, clerks, compounders, and tea tasters in the estates there.[2] Here again, it was the association with missionaries that gave the villagers the advantage. The Noels (and some of the other missionaries) helped a lot of the English-educated people obtain jobs in Malaysia and Singapore, through their contacts with counterparts of their denomination in these countries. Migration to the Gulf countries began very early, too. According to Raju Kurian (1978, 24), migration to Iraq from this region took place through British contacts as early as 1918. The first large-scale migration out of the region around Kembu took place during the depression, as hundreds of people left for Malaysia and Singapore. By the post–Second World War period, there were several streams of international migration from Kembu: to Singapore and Malaysia (where the migrants worked as clerks and estate supervisors), the Persian Gulf countries (dominated by clerical workers and nurses), and to Africa (comprised primarily of schoolteachers, surveyors, and clerks). Most migrants (both internal and international) took their families with them. Some who were in parts of the Middle East and Africa where the educational system was not considered to be of good quality sent their children back to boarding schools for their middle and high school education. Those in Malaysia often sent their children back for college education.

Not surprisingly, given the returns to education that villagers were able to obtain, sending children to English medium schools and colleges became an important community value. Over and over again, several of the older generation told me that their parents and grandparents had believed that "education was more important than wealth" and had, therefore, gone to great trouble to educate their children. "We children would get up before dawn, get ready hurriedly, and then set off for the two-hour trudge to school. By the time we got home in the evening, the light would be fading. When the situation at home was bad, *Ammachi* [mother] would sometimes not be able to provide us with lunch and so we would do without food for the whole day," Abraham Thomas, a middle-aged Gulf migrant recounted. I heard several such stories from Kembu villagers. Or children would be sent off to stay with relatives who lived in areas where there were good educational institutions. Many youngsters would go to faraway cities (outside Kerala) for their college education, and families would make a lot of sacrifices to make sure that their children received at least a basic undergraduate degree.

I discovered that careful money management and frugality was another important community ethic, something that Susan Visvanathan's study of Syrian Christians also corroborates. She writes, "Accounting, the keeping of careful ledgers with regard to daily expenses, is a prevalent custom among the Syrian Christians . . . Such account books can explain every major expenditure for several decades including sons' education, repairs to the house, births, marriages, hospitalizations, dowries sent out and brought in" (Visvanathan 1989, 1344).[3] Later she goes on to say that "thrift and economy are very specifically values associated with the Syrian Christians" (Visvanathan 1989, 1345). The local church tradition in Kembu placed a great deal of emphasis on saving and household budgeting (in fact, the churches themselves organized chitties).

As the home of missionaries and denominations from a variety of backgrounds, Kembu was also a highly religious community. Religiosity in this area was expressed primarily through daily family worship, which involved hymn singing and a reading from the Bible in addition to prayers. Jacob Chandy, a retired school headmaster and a prominent community figure, told me: "Thirty, forty years ago, one could hear the loud singing, the Lord's prayer and the 'Amens' from every household here in the morning and night. Now one can hear it from one or two houses, if that." Regular attendance at church and prayer meetings, as well as giving generous donations for religious causes, were the other attributes considered to be the mark of a good Christian.

Affiliation to a church denomination formed a strong bond between members. Marriages were generally arranged between men and women of the same denomination. Next to relatives, church members and immediate neighbors formed the social community for individual families. Due to the high rates of family migration, there was less of a community ethos and a greater degree of anonymity and impersonality than in either of the other two villages. However, there were many kin and affinal networks among the community which knit members together. As a high-status minority community, the Syrian Christians had a strong sense of ethnic identity and exclusiveness and this in turn led to a certain feeling of mutual obligation toward fellow members.

There was a sharp division between the Syrian Christians and the Backward Class Christians (who were largely Harijans converted by British missionaries).[4] The Syrians subscribed quite meticulously to the Hindu practice of avoiding low-caste members. "People from Kembu tried to live without mingling with other castes and religions," as one elderly Syrian Christian candidly admitted. Even after conversion, the Backward Class Christians had separate churches. Thus, in many ways they were in the same position as their Hindu counterparts, but over time they gained some improvement as missionaries and evangelists took an interest in them, urging their education and giving them jobs (though mostly of the low-status variety) in Christian institutions.

The extended family formed a corporate unit, and although the households were often nuclear, they were situated adjacent to each other on the family property. The Syrian Christian family was male dominated and patrilineal and followed the nuclear pattern with sons moving out of their father's house to one nearby (on the patrilocal property) when their children started growing up. For the most part, women were subordinated to the men. However, the education of women was stressed. Many were highly educated and a minority even obtained jobs, mainly as teachers and nurses in mission institutions. Dowries were given at the time of marriage. Dowry rates among Syrian Christians were traditionally higher than those of other communities in Kerala. However, during this period of time, the amounts were not too large. Due to patrilineal inheritance, they were also much less than a son's share of inheritance.

I have mentioned that the tradition of young people migrating to cities for education and subsequently finding jobs there and staying on or going to another city in search of jobs was established quite early in Kembu, as was the tradition of international migration. Since the nuclear household pattern was prevalent, the immediate family also migrated. Marriages of city-educated men were generally arranged with city-educated women from the same denomination so that the women would "fit in" with their husband's social circle. Thus, the combination of Western education, urban life, and the physical distance from the extended family in the village created the structural conditions for a stronger relationship between spouses. Since these people were deemed "successes," their lifestyles became the positive reference point for the community at large.

Gulf Migration, 1950–1990

Early Migration

In addition to the international migration streams to Malaysia, Singapore, the Middle East, and Africa, several villagers also started to emigrate to the United States and the United Kingdom from around the 1970s.[5] Some went to Great Britain directly from Singapore, with the British passport that they obtained, others went for an education and stayed on. Many villagers arrived in the United States to study in Bible colleges and then found work. From the mid-seventies, there was a big demand for nurses in the United States, and several women from Kembu were able to emigrate on that basis. Unlike the migration to Africa and the Middle East, and even to Malaysia and Singapore, migration to the United States and Great Britain tended to be permanent. Immigrants to these two countries also went on to sponsor their relatives. Because of these sponsorship chains, there were many Kembu villagers in both these countries. Thus, of the three areas studied, Kembu had the longest tradition of migration and the greatest diversity of destinations. A corollary to this is that there were proportionately fewer Gulf migrant households in Kembu when compared to the other two areas. However, it was still the case that about 75 percent of the Syrian Christian families in this area had at least one relative in the Gulf in 1990.

The first migration to the Gulf from Kembu began around 1930 but only a few people left at this time. Many of the first migrants responded to job advertisements in the newspapers and were subsequently selected on the basis of interviews. Since it was the professionally qualified people who went first, most were directly recruited by companies or their representatives (i.e., they did not go through agents) and so not only did they not have to pay for their job contracts, often even their airfares were paid for by their employers. As professionals, they were also given family housing and most of the migrants took their families with them. In addition, their contracts were automatically renewed until they were ready to retire. Thus the experiences of the early migrants from Kembu were very different from that of those from Veni and Cherur. The first migrants from Kembu in turn took over several of their relatives and friends (i.e., they arranged for job contracts for them); this was not at all difficult in this period.

A larger outflow to this region started after the Second World War.[6] From my discussions with older migrants and my household interviews, I gathered that the majority of the post–World War wave of migrants had been from lower-middle-class agricultural families. Obtaining their education had been a big economic struggle. The girls were sent off to mission-run nursing schools (which at that time paid them a small stipend) so that they could earn money and save up for their dowries. The boys trained at the technical school in Kembu or studied shorthand and typing. In short they came from frugal, hard-working, education-oriented families. There were also some professionally qualified migrants such as lawyers and engineers and one or two doctors among the early group who were from the middle classes. Conditions in the Middle East were not easy in this period since the area was still very underdeveloped in terms of the availability of infrastructural facilities and amenities. The migrants were careful with the money earned and planned their expenditures and investments carefully. From relatively lower-rung positions (petty clerks, for instance) the migrant villagers were able to rise to high-ranking ones like managers of the concerns. These early migrants also provided a lot of financial help to their parents, siblings, and other relatives. The case of Thomas George is typical.

My father was a postman. I was the eldest son and was interested in my studies, but my family could not afford to send me to an English medium school. So I went to the vernacular school for a few years and then quit school to take up a position as a shop assistant so that I could help my family. In the meantime I got married. We were struggling financially and an uncle who was already in the Gulf took me over there. (This was in 1955.) But I failed my first interview since I did not know enough English. So, my uncle got me a low level position in the bank where he was working (in Doha, Qatar). I was paid only Rs. 400 a month in the beginning and struggled for several years to save money and send it to my family. I gradually worked my way up and was able to have my family with me. I retired in 1982 as a senior officer, earning around Rs. 23,000 a month.

Ninan Koshy's story was narrated to me by Abraham, a relative. "Ninan completed his schooling and then went and studied to be a surveyor. He went to Quatar through the help of relatives in 1954 and worked there for thirty years. The family is now very, very, wealthy. The four children—three girls and one boy—are all doctors. The three oldest have M.D.'s. The youngest daughter and her husband have now gone to England to do their M.D. degree."

The story of "Toyota" Cherian was the most remarkable and the best known in the area. Cherian was from a middle-class family and, like Ninan, Cherian went to the Middle East through the help of relatives. He started out as a worker in the Toyota factory in Kuwait. He gained the liking and trust of the owner who entrusted business to him when he went to the United States. Cherian managed it so well that when the owner retired, he handed it over to him. Cherian also started branches in other areas so at the time of my fieldwork, he was known to be fabulously wealthy. I was told that besides arranging jobs for about sixty to seventy of his relatives, "Toyota" Cherian had also taken around 250 poor people from the area (paying their expenses and then deducting it from their salary later) to work in his factories.

As the migration became more institutionalized, several institutions sprang up in Kembu to qualify people who wanted to migrate or to aid migrants in other ways. The Technical Engineering School was started in 1940 (this was the first such school in the region) and was partly responsible for the large number of migrants leaving from Kembu. According to the founding director, the school was sending up to 350 students a year to the Middle East before 1960. After 1960 the number fell to around forty-five a year due to government regulations and because several such institutes had been started in the area by then. A nurse training school opened in the seventies. Several secretarial schools teaching typing, shorthand, and basic accounting were also set up at this time. A cooperative bank (which at the time of my fieldwork was the biggest in Kerala) opened nearby in 1953. According to the president of the bank, around one-third of the early migrants from the area had financed their trip by taking loans from the bank. (Since 1986, banks in Kerala had been forbidden by the government to give travel loans to potential migrants.)[7]

Migration Patterns

Due to the presence of these institutions, the migration gradually spread in Kembu and the surrounding villages. As the conditions and salaries in the Gulf improved, more and more people started migrating. The mass migration from this area began in the 1960s. These migrants went almost entirely through the contacts that were already built up (mainly relatives and friends) and very few went through professional agents.

The owner of the only travel agency in Kembu told me that there were no unskilled labor migrants from this region in the late eighties (and probably before that as well).[8] Professionals like engineers and doctors were also relatively rare. He estimated that around 50 percent of the migrants were clerical workers and a large proportion were bank employees and nurses. Only around 10 to 15 percent of the migrants were technicians or skilled workers. Again, according to him, close to 95 percent of the Gulf migrants from this area went on regular (legal) work visas.

On the basis of my household survey, which gave me information on the types of jobs (and the countries of migration) of the villagers, I estimated that the monthly income earned by most migrants from Kembu in the late 1980s was between Rs. 7,000 to Rs. 50,000. In addition, most of the migrants had perquisites such as free or subsidized housing, an annual home visit allowance, and so forth. A nurse could earn between Rs. 10,000 to Rs. 30,000, depending on whether she had a diploma or degree and on the country in which she was employed. (A nurse in Kerala would have earned only between Rs. 800 to Rs. 1,500.) The highest salaries were received by those with nursing degrees working in Kuwait (around Rs. 30,000). Doctors and highly placed bank employees earned at least around Rs. 50,000 a month (in Kerala, salaried doctors and bank employees would have received from Rs. 2,000 to Rs. 6,000 per month), together with a lot of perquisites like rent-free, luxurious housing. Since both spouses worked in many of the cases, the family income was considerably higher than the figures mentioned above. There were some very wealthy businessmen from the area (such as "Toyota" Cherian) whose monthly income must have been in the hundreds of thousands. In addition to their relatively high salaries and benefits, stable positions, and regular salary payments, migrants from Kembu also seemed to have the greatest extent of job security among the three areas studied. Although many villagers experienced some salary cuts after 1983, and there was a slight decrease in conspicuous consumption, because of their high incomes and stable positions, most were not badly affected by the crash in oil prices.

Due to the early migration, there was a large concentration of people from Kembu in the Gulf countries where oil exploration was started early as in Kuwait,

Qatar, and Bahrain. I have mentioned that the migration to the Middle East from this region took place largely through the help of relatives. Thus, during the Kuwait crisis of 1990, a local newspaper reported that there was an extended family in Kembu which had eighty-two members in that country. Another family eight miles away reportedly had one hundred and fifty members in Kuwait. This area was one of the largest Kuwait migrant belts in the state and probably the country as a whole.

A further corollary to the fact that people from this area had been in the Gulf the longest of the three communities was that in Kembu migration was two full generations old (unlike in the other two communities where it was only around one generation old). A good proportion of the young adults (thirty-five years and younger) had always lived in luxury and tended to pretty much take it for granted. "What do they know about hardship and financial problems? They have grown up in great comfort and were able to get into well-paying positions in the Middle East without any effort on their part. They have no concept of money management or saving. Maybe this misfortune will be a blessing in disguise and will teach them to be more careful in the future," said a first-generation migrant about his two sons during the Kuwait crisis.

I estimated that about 75 percent of the migrants from Kembu and its environs managed to have their spouse and children with them, at least for a few years. Only 25 percent of the migrants could not afford to do this.[9] These two categories made up the two streams of Gulf migrants from the village in the eighties.

The first stream were those who were at least moderately well off (mainly because they were second-generation migrants). Their expenses to go to the Gulf were low (since a close family member made the arrangements for them). The airfare and other expenses were met through personal savings. The migrant obtained a good job, with a high-paying salary and several perquisites, and could take his or her spouse over. Since the migrant's family (parents and siblings) was not in financial need, none of the earnings had to go toward their support. Thus, there was no need to send money back to redeem family debts, to support the parents, or to marry off sisters. As a result, migrants could afford to have their children educated in schools in the Middle East (despite the often considerable expense), and the family could live in comfort. The migrants did not have to save very much of the monthly salary, either, since both spouses would get a share of the family property (the dowry of the woman and the inheritance of the man). At most they would have to spend some extra money to build themselves a house. They could also count on having their jobs in the Gulf until the end of their working lives (barring such catastrophes as the Kuwait crisis) with a large lump-sum gratuity (in lieu of a pension) at the end worth between Rs. 500,000 to 5 million, which they could then invest to provide a good income for their retired lives, or which could be used for large expenditures such as dowries or weddings.

I found that both spouses were working in the Gulf in 75 to 80 percent of cases of those younger migrants who were there as a family. (This was a much higher proportion than among the earlier migrants.) The nonnurse wife was typically a graduate and generally migrated on a spouse visa, but she eventually got some kind of clerical job in the Middle East. As mentioned, children were usually sent to schools in the Gulf—often till they graduated but at least for the primary and secondary classes. They were sent to residential schools and colleges in Kerala for the rest of their education or, sometimes, the mother returned at this point. Another common arrangement was to leave children in the care of grandparents.

The second, smaller, stream was comprised generally of first-generation migrants and migrants from poorer families (though rarely from the "coolie" or laboring classes since such families usually belonged to the Backward Class Christian group which had hardly any migrants). The second stream of migrants also generally went to the Gulf with the help of an established Gulfite (i.e., they did not use agents) who was a relative or friend. But finding the money to pay for the airfare and other expenses, and possibly even for the job contract, was a bigger problem for this group. The money was usually obtained through a bank loan (by pledging land), by selling jewelry, by using a wife's dowry, or by borrowing from relatives. Such families also had other family debts to repay and the migrant had to assume these responsibilities. In addition, the migrant usually had to send remittances for the support of parents, and perhaps siblings, to get a sister or two married, or to renovate the parental house.

Migrants in this category were usually men who generally had to leave their wives behind (due to the economic factors mentioned, together with the fact that their wives generally did not have the education necessary to obtain a white-collar job in the Gulf). Kembu being a strongly patrilineal society, the wives were usually left in the care of their husband's parents. According to the villagers, this in turn could create in-law problems (such problems were usually greater in poorer and less well educated households where the daughters-in-law were not treated with respect) which hastened the need to build a separate house. But the man had to first earn enough to buy a plot of land and then save to build the house. On top of all this, the people in this category did not have jobs as good as those of the first group, so the earnings were also much lower.

All this might suggest that the odds of their being even reasonably successful were very low. But I must stress that most did manage to improve their economic standing, and several were able to do quite well. I came across many such cases. Often, their houses were pointed out to me by people in Kembu who belonged to the "old rich" group.

Annamma John, whose husband had retired from his position in an international foundation, told me about the case of her immediate neighbor who now lived in a new two-story house. "Their family had been very poor but the man went and did some course in the technical school and then went to the Gulf. He was able to save well, build the house and also put money in fixed deposits in the names of his children. He has now returned and bought a lorry [truck] and a taxi and has also started a chicken farm." Mathai, an *auto-rickshaw* (three-wheeler taxi) driver in Kembu, was the son of the servant of one of my distant relatives. He told me that he had gone to Muscat for eight years and during that time had got three sisters married and had himself married. He now had two children. He said that he came back from the Gulf because he "had made enough money" and wanted to be with his family. He had used his Gulf money to buy the auto rickshaw for Rs. 40,000 and now earned around Rs. 150 a day, enough to maintain his family in a comfortable lifestyle.

Was the greater economic success of migrants from Kembu (when compared to their counterparts in Veni and Cherur) due to class or ethnicity? Certainly, the primary reason for the success of the first stream of migrants had to do with their relatively privileged economic background (but this in turn was because most were second-generation migrants). The second, poorer group of migrants from Kembu were in a fairly similar economic position to some of the migrants from both Veni and Cherur. Yet, the outcome of the migration was very different when compared to that of their counterparts in the other two villages. I argue below that the difference had to do with ethnicity—specifically the differences in educational background, social networks, and gender norms.

Due to the emphasis on education in the area, many of the Kembu migrants were better educated than migrants from Cherur and certainly from Veni who were from similar economic backgrounds. Thus they could obtain well-paying jobs in the Middle East. Even if this were not the case, the contacts Kembu migrants had with high-placed migrants in the Gulf made it much more likely that they would get better, more-secure jobs than migrants from the other two villages. Finally, differences in gender norms between Kembu and the other two areas meant that male Syrian Christian migrants could use their money to have their sisters trained as nurses or lab technicians. Because of the high demand for such jobs in the Gulf, the women were able to find jobs fairly easily after the training was completed (through community contacts), which helped to distribute the burden of family debt, support of parents, and dowry (smaller dowries were expected if the woman had a lucrative Gulf job). Unmarried male migrants from Kembu also had the option of marrying a nurse, ideally one who was already in the Gulf but if not, a local nurse whom he could then take to the Middle East. This would lead to a dramatic increase in the net income of the family. If this was not possible, he could still look for a woman who had a local job.

Since the immediate family was in the Gulf in a majority of cases, most of the money earned by migrants from Kembu was deposited in banks in the Middle East and only transferred back to Kerala around once a year. Even when the family was left behind, they often had some local sources of income such as agriculture or the salary of the wife, if she was working. Thus, compared to Veni and Cherur, there was less dependence on remittances for routine expenses. According to local bank officials, villagers in Kembu manifested a shrewd awareness of exchange fluctuations and the stock market. Money was transferred directly to local banks at optimal rates and was then distributed in securities and shares in such a way that returns were maximized. The high education of the villagers, together with the employment of many of them in the banking sector in the Middle East and in Kerala, allowed such information to be available as part of the ethnic resource of the community at large.

The Fieldwork

Through the help of some distant relatives in Kembu, I was able to arrange for my stay as a paying guest of a widow who lived in a central location in Kembu. The ancestral home of my mother's family was in a nearby town and my maternal grandfather (who had been a bishop) had been well known in the area, so I was as close to being on "home ground" as I would probably ever be. I was not conspicuous as I had been in Veni and in Cherur, since there were other women with short hair in the area. Quite a number of villagers had relatives living in the United States and several people had lived in other cities in India. Again, since most of the villagers were well educated, my study was not regarded with any particular alarm or interest. But precisely for these very reasons, my reception was cooler and more formal in Kembu than in Cherur. The villagers were generally familiar with social research, so it was not difficult to go to a household and explain that I was doing a study. But because their paradigm of social science research was the survey, the conversations in many cases were more structured with individuals giving brief, focused answers to my questions. In many cases this made it more difficult to carry out an informal participant-observation type of research where I could stop by for a friendly visit and have longer, more relaxed, less focused conversations.

Due to the family migration from the area, many migrant families were away for years at a time, leaving vacant houses behind. Others had moved out permanently to cities around the country or to the United States. So, the situation in Kembu was unlike that in Veni and Cherur, where almost all households with migrants had some members left behind in the village. This meant that in many cases, I was not able to talk to a member of a migrant household in Kembu and had to make do by talking to neighbors, parents, siblings, and relatives of migrant families. Because of the Kuwait crisis, however, several families who would not have been in the village returned while I was living in Kembu, and I was able to talk to many of them. I visited a total of sixty-one households in Kembu for my household-level interviews and survey (forty-five among the Syrian Christian group and sixteen among the Backward Class Christians, who lived in separate "colonies") and obtained information about several more during the course of my fieldwork.

My relatives and family friends were very helpful in providing information, introductions, and contacts. Most of them were nonmigrants, so I was also able to obtain their perspective on the changes brought about by migration. I developed close relationships with a few other villagers during the course of my fieldwork. One of them was Mary Mathews, the outgoing wife of a prominent local doctor. She took a personal interest in me and in my study and introduced me to several of her neighbors.

My marital status came up a couple of times in Kembu. On one occasion, Mary asked me how old I was and why I was not married yet. I mentioned my age and told her that the main reason I was still single was because I did not want an arranged marriage. She said, "Fine, why don't you find someone and get married? After all, you are not getting any younger." I replied that I had not met the right person yet and that I was particular about marrying someone who would consider me an equal partner. She expressed skepticism that I would come across a man like that. We were walking to a neighboring house during this conversation and when we got there Mary introduced me to her friend, saying in Malayalam, "Her name is Prema [which means love], but poor thing, she doesn't know how to get it!" In subsequent conversations she urged me to put aside my idealism and get married, telling me in particular about a friend of hers who had similarly put off marriage for the sake of her career (as an attorney) but had regretted her decision subsequently, by which time it had been "too late" to get married.

Although villagers in Kembu saw the Middle East as a desirable place to migrate to temporarily, it was the United States that was viewed as the "promised land" due to its educational system and the possibility of permanent residence and citizenship and because it was a "Christian country." The villagers were willing to go to great lengths to obtain a green card sponsorship. Many villagers asked me (and only half in jest) whether, when I got a job and a green card (when, not if), I would sponsor them. In the early period of my fieldwork in Kembu, most people assumed that I was a green card holder and even tried to arrange marriages for me through my relatives, which stopped abruptly when I told them that I only had a student visa.

Kembu and the Kuwait Crisis

I arrived in Kembu in mid-July 1990, just a few weeks before the invasion of Kuwait by Saddam Hussain on August 2. Particularly after the invasion, everyone was tense and anxious since many of their family members and friends were in Kuwait. There were long lines outside the local international phone booth (located in the home of a villager) as people tried to establish contact with loved ones in Kuwait, sometimes without success. Special prayer meetings were held in houses that had members in Kuwait and at many of the local churches. More informally, a friend or neighbor would go over to a "Kuwait house" to pray with family members and comfort them. Newspapers were full of accounts of the atrocities that were taking place in Kuwait by Saddam Hussain's troops. Foreign workers often had to leave most of their possessions behind (including the money they had in Kuwaiti banks which they could not access after the invasion) and had to make their way across the desert to Amman in Jordan to catch a flight. Several Indians were forced to stay in makeshift camps in Jordan as they waited to be evacuated. Newspapers carried stories about the terrible conditions in the camps. Under pressure from Gulf migrants, the Indian government organized special flights to airlift Indian nationals in Kuwait back to India. Since most people did not have the money to pay for the flights, they were required to post a bond, the condition being that they could not leave the country again without repaying the bond. From the middle of August to the middle of October, 113,614 Indians were evacuated from Amman by Air India (Indian Express 1990). Others left by ship or by alternate airlines. According to estimates, around 170,000 workers returned from Kuwait and Iraq to India between August and December 1990 (Battistella 1991, 25). However, many chose to stay on in Kuwait rather than face poverty in India, in the hope that they would be able to secure employment once the situation had normalized.

The invasion of Kuwait created instability in the entire Middle Eastern region, and many migrants in other Gulf countries had their salaries cut. Newspapers in Kerala reported that remittances from the Gulf had gone up several fold in the wake of the Kuwaiti invasion as migrants in neighboring countries sent back their savings, something I was able to corroborate from the banks in Kembu. There was a big drop in spending by Gulf families, which affected businesses throughout Kerala, but particularly in the Gulf pockets.

The Kuwait workers and their families started returning while I was in Kembu. Most people arrived in September. In the Kembu region, estimates put the number of returnees at 750 to 2,000. I heard (both directly from the returnees and indirectly from neighbors and relatives) about the problems that many of the families faced in Kuwait and in Kerala. Returnees described how most people had locked themselves in their houses in Kuwait after the invasion. They feared that there would be a food shortage. The army was around the banks so they could not withdraw their money. In any case, the value of the Kuwaiti dinar had fallen sharply in the wake of the invasion, so their bank accounts had become practically worthless. Taxi drivers were charging exorbitant amounts to travel through the desert, which made it even more difficult for people to make their way to Amman. Families who had most of their money in Kuwaiti banks lost their life savings. In some cases, families had not saved much because they were counting on obtaining a large gratuity payment when they retired. Many had debts, others only had a big house and some land in Kembu, several had daughters to marry off (with large dowries) and children who were studying in expensive boarding schools in India. I heard of the case of one man who tried to commit suicide after returning from Kuwait because he had three unmarried daughters and a lot of debts. Many returnees were staying with parents or siblings in crowded conditions. Despite all these problems, however, returnees in the Kembu region were in a much better situation than those in other regions of Kerala. Most had some savings and assets in Kerala, or at least had parents and siblings who were wealthy and could support them for the short term. Because of their educational and professional qualifications, they could also be assured of eventually securing a reasonably well-paying position in India or in one of the other Gulf countries. Newspapers in Kerala reported that there were two strata of Kerala migrants in Kuwait: the professional and white-collar migrants from central Travancore (the larger Kembu region), and the unskilled migrants and business people from Malabar (the larger Veni region) and some of the coastal areas. (In a subsequent trip to Cherur, I verified that there were no Kuwait returnees there.) It was the unskilled group that was facing the greatest difficulties, in many cases, even the prospect of starvation, as they had no savings or sources of income. Fortunately, however, the Kuwaiti situation proved short lived. Since I left India in January of 1991, I could not verify this personally, but newspaper accounts and my correspondence with people in different parts of Kerala indicated that a return migration started in March 1991.

Consumption, Investment, and Exchange Patterns

Due to the family migration, most of the money earned by Gulf migrants from Kembu was spent in the Middle East. Professional migrants lived lavish lives, adopting the latest fashions and going on holiday trips to Europe and the United States. The children of such migrants were often sent to England or the United States for their higher education. White-collar workers, semiprofessionals, and technical workers (who comprised the bulk of migrants from Kembu) lived comfortably. In the following section, I will focus on the larger expenditure items of Kembu migrants.

Although several new two-story houses had been built in Kembu by Gulf migrants, surprisingly, I did not find the huge palatial mansions that I saw in some coastal Gulf pockets. Next to house building, the largest items of expenditure were education and dowries. Donations in the order of several hundred thousand rupees were given as "capitation fees" to secure seats in private professional colleges. The Gulf migration had also led to a tremendous escalation in dowry rates. At the time of my fieldwork, I was told that a minimum dowry of about Rs. 100,000 had to be given "among average folks." Middle-class families generally had to provide a dowry of Rs. 300,000 to Rs. 500,000. Among wealthy families, there were cases where the dowry was as high as two million rupees; "for instance, if the boy is a doctor and comes from a wealthy family and the girl is a graduate with no job from a Gulf family." Even poor families had to provide a dowry of Rs. 10,000 to Rs. 15,000. The dowry excluded the gold jewelry that was given to the bride at the time of her marriage, which again could be worth from tens of thousands of rupees to several hundred thousand rupees.

Even though the dowry rates were very high, except in the case of poor families, the value of the dowry continued to be less than the value of the inheritance given to the son. Compared to the huge dowry rates, the expenses of the wedding were relatively modest, about Rs. 13,000 on average. Wedding gifts were also not large unless it was a close relative, and even here, the amounts were relatively small compared to the financial standing of the families involved.

Unlike the other two communities, a good proportion of Gulf money was invested in financial instruments (bank deposits or stocks and bonds) and in property such as rubber estates. Having a large inheritance to pass on to one's children was an important value in the area. A lot of the local gossip consisted of attempts to speculate about how much individuals had "locked up in the bank" based on stray remarks made by the person, by friends, or by bank employees. Status in this community accrued from having a large bank balance, having professionally educated family members (the large dowries were often ways of securing such sons-in-law), and being a devout Christian.[10] The pastors of the area, however, remarked wryly that the material prosperity of the villagers had "often led them to turn away from God."

In general, the tradition of familial migration that had been created in the community had resulted in the loosening of community bonds and the development of a greater individualistic ethos. Due to this factor and the general affluence of the community as a whole, there was very little reciprocatory or redistributionary activity in this area. Remittances were mainly used for the needs of the immediate family. A certain amount would be sent to parents and young siblings but this was also not generally needed. Unlike in both the other communities, in Kembu there was also little gift giving on return except small token items like foreign chocolates. Some money and foreign goods would be given to the families of house servants and to the poor people in the neighborhood who generally approached the migrant. Thank offerings and donations were also made to the church.

The Status Struggle

Between 1950 and 1990, the situation of the "old rich" families in Kembu had rapidly declined. The land reforms of the Kerala government had a big impact on such families, drastically reducing their landholdings. However, it was the Gulf migration that affected them particularly badly. As in other Gulf areas, agriculture was gradually abandoned as it became less and less profitable and as such families sold portions of their land to the new migrants. But migrants were only interested in house plots and there was no one to buy land in large amounts. So those whose wealth was in the form of land had to work hard at agricultural cultivation for very little returns. Jacob Chandy told me about his own case. His father had been one of the very wealthy in Kembu with sixty acres of land. At the time of my fieldwork, Jacob owned ten acres of land worth a potential four million rupees. If that money had been invested, it would have yielded an interest of about Rs. 40,000 a month. Since he could not sell the land, however, Jacob said that he was only able to eke out an income of Rs. 2,000–3,000 a month from cultivation.

Because of the large salaries earned by Kembu villagers in the Middle East compared with the salaries of even good professional jobs in Kerala, and the presence of several "old rich" people in the area, the status struggle between migrants and the wealthy nonmigrants seemed to be more intense in this area. Many of the traditional elite in the area like Jacob Chandy found themselves vastly out-spent by newly rich Gulf migrants. They talked about how Gulf migrants ate fish or chicken for every meal, the cars and electronic gadgets they owned, the huge dowries they gave or received, and the way their "not very bright" children were able to get into private professional courses (medicine or engineering) by giving huge donations. In many cases, newly rich migrants had even been able to marry members of their extended family.

Several members of the former upper classes had moved out of the area since they could no longer keep pace with the lifestyles of the migrants. A relative who had lived ten miles from Kembu and had recently moved to Trivandrum, the capital city, said, "We are so glad we moved out of the region. Here we are surrounded by those with salaried jobs like us—just legitimate money. In Kalloor it was so difficult to keep up with the lavish expenditure of Gulfites around us."

I met Kuttan, a young man in his late thirties, at the home of another distant relative. He told me that he had grown up in the area and had then gone away for several years to study and work. When he returned, he found that the people he used to "kick around" were now "big people" and very wealthy. He could not compete with them, and it was humiliating, so he moved from there to a city about fifty miles away.

In typical old rich fashion however, members of Kembu's traditional elite continued to maintain that wealth did not confer status or respect in Kembu and that most migrants lacked the culture and the refinement which came with good breeding and real class. Thankamma Philip, a retired college professor, was telling me about the big two-story houses that the nouveau riche were building (two-story houses were a postmigration phenomenon in the area) and added, "I haven't been inside any of them but I wonder whether they will also be able to build a cultured life." In a discussion about some Kuwait returnees who found themselves left only with a big house which they now had difficulty maintaining, Ruby Chacko, the wife of an attorney said haughtily, "Who asked them to build such mansions?" She went on to tell me that the moral life of the area had deteriorated after the Gulf migration as people had become very materialistic and money minded. According to her, even the church donations were given by Gulf migrants "as a bribe so God won't take the money away from them."

The old rich also had several anecdotes to illustrate the foolish behavior of their newly rich neighbors. Sally Easau gave me the example of the nurse in the house opposite hers: "They went and built a big two-story house because her brother and sister had built such houses before them and they said they must do the same. But now they regret it. The wife is enormously fat and so can't climb up the stairs. So she hasn't seen the upstairs for years!" Breaking into peals of laughter, she went on to illustrate how "crude" many of the Gulfites were by telling me about the woman she had overheard recently: "She was in the market to buy oranges [which depending on the season, could be quite expensive] and the orange seller asked her how many she wanted. Raising her voice a little to make sure everyone around her heard, she said, 'Oh, give me two dozen. My children—they chew and spit, chew and spit, chew and spit, and it is all gone in two days.'"

Sarah Varghese had a "new rich" story from her friend, Elsie Joseph, a general practitioner. "An older woman came to see her [Dr. Joseph] with a baby swathed in a woolen cap, booties and coat. The child was obviously uncomfortable in the heat and so Elsie said, 'First, take off those things. They are not suitable to wear here.' The grandmother was indignant and retorted, 'I'll have you know that these clothes are from America, sent over by my daughter from there.'"

In Kembu even more than in Veni and Cherur, migrant households considered it a matter of prestige to obtain the best and most expensive medical treatment. Mary Mathews, the doctor's wife, told me about two instances where this arrogance had resulted in tragedy. In both cases, the migrant relatives of gravely ill family members had flown in from the Middle East. "In a speech laced with high-flown medical words they demanded to know if *Achayen*[11] [her doctor husband] had performed this procedure or that, and whether he had this equipment and that. When they realized that he did not have the 'latest technology' they got upset and told him rudely that they were going to take their relatives to a hospital in Cochin [a city that was over two hours away by car]. Unable to take the strain of the journey, the patients died in both cases—one en route, and the other after getting to the hospital."

Migration and Gender

Several women who were schoolteachers had migrated to Africa (and sometimes to other countries like Sri Lanka, Malaysia, and Singapore) to work, occasionally on their own, but most often with their husbands. However, the group that was able to benefit most from migration were nurses. Within Hindu culture, nursing has traditionally been considered to be a stigmatized occupation for women (very few men went into nursing) because of the "inappropriate" and intimate contact with male strangers that it entailed. Although Syrian Christians were less bound by Hindu ideology, some of these ideas spilled over into the community. Thus, the Syrian Christian women who went into nursing during the colonial period and immediately after were largely from the lower middle classes. One of the attractions was the stipend that was paid to nursing students during this period. Occasionally, some women from "good families" also became nurses, sometimes against their parents' wishes, due to the economic difficulty their families had fallen into or the desire for independence. Annie Thomas was a middle-aged nurse who had retired after working in the Middle East. She told me that she was from an upper-middle-class family but went for nursing because she had been rejected for a couple of marriages on account of being dark complexioned. This upset her, so she decided that she would stay single, become a nurse, and then do missionary work. After working as a nurse in India for a few years (during which time she got married), she migrated to the Middle East.

As nurses came to be in big demand in the Middle East and the United States in the sixties and particularly the seventies, more and more women from Kembu and other Syrian Christian areas went in for nurse training (even though the payment of the stipend had been discontinued by this time). The highly lucrative salaries offered to nurses in these countries provided women the opportunity of being the primary income earners in their family, a position which greatly increased their power and autonomy. Over time, nurses became much sought after as brides. Thus they were often able to marry professionally qualified (occasionally even younger) men from good families for little or no dowry. "Lizzy's brother went first. He financed her nurse training and then took her over. After a few years she got married to a lawyer who was also in the Gulf. Imagine that, a lawyer! In the old days, it would have been unthinkable for a lawyer to marry a nurse," said Reeni Philip, about one of her neighbors.

Since the norm of the nuclear family being together had been established by this time and most villagers were also able to obtain stable, well-paid jobs, both male and female migrants took their spouses to the Middle East after marriage. Marriages were often arranged between migrants. As the cost of living in the Gulf increased (and as the income cutoff for migrants to have their families with them went up), male migrants became increasingly particular that their spouses should also be able to work in the Middle East (female migrants would generally only marry such spouses). Because marrying a man from the Gulf was prestigious, this increased the emphasis on women getting a good job-oriented education. Family migration also generally resulted in a closer relationship between spouses as they were separated from family and friends and thus were more dependent on each other for companionship.

Many Gulf families from Kembu were able to have their children complete their entire schooling in the Middle East. At that point, they were sent back to India for college education (often in private medical or engineering schools). In other cases, the children were sent back to Kerala after their primary schooling and left in the care of grandparents or sent to residential schools. If the mother was not working (or did not have a well-paying job), she often returned at this stage to look after the children. But in those cases she lived in a separate house with her children, remittances were sent to her, and she was in full charge of household and often even financial decisions. The case of Gracy Joseph is illustrative.

> He [her husband] would keep enough for his expenses there and send the rest back to me. I put some money in savings deposits, some in Units (bonds) and then I wrote to him and said that we should put some money in the names of each of the children. He agreed, so I did that. I was the one who supervised the building of this house. Some five years ago, rubber plantations became very lucrative so I thought that it would be a good investment to buy a few acres in the hills with some others in the village. When I wrote to my husband about this he said, "Gracy, I leave that to you. You know more about the local situation than I do." I did [buy some land in the hills] and it turned out to be very profitable. So you see, he leaves everything to me!

Even in the cases where the man had to leave his wife behind with his parents, they usually looked after her well, since the norm in middle- and upper-class families was that a daughter-in-law was to be treated with greater care than one's own daughter (it was considered shameful if she complained to her husband or parents about any deprivation in her in-laws' house). The relationship between the spouses was respected and letters and phone calls between them were private. The man sent the money for his family's personal expenses to his wife, and the rest of the money for the maintenance of the joint household was sent to his parents. Many such men also tried to take their wives over for at least short periods of time (on visitors visas).

It was the youngest son who traditionally inherited the ancestral house and who looked after his parents during their old age, so wives of youngest sons usually returned fairly soon to be with their parents-in-law. I came across many cases where, even though the father-in-law was nominally the head of the household, the daughter-in-law was the one in charge, since she had proved herself to be capable and the parents-in-law were elderly.

All this is not to say that the Gulf migration had a positive impact on all women. I did hear of cases where there were tensions between parents-in-law and the daughter-in-law, mostly among poorer families (the second stream of migrants). The most poignant case was that of Bindu, a young woman with two children, whose husband, Raju, had been working in Kuwait since 1980.

Raju came from a relatively poor family but was taken over by Toyota Cherian, a relative, who therefore did not charge him even for his airfare. Raju's job paid him Rs. 12,000 a month, not enough to have his family with him, so Bindu and the children remained behind in Kembu, first at his parents' house, and then when problems developed there, at Bindu's parents' house. As the only migrant in the family, all the responsibilities fell on Raju's shoulders, and he had to take care of his parents and his sister's dowry and wedding expenses. In Kuwait, Raju shared a room with several other men, so that he could save the maximum amount of money (Rs. 10,000 a month). Except for the amount that he sent to his parents, Raju sent the rest of the money to Bindu, who used it to buy a house plot (for Rs. 275,000) and build a house (for Rs. 200,000). When the house was nearly completed, she moved in with her two children. Soon after that, however, the problems with her in-laws increased (Bindu said that they were envious of her house) and they wrote to Raju saying that Bindu was having an affair. Raju believed them and stopped sending money to Bindu (he kept the money in Kuwait) and also wrote her several nasty letters. Bindu told me that she had gone through a very bad period and that she had survived only through her belief in God and the support of church members and neighbors (her father supported her financially). Two years later, Raju realized that his wife was blameless and that he had been wrong. He sent some money to her and was just getting ready to transfer a large sum to complete the house (it was unpainted and the flooring was unfinished) when the invasion took place in Kuwait. When I visited Bindu in August, she told me that Raju was trying to come home. He had lost the savings he had in the bank in Kuwait and told her to try to borrow money for the time being and that he would repay the money as soon as he could.

Wives like Bindu who remained behind in Kembu also had to face the problems of loneliness and bringing up children on their own. Amy, another young woman whose husband was in the Gulf, told me that she and her husband felt very bad about being apart. He missed her and the children, and she in turn had to deal with several problems because she lived alone. Not having her husband there even for Christmas and other special occasions was particularly difficult. Both Amy and her husband wanted to save money quickly so that the husband could return and the family could be together. They had bought some land near a busy intersection hoping to start a shop. Amy told me that she and her other friends whose husbands were in the Middle East got together periodically and that the conversation was always about the difficulties of living apart from their husbands.

Amy added, "Of course, if the alternative is poverty, that is not good either since poverty is even worse for family relationships. So they [the men] should go, save as much as possible in as short a time as possible (enough for a moderate standard of living), and then come back." She told me of several neighboring families who had been able to do just that. So in Kembu, husbands and wives generally seemed to have a much closer relationship, when compared to Cherur and certainly Veni, which in turn shaped their migration patterns. I know of several cases, for instance, where men had the opportunity to take up good jobs in the Middle East but turned it down because they could not have their families with them (either the salary was not sufficient, the wife had local commitments and could not migrate, or the place or job was not suitable for family life).

There was a lot of talk about the rise of hypogamous marriages due to the Gulf migration and some of the problems created by such marriages. By this time, interdenominational marriages had become common and parents had also started looking far and wide (within the Syrian Christian community) for suitable marriage partners for their children. Because of the tremendous increase in dowry rates that had taken place as a result of the migration, there were several nonmigrant families who found that they did not have enough money to get their daughters married to men from equal-status families. In such cases, they were often married to Gulf migrants who had well-paying jobs but who were less educated and from lower-status families. Sometimes the difference in the backgrounds between the two sides created tensions: between spouses or between daughters-in-law and parents-in-law. Frequently, problems developed because the wife was lavish in her spending habits (often in order to justify the marriage to relatives and friends). A bank employee narrated a funny story about a friend who had been in such a situation but had managed to "cure" his wife of her extravagances: "Simon's wife was a spendthrift. However much he sent back, it was never enough. So Simon decided that he had to try to curb her spending. He took her to the Gulf on a visitor's visa for a few months. He was a pipe fitter there and used to come home from work with grease on himself and with his mouth full of sand. Simon didn't say a word but the wife saw all this and was shocked. Without his saying anything, she herself became very careful with money (seeing how hard he worked to make it). Since she returned she has cut down on fish, and takes the bus instead of an auto-rickshaw. Simon now says that life is very good!"

In another case, I was told about a well-educated woman from a good family who used to ill treat her uneducated mother-in-law. However, the greatest tensions developed in cases where the bride's side had been deceived about the type of job that the man had in the Gulf. I heard of several instances where men who were technicians in the Gulf passed themselves off as "engineers" and got married to women from good families. In other cases, men who had lost their Gulf jobs did not reveal this to their prospective brides. When the women and their families discovered the truth they were very angry and upset, in a few cases resulting in the breakdown of the marriage.

In Kembu, as in Veni and Cherur, the changes in the position of women brought about by migration were not confined to migrant households alone and there was a more general effect on the community at large. A great stress was put on education and job training, and working wives had become the norm, increasing the status and power of women within the household and in the community at large. Several women in the community were doctors, engineers, bank officials, and well-placed government employees. Older women told me that the younger generation of women were more confident, outgoing, and independent than they had been at the same age.

At the same time, the escalating dowry rates meant that daughters were frequently seen as a burden. Unlike among the Nayars and Ezhavas, families of Syrian Christian brides had little control over the way the dowry was spent. Most of the time, in keeping with custom, the money was handed over to the parents of the bridegroom for them to use as they pleased.[12] In a few cases, families of brides had been able to insist that the dowry money be put in the name of the couple. (I was told that having the money in the name of the woman was extremely rare.) Again, the formal superiority of men and particularly of the husband was institutionalized and continued to be maintained in a variety of ways, to a much greater degree than in Cherur. I also detected a new trend among second-generation migrants in Kembu, which suggested that some of the gains made by the first-generation women migrants might be reversed.

Among the second-generation migrants, young women (even daughters of nurses) were almost never sent for nurse training. Of the more than dozen cases that I was acquainted with directly or indirectly, I did not come across a single instance where the daughter of a nurse became a nurse herself. This was due to the stigma that was still (though to a lesser degree) attached to nursing. Thus the profession continued to be perceived as one entered into by poorer women unable to afford a college education (which was considered far more prestigious).

Girls of the community were being sent to "reputed colleges" for a general education (a small minority went to medical school and became doctors) and were married off (with large dowries) to professionally qualified Gulf grooms. These women then worked in white-collar positions in the Middle East, and their jobs and incomes were to supplement the primary income earned by their husbands. The phenomenon of women going as primary migrants was increasingly being viewed as an aberrant, or at least a less desirable, pattern. Thus, the preferred situation was when the family could obtain a bridegroom who had higher educational qualifications and a better occupational position than the bride (this was done through giving large dowries).

Recall that many of the gains in the status of women were made as a consequence of the numbers of female nurses who went abroad from this area. However, the changes in gender ideology and practice brought about by their opportunity to be the primary economic earners in the family could turn out to be temporary. During the period of my fieldwork, only poorer families (whose numbers were decreasing) were still sending their daughters to train as nurses. In a period of one generation, though nursing as a profession had become more respectable, it was still not seen as prestigious and therefore, wealthier families (who were now a significantly larger proportion of the population) had lapsed back into the conventional pattern of status acquisition, where women were educated to be appropriate social partners of men holding professional jobs.

Migration and Caste

The term *Backward Class Christians* was the official designation of converts from the Harijan castes. Such conversion did not bring about much change in their caste status. The Syrian Christians called them "Pulaya" (the name of the Harijan caste) Christians and the relationship between the two groups was similar in many respects to that between Harijans and upper castes in Hindu communities.[13] In Kembu, most of the Backward Class Christians continued to live in "colonies" and attend separate churches.[14] Many of them worked as servants in Syrian houses. In general, Syrians avoided close social contact with them in anything other than a master-servant relationship and would not eat or drink in their houses. However, there was a feeling of obligation to them as fellow Christians. The Syrians of Kembu recognized that, to keep converts and to garner future members, it was important to emphasize the spiritual, social, and material benefits of church membership. Thus, pastors and Christian social workers took a very active interest in this congregation, encouraged the Backward Class Christians to pursue education, and often helped educated members to get jobs (mainly in the Christian institutions). They were exhorted to spend their money carefully and to save. Again, the Syrian church also helped needy households with loans. For all these reasons, their situation was better than that of the Harijans of Cherur. At the time of my fieldwork, several families had members with salaried jobs. For this group, education was the route to a certain degree of social and economic mobility.[15]

Despite the fact that the Backward Class Christians lived in an area of very high migration, they were not able to participate to any significant extent in the international exodus. As in the case of the Harijans, the few migrants who were able to go to the Middle East only managed to pull themselves out of poverty and also did not (or were not able to) take anyone else from the "colony" over, so the migration did not spread.

I have indicated that most of the migrants from Kembu migrated through the help of family and friends. Although some Syrian Christians did help their servants migrate, this was quite rare. As one bitter Backward Class Christian man put it, "Then who will stand in the front yard?"—a reference to the fact that Backward Class Christians generally stood on the ground in front of the steps of an upper-caste member's house (i.e., they were not invited inside) when they went to see him or her for a favor. He meant that Syrians would be reluctant to help Backward Class Christians migrate since migration would have undermined the economic and social hierarchy between the two groups. Some of the Syrian Christians themselves admitted to me that many of them would not help "take a Pulaya over and run the 'risk' that he would end up earning half as much" as they earned. Mary Mathews also mentioned that several villagers had scolded her for educating the children of her servants "because they would not be willing to be servants after getting educated."

Caste operated in an indirect way as well. Since helping someone obtain a job in the Middle East involved some effort (to find a suitable position and get the visa), risk (of the migrant defaulting the loan), and responsibility (for the migrant's conduct and performance once in the job), people preferred to take over relatives and friends. The traditional dependence of the Backward Class Christians on the higher castes may also have made it psychologically more difficult for them to choose the migration option. As one Backward Class Christian woman put it, "We just did not think about it. People in our group have always depended on the Syrians for work." Another possible factor could be difficulty they experienced in mortgaging their land (since they lived in lower-caste colonies) to raise money for the passage.

To some extent, the migration only increased the economic and social distance between the Syrians and the Backward Class Christians. This was due to several interrelated reasons. Food crop cultivation, which this area had specialized in earlier and which was also very labor intensive, had largely been abandoned. Since the Backward Class Christians specialized in agricultural labor, they lost their primary source of income. During the period of Gulf migration, there was a labor migration into the area by large groups (predominantly men) from the neighboring state of Tamil Nadu, where the economic situation was far worse. The Tamilians were willing to work for lower wages and were also considered to be more docile (workers in Kerala were believed to be militant due to the Communist influence). Thus, they were taking over many of the labor opportunities in the area and had begun to specialize in the most lucrative unskilled and semiskilled jobs: the tasks connected with house construction. As a result of both these developments, the Backward Class Christians of the area were forced out of their traditional occupational niche. The families that had salaried earners were able to get by but the rest found it difficult to cope with the huge price increases in the area.

Conclusion

Although Kembu was also an agricultural area like Veni and Cherur, the key factor that differentiated Kembu from these two areas and fundamentally shaped its migration pattern was the fact that it was a strongly Christian area. Religion did not shape migration patterns directly, but indirectly, through the ties the villagers had with Western missionaries and British colonialists. These ties helped them obtain a good English education and positions in mission-run organizations. The women of the community were also well educated and many worked as teachers and nurses. The educational and occupational training of the Christians and their relationship with the British enabled them to migrate to cities around the country, and to other countries right from the turn of the twentieth century, for white-collar and even professional positions. Their occupational profile and nuclear family structure permitted family migration which in turn deepened the nuclearization of families and weakened community ties.

The community ethos was reflected in the consumption, investment, and exchange behavior of migrants from Kembu. Remittances were mainly used for the needs of the immediate family and the stress was on accumulating family wealth and professional status. Thus, the relationship between individual acquisition and community reproduction was tenuous in this community. The value placed on religiosity and the preservation of the church partly counteracted the weaker social bonds. Time and effort were often spent on religious activities upon return from the Middle East, which resulted in frequent interaction with fellow church members. Migrants were also generous with church donations. However, since there were so many churches in Kembu, each had fairly small congregations, limiting the size of the community.

The relationship between religion, status, and gender can be seen by the abundance of nurses in the area. As Christians (and as people who had close ties with mission-run hospitals and nursing schools), women in Kembu were able to go in for nursing despite the stigma attached to the occupation within the wider society. Syrian Christians were also among the first groups in Kerala to provide higher education for women and to have women working in white-collar and professional jobs. While this nexus between religion, status, and gender fundamentally shaped the migration patterns from this area, since it permitted many women to be the primary migrants in their family, I have argued that it was also transformed by migration. Very few second-generation migrant women went in for nursing or became primary income earners. Instead, they were married to professional men and went with them to the Middle East as secondary migrants.

Migration brought about several other changes in the central defining features of Kembu. From a community of devout, hard-working, frugal farmers, the villagers had metamorphosed into wealthy international migrants who worked in professional and white-collar occupations and lived in luxury. As pastors and villagers told me, the economic prosperity had changed their earlier Puritan-like ethic to one which tended to be more complacently religious, and which viewed their economic success as a sign of divine favor. With the deepening of the nuclearization process, the links between extended family (which had traditionally been very close) were being weakened. Although migration erased many subgroup differentiations, such as those based on denominational background and family ancestry, caste cleavages were reinforced as the Backward Class Christians were unable to benefit from the economic prosperity of the Syrian section of the community.

CHAPTER 8

The Ethnic Kaleidoscope and International Migration Revisited

$\mathcal{T}$he portraits of Veni, Cherur, and Kembu have provided vivid examples of everyday ethnicity at work. Since I chose regions that were almost entirely inhabited by one ethnic group, the differences between the Mappilas, Ezhavas, and Syrians are clearly evident. I found many of these differences even in areas of Kerala where members of the three groups lived intermingled with one another (except in a few highly urban pockets inhabited by professionals and salaried government employees), since close social interaction was still confined to members of the same ethnic background. As in the case of the Muslims of Kuttur, however, the ethnic characteristics that were so prominent in Veni, Cherur, and Kembu tended to be more muted in ethnically mixed areas. This is not surprising since ethnicity, although inscribed in individuals, is a group-level phenomenon and is thus most visibly manifested in ethnic *communities*. It is in the context of community living that the norms and behavioral patterns that go into making ethnicity can be most easily ratified and naturalized, since this can be done publicly, in the community (by neighbors, friends, and even strangers), rather than privately, in the home.

For instance, I have discussed the way gender norms were assiduously enforced by the community in Veni, through gossip, innuendo, and (as in my case) direct verbal harassment. In Cherur, villagers were forced to part with large sums of money they could often not even afford for life-cycle celebrations and temple festivals, through the tactic of "shaming" those who did not contribute the expected amounts. In Kembu, I observed the many subtle ways in which most

Syrians maintained the distinction between themselves and lower-caste, "recent" converts to Christianity, and how these norms were inculcated into newcomers (such as the children of Gulf migrants who had grown up in the Middle East) by well-meaning relatives and neighbors.

At the same time, I must emphasize that the development and maintenance of ethnicity does not depend on community isolation but on structured interaction with ethnic "others." It is only in the context of such interaction that boundaries between groups and norms of exclusivity and distinctness are formed, as the discussion of the historical background of the groups in chapter 3 illustrated. All three groups became "ethnicized" as a consequence of their encounters with Western colonialists, although for different reasons.

Islam became the basis of identity and community formation for Mappilas during and after the brief Mysorean interregnum (which gave them the basis to construct a positive and oppositional Islamic identity), primarily because the policies of the Portuguese and the British deprived them of their sources of livelihood (trade and land) and, along with the policies of the Mysorean rulers, created cleavages between them and the Hindus. These cleavages had begun to slowly erode in the postcolonial period, and as I indicated in chapter 5, the prosperity and increased contact with Hindus brought about by international migration had made many of the Mappilas in Veni more outward oriented.

Unlike the Mappilas, both the Ezhavas and the Syrians benefited from colonialism. In the traditional caste structure, groups were clearly differentiated, but the hierarchical nature of the system meant that relationships between lower and higher castes were generally emulative (to the extent that this was permitted). The process of commercialization initiated under colonialism brought prosperity to many Ezhavas and also freed them from many of the traditional caste restrictions. Initially, the Ezhavas attempted to Sanskritize and imitate the Nayars, but as they became more prosperous than the latter through international migration, they had started to formulate a distinct social and cultural identity.

Due to the proselytizing and confrontational behavior of the Portuguese, the Syrians emphasized their distinct identity as a group that was "Hindu in culture, Christian in religion and Oriental in worship" (Podipara 1973, 107) and continued to maintain their traditional Nayar-emulative practices. In the early British period, they abandoned these practices as they lost their position as warriors (the reason they had been categorized as quasi-Nayars) and went on to adopt several Brahminical rituals and practices such as vegetarianism and strict gender segregation. Colonial patronage created a wedge between Syrians and upper-caste Hindus (whose fortunes had declined over the colonial period) and brought about a greater degree of Westernization by the Syrians, which was reinforced by the white-collar and semiprofessional international migration. It is only at this point that Christianity became the basis to construct an *ethnic* identity which was not just religious but also cultural.

I argued in chapter 2 that ethnicity has a dual function. Ethnicity is one of the most successful ways in which competing groups can organize to try to gain access to resources. It is also one of the ways in which competing groups express, maintain, or try to compensate for their differential access to resources. Both of these functions of ethnicity can be seen in the three cases that are the focus of this book.

The development of ethnicity among the Mappilas took place with their movement to the interior and the realization that they had special privileges to gain as Muslims under the Mysorean occupation. When they lost their privileges under the British, the introverted and separatist identity they developed was clearly an attempt to compensate for their loss of resources by emphasizing community solidarity. As a privileged group with Kerala society, the Syrian Christians resisted Portuguese attempts to categorize them with the recently converted and lower-caste Latin Catholics. Later, when they lost their status as warriors, they adopted Brahminical customs and still later, under the patronage of the British, became more Christianized and adopted Western education. Each of these strategies was an attempt to maintain their privileged position vis-à-vis the ruling class under changing circumstances. Ezhavas organized and mobilized under the leadership of Sri Narayana Guru and other leaders to obtain access to the social, economic, and political resources that had become available as a consequence of the dismantling of the traditional caste system. The socioeconomic position the group was able to obtain as a consequence of migration was expressed through the new marriage rituals and practices that wealthy Ezhavas had introduced.

In other words, as long as there are significant differences between groups in the access to social, cultural, economic, and political resources, these differences are legitimized as being an outcome of ethnic variations. Since the distributional access of different ethnic groups keeps changing, the content of ethnicity is always being reformulated.

In chapter 3, my central argument was that the Ezhavas, Mappilas, and Syrian Christians emerged as ethnic entities with distinct social boundaries and cultural characteristics over the period of colonialism. Ethnic groups also experience changes in composition and size over time. Sections of a group may split off and form a new group or may merge with another group. For instance, Gulf migration permitted economically successful "Ten" Muslims to separate themselves from their fellow fisherfolk and in some cases merge with the higher-status Muslims. Thus the boundaries of ethnic groups are fluid and porous. But in general, boundary changes are small and at the fringes, and are also quickly naturalized, allowing groups to maintain the appearance of continuity and stability over time.

As a group-level phenomenon, ethnicity both enables and constrains individual members. These effects in turn work through subjective and objective means. Subjectively, ethnicity shapes the outlook of individuals by defining goals and the paths to be taken to achieve them. Thus, materially or educationally disadvantaged individuals might be pushed into aspiring toward a high-achieving trajectory by successful ethnic groups. Conversely, even high-achieving individuals may be constrained by the "leveled aspirations" (MacLeod 1994) of ethnic groups that are not successful. Since the Syrian Christian community had established a white-collar and professional migratory tradition, many lower-class members, both male and female, were able to aspire toward obtaining such positions. In Veni, however, young boys and girls had very limited educational aspirations and most girls had no occupational aspirations at all.

The material in this book has also demonstrated the extent to which the social and economic resources of ethnic communities were objectively important for individuals. Migrants from all three groups used the resources of their respective communities to institutionalize and facilitate international migration. However, we have also seen how ethnicity can be a negative resource, preventing access to and utilization of opportunities. For instance, due to gender norms and practices which defined women primarily as homemakers and restricted their education and job-oriented training, women in Mappila Muslim and Ezhava Hindu communities were not able to participate directly in the Middle Eastern migration. Again, while moderately educated Syrian Christians were able to obtain white-collar positions in the Middle East, equally educated Mappila Muslims and Ezhava Hindus were not able to take advantage of many of these opportunities because they lacked the necessary social and cultural resources. Thus we see the critical importance of social background in affecting the likelihood of individual success, something that tends to be completely obscured by the meritocratic discourse that is so widely prevalent today (even in contemporary Kerala).

Is ethnicity primarily a matter of culture, of structure, or of both working together? By elongating the time frame, this study has shown the dialectical relationship between culture and structure in the development, maintenance, and transformation of ethnicity, something that most literature on ethnicity has overlooked. Certainly, much of the variation in the patterns of migration and utilization of remittances that the three communities manifested was due to the educational and occupational differences of the communities. However, as I have argued, the educational and occupational profiles of the communities were themselves a product of the differential ethnicity of the groups. Mappila Muslims had low educational levels and turned to business ventures since community leaders such as the Tangals had actively discouraged participation in the educational and occupational sectors of the wider society. Although Ezhava leaders like Sri Narayana Guru stressed the importance of education for the upliftment of the community, educational levels still remained fairly low in the first half of the twentieth century. After centuries of exclusion because of their caste status, the Ezhavas did not immediately have the social and cultural capital to succeed in the educational system. In the Syrian Christian case, it is likely that they first turned to education when they lost their position as warriors and started emulating Brahmin practices. This process of course was greatly accelerated under the active patronage of British regents and missionaries. It is clear, therefore, that to understand ethnicity, it should be viewed as a *process* and thus, the manifestation of ethnicity at a point in time should not be divorced from the dynamic historical background that created it. Fluidity and future change should also be factored into the study of ethnicity in the present.

The Nucleus of Ethnicity

I have argued that a nexus of religion, status, and gender comprised the core of the ethnicity of the three communities under study (this may vary in other locales). Religious identity defined and shaped the character of the three groups and set the parameters for intergroup interaction. Religious beliefs and practices were also an important part of the everyday lives of individuals in Veni, Cherur, and Kembu. Although religious identity, belief, and practice had a powerful and constraining effect on individuals, over time, community members who had access to new resources were able to modify the social meaning of belonging to a particular religious community, the interpretation of religious doctrines, and the types of religious behaviors deemed important. I have shown how these new resources could arise as a result of international developments which changed the global alignment of countries identified with particular religions (colonialism, the monopoly over oil), or as a consequence of regional developments which resulted in changes in the socioeconomic position of local religious groups (commercialization), or a combination of the two factors (the discriminatory treatment of groups by colonialists, the differential participation of communities in international migration).

An important way in which the identities of the Mappilas, Ezhavas, and Syrians were embodied were through distinctive concepts of honor and shame, in turn manifested through unique symbols and behavior. Correspondingly, redefinitions of identity were accomplished through changes in these symbols and behavior. Status in Veni, Cherur, and Kembu was closely tied in with religion. Thus, in all three communities, members who were religiously devout, ethical, and active in the respective religious institutions of the community (the mosque, temple, and church) had a high status. Differential concepts of normative gendered behavior, particularly that of women, also distinguished the three communities. In the Mappila community, seclusion and veiling of women was viewed as prestigious, while among the Syrians, having well-educated, professionally employed women in the family who knew how "to mingle with people and to talk well" was highly regarded. As women's rights came to represent an indicator of modernity and progress, the matrilineal heritage of Nayars and Ezhavas and the greater freedom that women in the community enjoyed had become a source of pride for members, an ironic reversal from a few decades earlier when the same heritage had been a cause for shame (in the colonial period).

Most analyses of ethnicity do not discuss the fact that gender ideology and practice are central to the culture and social organization of ethnic groups. Veni, Kembu, and Cherur had three different patterns of gender relationships, and this led to fundamental differences in the organization of the household and extended family, marriage practices, educational patterns, economic behavior, concepts of status, migration, and remittance flows, as well as my reception as fieldworker in each of the areas. The centrality of gender to ethnicity is also demonstrated by the fact that changes in status and identity are often signified by reconstructions of gender.

Ethnicity and International Migration

Drawing on the work of cultural sociologists who have analyzed economic processes, I have argued that it is important to understand that the economy and individual economic behavior are not autonomous of the social context but are shaped by it. By using this approach to the study of migrant economic behavior, I was able to demonstrate the dialectical relationship between ethnicity and international migration. In this section, I will return to the schema of Parry and Bloch (1989) that I introduced in chapter 2, and show how the "short-term cycle" of acquisitive individual economic behavior was constrained by and articulated with the "longer-term community cycle" that reproduced the "social cosmos" or the ethnicity of each of the communities.

The Middle Eastern region offered a range of possible occupations for which migrants were needed, and the migrants from each of the three communities were tracked into different economic niches. Thus, migrants from Veni largely obtained jobs in the nonformal sector, those from Cherur took up formal contractual positions as technicians, while clerical workers and nurses dominated the outflow from Kembu. In every case, the organization of the migration and remittance process was also distinct and reflected the cultural ethos and social organization of the community.

While ethnic networks were crucial to both the organization of migration and the remittance process, they were used in different ways by each community. The long history of social and economic interaction between the Arabs and the Mappila Muslims provided the initial impetus for the Middle Eastern migration, and the first Mappila migrants from Veni used their connections to obtain (illegal) passage on returning merchant ships. The solidarity of the Mappilas enabled the community to sustain a large, frequently illegal migration and provide for members in the Middle East who were sometimes unable to obtain regular work for months on end. Migrants were also able to use their networks to maintain chitty groups and to send back remittances in the form of tube money, which increased the financial gains of the migration.

Ezhava migration from Cherur was initiated through the professional agents who had established themselves in the area. Since Ezhavas lacked the group cohesiveness and the ties to the Arabs of the Mappilas, even later migrants had to use agents and pay their exorbitant fees. Social networks helped direct Ezhava migrants to agents who had established a reputation of being trustworthy. As many of the chitties established by early migrants had collapsed, later migrants had to depend on formal mechanisms to save money and send back remittances. Most sent remittances back in the form of postal drafts.

Middle Eastern migration from the Kembu region first began through the British contacts of Syrian Christians. Many early migrants were directly invited by companies who paid for their travel expenses. Subsequent migrants went through the help of close relatives who were well placed in the Middle East region. Remittances were generally transferred back to Kerala through bank drafts on an annual or semiannual basis.

Consumption, Investment, and Exchange

It is important to keep in mind that consumption, investment, and exchange patterns are affected by two important variables: the way the income is obtained and the characteristics of the community within which the income is spent. Thus, in Veni, Cherur, and Kembu, similarities in the way in which income earned from international migration was perceived (as having some of the qualities of windfall income), together with the variation in the communities' ethnic structures, account for the similarities and differences in their consumption, exchange, and investment patterns. While there was a pronounced change of lifestyles marked by status spending, cultural entrepreneurship, and public generosity in each village, the relative balance between these factors varied, as did the specific income-generation activities into which the savings were channeled.

I have argued that the crucial factor differentiating the economic behavior of the three groups was the variation in the definitions of status. Status within the Mappila Muslim community in Veni accrued from being a donor. Thus, wealth was distributed to a large circle of people within the community and was also used to support religious causes. In Cherur, being able to celebrate functions on a large scale was prestigious, so much of the migrants' savings were spent on lavish gifts and entertaining for life-cycle celebrations. The gains of migration were mostly distributed within the extended family. Since Ezhavas viewed educating children as important, money was also spent on this goal. While Syrian Christian migrants sent some remittances to support the church and religious causes, they saved most of their wealth to finance the professional education of sons (and sometimes daughters) and the dowries of daughters. For the most part, therefore, the Syrian Christian migration only enriched the immediate family.

Variations in the gender norms and practices of the three communities also resulted in economic control being passed to different sets of individuals. Married Mappila Muslim migrants generally entrusted the economic and social supervision of their household to their father or other male relative; Ezhava migrants often put their fathers-in-law in charge; while most male Syrian Christian migrants left their wives in control.

Although the character of the communities constrained individual responses to migration, these responses had the eventual result of reformulating the ethnic structure of all three groups. Thus, there was an evolving dialectical relationship between ethnicity and individual migrant behavior. Conventional studies of the economic consequences of migration have generally been informed by the neoclassical perspective, which ignores cultural context. Because of this, they have been unable to explain some of the ways in which international remittances have been used. Since policies are usually guided by the neoclassical perspective, many of them have also been ineffective. An understanding of the larger social order of which the economy forms a part helps us to understand why economic behavior often deviates so far from the conventional axioms of atomized and self-interested decision making, why the same people can manifest quite different economic behavior under different circumstances, and why the same economic situation can result in completely divergent types of behavior. By thus integrating social factors into the schema, we can try to produce a theory that conforms more closely to reality and which will, therefore, have more explanatory and predictive capacity.

Migration and Caste

There were significant differences in the impact of the migration on the lowest castes of the three communities, between the Muslim pattern on the one hand and the Hindu and Christian patterns on the other. It is only the Pusalar Muslims of the coastal areas (the "Ten" group in Pullad) who were able to migrate to the Middle East in large numbers and make substantial social and economic gains. As a consequence of the migration, the social boundaries between the Malabari Mappila Muslims (the "Eleven" group in Pullad) and the Pusalar Muslims were gradually eroding with increased interaction and even intermarriages. The impact of the migration on the Harijans and the Backward Class Christians was very different. A few people had been able to migrate in these areas and some had even done well, but the migration did not spread among these groups and the economic and social distance between the upper- and lower-caste groups in the Hindu and Christian areas had only increased as a result of the Ezhava and Syrian migration.

What accounts for these differences? Although I have touched on several possibilities while discussing the three cases, the most likely cause is the variation in caste ideology between Kerala Muslims on the one hand and Hindus and Christians on the other. I would argue that it was the weaker-caste ideology of the Muslims that allowed the Pusalars to take advantage of the ethnic networks of the higher-caste Muslims, something that the Hindu and Christian Harijan groups were not able to do.

Studies of caste among non-Hindu communities in India are relatively sparse. Conventionally, scholars have viewed such structures as being similar to the caste system of the Hindus (Dumont 1970, 210; Fuller 1976, 58). However, other scholars dispute the appropriateness of using the term "caste" for the stratification patterns manifested by non-Hindu groups, particularly Muslims (see Vatuk 1996, 228–230). They point out, for instance, that Muslim status groups provide more scope for individual mobility (Mandelbaum 1970, 544–559) and intergroup marriage (Ahmed 1973). I found that there were some variations in the caste system of the Mappila Muslims and Syrian Christians, when compared to that of the Kerala Hindus. Caste distinctions among the Mappilas seemed to be less formalized and institutionalized with the primary basis for the separation between the Pusalar and Malabari Muslims being differences in occupation, income, and culture, rather than heredity. Among the Christians, it was only the distinction between the Syrians and the Harijan groups (Backward Class Christians) that was sharply drawn. Ezhava converts, for instance, were gradually absorbed within the Syrian category.

It is likely that the Malabari Mappilas (and Arab Muslims) were willing to help Pusalar Muslims because caste distinctions between the two groups were not as rigid as in the Hindu and Christian cases. More importantly, the fluid caste ideology of the Muslims provided an "escape hatch" for successful individuals to overcome their low social status and be absorbed into the Malabari category. The unprecedented opportunities brought about by the Middle Eastern migration made this possible for significant numbers of Pusalar Muslims. In the Cherur region, there did not seem to be much interaction between the Ezhavas and the Harijans, so there was little opportunity for the dissemination of information and the spread of migrant networks between the two groups. In Kembu, however, Syrians and Backward Class Christians interacted on a fairly regular basis, but as I have mentioned, there were several social mechanisms that maintained the social and economic hierarchy between the two groups and excluded the Backward Class Christians from the migration networks of the Syrians.

Migration and Gender

Perhaps the most dramatic difference between the three communities was the impact of the migration on women. In Veni, migration resulted in their earlier marriage and greater seclusion and also hindered the development of a personal relationship between spouses, thus contributing to a higher divorce rate. Young wives were generally placed under the direct supervision of their in-laws who tended to be strict about enforcing rules regarding seclusion and participation in housework. Male migration also delayed the family's move to an independent house. Even after moving to an independent house, wives of migrants had to guard against giving rise to any rumor regarding their behavior. Many women in Veni seemed to manifest signs of psychological stress.

In the Cherur Ezhava community, the long tradition of male migration had strengthened the position of women since they were able to remain in their parental homes even after marriage, and remittances were sent to them. Many older migrant wives continued to perform the economic tasks that had traditionally supplemented the household income (raising cows and chickens, growing vegetables and fruit in the land around the house, weaving coconut fronds), which gave them some economic independence. Women were in charge of lending out a portion of the remittances and collecting the interest. Wives of migrants often played an active role in supervising the construction of the family home. As a consequence of the migration, Cherur had become a female-dominated village, with women being very visible and active in local affairs and politics. Migration resulted in a greater emphasis on education for both boys and girls. The rise of hypogamous marriages had also raised the status of women and their families.

There were many female migrants from Kembu, and international migration provided such women the opportunity to become the primary economic earners in their families, or at least important income earners in their own right. Family migration strengthened spousal bonds and correspondingly weakened the power of the extended family to regulate female behavior. Male migrants who were not able to have their families with them sent their remittances to their wives. Many women played a major role in deciding how the money was to be invested and in supervising the construction of the family home. White-collar migration had increased the emphasis on women's higher education and employment.

I have indicated that the institutionalization of migration and the increased prosperity of the three areas seemed to be bringing about some changes in the gender norms and behavior of the younger generation. In Veni, for instance, decades of migration (and the corresponding decline in agriculture) had resulted in parents becoming increasingly economically dependent on their migrant sons, which strengthened the position of young men within the family. This meant that young men were able to develop close relationships with their wives if they wished to do so and to go out with them much more freely than in the past. In Cherur, hypogamous marriages had brought some college-educated women into the community, but they were not allowed to take up paid employment or do the traditional economic tasks which had given women of the older generation some independence and freedom of movement. In Kembu, the nursing profession which had provided the older generation with the opportunities to become the primary migrants and income earners of the family was closed off to daughters of migrants who were mostly provided an undergraduate education and then married to professional men. Unlike their mothers, therefore, they became homemakers or supplementary income earners.

Although I have argued that international migration brought more benefits to women in Cherur and Kembu when compared with women in Veni, I have tried to qualify this in many ways in the earlier chapters. The reactions of the women of Veni, Cherur, and Kembu to my own situation made me see how much I myself was a product of my urban, Westernized upbringing and also cautioned against any monolithic concepts of gender oppression and resistance. The people that I considered oppressed pitied my own subjugation to idealistic modern ideas of womanhood, equality, and romantic love. Many women considered it a privilege to have their husbands chosen for them by their parents, to be able to stay at home, and not have to worry about earning a living. Again, when Mary Mathews urged me to give up my idealistic vision of an "equal marriage," she was only being realistic in pointing out to me that such marriages are very rare.[1]

Methodology, Ethnicity, and Migration

By being both ethnographic and comparative, this study has revealed the powerful ways that ethnicity shapes the lives of people and mediates the sociocultural impact of migration. I have also shown how the ethnicity of the three villages affected the success of my own research. Although there is now much discussion about the need for "reflexivity" on the part of social science researchers who use qualitative methods, there has been little written about the ways in which research is understood by different societies and subcultures and the impact this might have on fieldwork strategies.

The strong minority consciousness of Veni villagers and their deep suspicion of strangers, together with their low educational levels, made it difficult to conduct household visits. The concept of social research was something that a lot of the villagers found difficult to understand and so many people were mistrustful of my motives. Because of the strong separation between male and female spheres of activity, it was often not possible to obtain even the most basic information about the male migration from the women of the household.

Cherur, however, was a different research experience altogether. Male migration had made the village a largely female space, and women were in charge of both community and household affairs. They were thus valuable respositories of information on a range of issues. Both women and men had some exposure and knowledge about the outside world and were welcoming and open. This, together with the high regard the villagers had for higher education, made them willing participants in my research. The curiosity of the villagers about my own background and experiences also made it easy for me to initiate informal conversations and obtain a variety of information about the community and migration patterns.

Villagers in Kembu were well educated and were aware of the concept of social research. However, since they assumed that all social research was survey based, many people did not understand my model of research and the type of information that I was looking for. So, while most villagers were willing to spare some time to answer my questions with short focused answers, quite often it was somewhat difficult to engage people in longer, more informal conversations and to make repeated household visits.

The varying experiences that I had in the three areas showed me the extent to which social research is an interactive process where the personal characteristics and social backgrounds of the researcher, and the researched, as well as the social context in which the interaction takes place, affect the kind of information obtained. It was clear to me that this was equally true of survey studies as well. I was in Kerala during the time that the 1990 pre-census survey testing (in preparation for the 1991 census) was being conducted, and went around with some pre-census enumerators while I was trying to find a suitable Hindu migrant area to study. I returned to some of the same households for my own research and realized that, in many cases, they had provided false information to the enumerators (even such basic information as the number of people in the household) out of fear that they might be assessed with higher house taxes. I have also mentioned the experiences of government survey researchers in the Veni area who had finally started resorting to "guesstimates."

Conclusion

Through studying the migration patterns of Veni, Cherur, and Kembu, this book has contributed to the understanding of ethnicity by showing what it is, how it affects the everyday lives and decisions of people, and how it changes. At the turn of the twentieth century, all three communities were poor and largely agrarian. All turned to migration over the next few decades, and since the early seventies, a large proportion of their inhabitants had migrated to the Middle East and were able to improve their economic position substantially. Despite these broad similarities, the actual patterns of migration, remittance use, and social change manifested by the communities were very different because, in each case, the three pieces comprising the kaleidoscope of ethnicity—religion, status, and gender—were distinctive.

An understanding of ethnicity is particularly important today when it has become such a powerful global force. I have argued that ethnicity develops as a means to obtain or maintain access to resources. Ethnicity has become particularly salient today because it is a significant political, economic, social, and psychological resource in multicultural welfare states since identities are recognized and benefits distributed on the basis of national ancestry. Furthermore, globalization has strengthened ethnicity by increasing the scale and scope of ethnic groups. Ethnic groups can develop, exist, and mobilize across national boundaries due to both large-scale international migration and the dominance and accessibility of the electronic media. The presence of wealthy expatriate communities around the world and the ease and speed of global financial transfers allow groups to mobilize and move resources very quickly in support of their causes. Deterritorialization has also stengthened the psychological need for home and homeland (Appadurai 1996; Gupta and Ferguson 1992; Robertson 1992, 30).

I have shown that ethnicity is fluid and constantly being reinvented. However, since the power of ethnicity rests in its ability to construct itself as a natural, ancient, and unchanging sociocultural unit that individual members have an obligation to uphold, its increased salience has also strengthened attempts at reification. Thus we now see several attempts to put forth or deny claims to entitlement on the basis of the inevitability and insurmountability of cultural differences.[2] The resuscitation and reconstruction of ancient history to showcase an idealized golden age as a blueprint for the future, or to point to past grievances against other groups as justification for current hostilities (Marty and Appleby 1991), are also based on this model of unchanging essences.

Finally, this study of ethnicity has contributed to the understanding of short-term international migration. We have seen that migration and remittance patterns often do not obey the type of economic and microlevel logic that scholars assume governs such behavior and that, therefore, many studies have missed important aspects of international migration. For instance, I have shown how the operation of ethnic networks in Veni, Cherur, and Kembu did not take place in the manner conceptualized by the social network theorists. Thus, the networks did not work uniformly in all three communities, nor did they eliminate group differences over time. The way the networks worked in each community was distinct, closely tied in with their history and social location, and also depended on the degree of solidarity of the community. We have also seen that there were mechanisms to prevent the expansion of social networks to those who were defined as being "outside" the community.

With the current backlash against immigrants in countries around the world, we are seeing more and more states turning to temporary contract migration as a solution for their labor shortage problems. The need for more studies focusing on the impact of such migration on host and sending countries is all the more urgent.

NOTES

CHAPTER 1   *Ethnicity and International Migration*

1. For instance, see Alba 1990; Conzen et al. 1992; Gans 1979; Rumbaut 1994; Steinberg 1981; Waters 1990.
2. Brass 1991; Horowitz 1985; Phadnis 1990; Schermerhorn 1978.
3. Census 1991 figures.
4. The term was coined by James Watson (1975) in his study of Chinese migration. See also Bloch 1984; Chen 1940; Pitt 1970; Van Velsen 1960.
5. The classic work is by Robert Redfield (1941). See Kearney (1986, 333–337) for a review of this perspective. See Brandes (1975) for a typical case study.
6. See So (1990) for a good overview of the approach.
7. See chapter 4 for a discussion of these studies.
8. One unpublished report from Nair's statewide survey indicated some differences in the educational and economic background of Muslim and Christian migrants (Nair 1986).
9. See Morawska (1990) for an overview of these studies.
10. See also Appadurai 1996; Eikelman and Piscatori 1990; Gardner 1996, 8–9.
11. Gordon 1964; Gibson 1989; Morawska 1990; Steinberg 1981; Waters 1999; Zhou and Bankston 1998.
12. Alba 1990; Gans 1992; Ignatiev 1995; Lieberson 1985; Tuan 1999; Waters 1990.
13. Significant exceptions include the work of Peggy Levitt (1995) and Luin Goldring (1992).
14. Studies of the Middle Eastern migration include Abella 1992; Abella and Atal 1986; Amjad 1989; Arnold and Shah 1989; ESCAP 1987; Gunatilleke 1986; Kerala Economics and Statistics Division 1987; Nair 1983 and 1986; Owen 1985; Saith 1992; and Serageldin 1983.
15. Chiswick 1978; Grebler, Moore, and Guzman 1970; Morales and Bonilla 1993; Portes and Rumbaut 1996; Reimers 1985.
16. A few of these studies have indicated that migration led to the transformation of ethnicity (Kallen 1982; Gardner 1995).
17. E.g., Abella and Atal 1986; Amjad 1989; Appleyard 1989; Arnold and Shah 1986; Gunatilleke 1986; Rashid 1989; Wickramasekara 1993.
18. The contracts were short term and jobs insecure, however many of the migrants could end up in a situation of net loss, not even able to recuperate their initial expenditure.

19. Gulati and Modi (1983, 58) and Nair (1989, 343).
20. In the migration "pockets" of the state, of course, the percentage would be considerably higher.
21. It is estimated that around 24 percent of the migrants from Kerala returned between 1984 and 1987 (Nair 1987a). However, many of these migrants were able to go back after a period of a few months to a year.
22. The situation eased, particularly after the Iran-Iraq war, but by this time, migrants from Kerala were faced with stiff competition from migrants from some other countries such as the Philippines and Sri Lanka, who, due to more favorable exchange rates, were willing to work for lower wages. (Information gained from conversations with migrants from different regions of Kerala and from discussions with scholars like P.R.G. Nair, who had conducted studies of the migration.)
23. According to estimates, around 170,000 workers returned from Kuwait and Iraq to India between August and December 1990 (Battistella 1991, 25).
24. Person whose ancestral language is Malayalam, the language of Kerala.
25. Behar and Gordon 1995; Narayan 1993; Visweswaran 1994.
26. I obtained affiliation with the Center for Development Studies in the capital city of Trivandrum and used the Center as my base during the period of fieldwork.
27. There have been many historical studies of the Mappila revolution of 1921. (See chapter 3 for a description of this event.) Miller's study (1976) is about the only one to describe some of the general social features of this community in the more recent period and even that was written in the early 1970s.
28. Identifying such an area took several weeks of travel and investigation. Here I relied more heavily on the accounts given to me by the village officers, health workers, creche teachers, and their records. In addition I visited fifteen households in the village and had some discussions with them about their own family and the community at large.
29. I found that this village had adopted a very different pattern of social change from that of Veni. I make passing references to the differences between the two villages during the course of this book. Since I did not study a control group for either Cherur or Kembu, however, I have not incorporated the data I obtained from this nonmigrant village into the main argument.
30. During the period of my stay in Veni, I also made a week's trip to a well-known Gulf pocket further to the south. This was one of the most written about Gulf centers in the state. It was an ethnically mixed area (mostly Hindu and Muslim) and more urban than Veni.
31. This was one of the differences between Kuttur and Veni. In Veni, too, there were women council members, but there this was a formality since it was required by law, and in actuality, it was the husbands who did all the house-to-house campaigning and subsequent house visits on their behalf.
32. This was in part because Kerala as a state manifests very little rural-urban difference. Another problem was that I was looking for a Muslim *neighborhood* and not just a scattered sample of Muslim households. In the heart of the city, however, Muslims lived intermingled with Hindus and Christians. I went to a few such houses and noticed that those families tended to differ very little from their Hindu and Christian neighbors, and thus bore no similarity to the average Muslim family in Veni.
33. I also made a quick one-week survey of another (predominantly Ezhava) Hindu community during this period.

34. Of course, these stages were not always that clearly sequenced or demarcated, and frequently, I would make a new discovery by pure accident, which would change the course of my investigations.

35. Often my initial impressions proved to be incorrect, particularly in the earlier stages of my fieldwork. For instance, from my preliminary visits to Kuttur, the urban Muslim area, I felt that the impacts of the migration were rather different from Veni, which is the reason that I decided to conduct the comparative study there. As mentioned, this impression changed after two months of intensive fieldwork in the area.

36. Of course, there were also the exceptional cases where the people involved insisted on my writing down everything they said.

CHAPTER 2   *The Kaleidoscope of Ethnicity*

1. Besides Barth (1969) and Leach (1960), see also Bonacich (1972) and Horowitz (1985).

2. See Park (1950) for a typical example. It was not until the early 1960s that growing social unrest effectively forced the recognition that these assumptions were faulty. Milton Gordon (1964) tried to modify the assimilationist perspective by arguing that there were several types of assimilation (he identified seven types) and that groups might assimilate in some ways but not others.

3. See Deutsch 1966; Enloe 1973; Glazer and Moynihan 1975; Horowitz 1985; Smith 1981; Van Den Berghe 1981.

4. The HarperCollins Dictionary of Sociology distinguishes the two forms of ethnicity as "cultural" and "political" respectively (1991, 151).

5. Richard Alba (1990) and Mary Waters (1990) characterize white American ethnicity in the contemporary United States this way.

6. I have drawn freely on ideas and suggestions of Dietrich Rueschemeyer, my dissertation advisor on this section, and I gratefully acknowledge his contributions.

7. I am indebted to Dietrich Rueschemeyer for these ideas.

8. See Eikelman and Piscatori (1990, 8–9) for a description of how the interpretation of Islamic doctrines have changed "according to prevailing economic, social and political contexts" (1990, 9). See also Visvanathan (1993, 34–40) for a discussion of how different subgroups of the Syrian Christian church offered different interpretations of key historical events.

9. See, for instance, Caplan (1987), Juergensmeyer (1993), Lawrence (1989), Marty and Appleby (1991, 1993a, 1993b).

10. See, for instance, Amjad (1989), Appleyard (1989), Arnold and Shah (1989), Gunatilleke (1986), Papademetriou and Martin (1991), Stinner (1982), and Watson (1975).

11. Over and over again, I heard economists, government officials and nonmigrants in Kerala discuss the wasteful and inflationary spending habits of the migrants. In the early period of the migration, there had been hopes that the remittances would fuel Kerala's economic growth, and when this did not materialize, some tentative attempts were made to try to divert a part of the remittances into Kerala's ailing industrial sector. These attempts have met with little success (See Nair, 1989, 360).

12. In emigrant villages, the migrant patterns tended to spread even to the nonmigrants due to the contagion effect. This will be discussed a little later in the chapter.

13. I must stress that money earned as a result of short-term international migration is

only one type of income that is seen to be serendipitous or unearned. As such, such patterns of consumption behavior are manifested in other such cases as well, for instance in the case of money that was obtained through a lottery, or through illegal means.

14. In a hybrid society, there are two coexisting domains of legitimacy—the traditional system and the modern system. Becoming modern and becoming neotraditional therefore should not be seen as incompatible strategies. Either or both could be adopted by the migrants as resources in their struggle for recognition and class status—depending on what is most appropriate for the local context and the particular situation.

15. Since this is the social distance that is sought to be bridged, it is not surprising that the first thing the migrants do with their remittance is to purchase land and build a house with concrete and mortar (as against the thatched roof houses of the manual labor class). Again, it is significant that even when the migrants remain unemployed on return, they are reluctant to return to manual labor.

16. The classic work is by Robert Redfield (1941). See also Kearney (1986, 333–337) for a review of this perspective. See Brandes (1975) for a typical case study.

17. See Bloch (1984), Pitt (1970), Van Velsen (1960), Watson (1975).

18. See Engelbrektsson (1978), Huguet (1989, 102), Rozario (1992, 122–126) and UNESCO (1984).

CHAPTER 3   *Colonialism and Ethnogenesis*

1. Based on 1968 figures, Malayalee Brahmins constituted around 1 percent of the total population of the state; Nayars constituted 15 percent; the Ezhavas 22 percent; and the slave castes 9 percent (including converts). Most of the Muslims in Kerala are Mappila, and of these most are Malabaris, but there are no figures available of the exact numbers or proportions. In 1968, Syrian Christians made up about 75 percent of the Christian population and about 16 percent of the total population of the state.

2. The description of the caste system given here is largely based on colonial accounts and on more contemporary studies, which also use the former as primary sources. In light of the recent studies (Bayly 1989; Price 1989; Washbrook 1982), which have demonstrated the influence of colonial sociology in systematizing and rigidifying many aspects of the caste system, any attempt of this kind that tries to paint a picture of a precolonial or early colonial caste system based on colonial accounts must be treated as tentative. Dirks (1989) has shown that the "invention" of caste took place even in the process of translation and transcription of precolonial texts. Though caste categories remained fluid in Kerala as elsewhere, Susan Bayly, for instance, points out that "status demarcation was more highly developed in the precolonial Keralan kingdoms than it was elsewhere in the south" (Bayly 1989, 248).

3. Pillai (1987, 81) notes that the term *Nayar* first appears only at the end of the ninth century.

4. According to the legend, the god Parsurama created Kerala by throwing his axe into the sea. The sea receded and the land that rose from it was given by him as a gift to the Brahmins. The Nayars in turn were ordered to be their loyal vassals. Scholars believe that this tradition was first floated at the zenith of the Brahmin control, between the eighth and twelfth centuries (Menon 1967).

5. See Nagam Aiya (1906), Innes (1951), Logan (1981), and Menon (1976) for descriptions of the early history of Kerala and the three groups.

6. See Susan Bayly (1989, 47) where she argues that "as of the late eighteenth century, the Nayars were still one of the loosest of south Indian status categories; virtually anyone, even non-Malayali military men, could be recruited into the armies of one of the region's new warrior rajas [kings] and endowed with Nayar titles and 'honors.'" See also K. Gough (1961) and E. Miller (1954), who both argue that this was particularly the case in northern Kerala.

7. In practice, it was generally only the women of the upper subcastes who married high-caste men. Cross-cousin sambandham marriages were generally practiced among the rest of the caste.

8. But in practice both polyandry and divorce were rare, at least after the late nineteenth century when the scribes of the colonialists studied the issue. See Logan (1981, 136) and Nagam Aiya (1906, 359–360).

9. Stephen Dale (1980) for instance states that these privileges were granted since their economic function was important to the local rulers.

10. Converts from among the fisherfolk are now called Pusalars (see Dale 1980, 29). See Koya (1983), R. A. Miller (1976), and K. N. Panikkar (1989) for other sources on the Mappilas.

11. There is a range of evidence to support the St. Thomas tradition (see the discussion in Pothan (1963, 9–30). Whether or not St. Thomas was indeed the founder of Christianity in Kerala, there is incontrovertible evidence that Christianity flourished in Kerala as early as the fourth century A.D.

12. One surmise is that this was done in return for the gifts of money bestowed by the Christians on the rulers who at that time were under siege by various invaders. See Ayyar (1926, 53).

13. Pothan (1963) points out that the Syrian Christians were given several princely privileges. These privileges and rights were inscribed on copper plates and included "the right to carry the curved sword, the right of proclamation, the privilege of forerunners, the litter, the royal umbrella, the ceremonial drum, the gateway with seats and ornamental arches" (1963, 34).

14. Susan Bayly argues, "By the later nineteenth century, . . . the loose and flexible corporate identities had taken on a very different form. Both the Syrians and their *savarna* (clean/upper caste) antagonists, particularly the upper Nayar caste groups, had begun to behave like the sort of communities which have often been described as 'traditional' that is as groups confronting one another across a set of fixed and exclusive corporate boundaries" (Bayly 1989, 294). Her conclusion is therefore that the processes unleashed by colonialism had resulted in the formation of communal groups. See also Menon (1994).

15. I am not arguing here, like Bailey (1963, 118) and Leach (1960, 6–7), that competition between castes did not and could not take place in the traditional caste order and that it was therefore this characteristic which exemplified the movement from caste to ethnic group. Group competition is only one manifestation (and not a necessary or sufficient factor) of the transition.

16. See Brass (1974), Laitin (1985), Lemarchand (1985), and Washbrook (1982) for other studies of this phenomenon.

17. Dietrich Rueschemeyer and Peter Evans (1985) discuss the complex relationship

between state autonomy (from the dominant class) and the transformative capacity of the state.

18. They argued that the universal church could contain many local churches with different customs and that the "law of Peter" and the "law of Thomas" could coexist (Ayyar 1926, 109).

19. Richard Fox (1985, 14–26) also makes a distinction between the two periods in India which he terms as the "development of underdevelopment" and the "development" phases. In the Kerala situation, the two periods do follow each other and can be distinguished empirically but this may not always be the case. The separation of the two phases is for analytical purposes with the argument that different types of ethnic consequences take place in each phase. In concrete situations of colonialism, however, these phases could overlap.

20. The model developed here is more applicable to British colonialism than it is to the colonialist strategies of other countries. See Ali Mazrui (1985) for a comparison between the political consequences of the "imperial ethnicity" of the British and the French.

21. And generally from a completely different culture.

22. This was common in Eastern India, which followed a different land tenure system.

23. Thirty-two such outbreaks took place between 1836 and 1921 (Dale 1980, 120).

24. The Mappila Rebellion was also influenced by the Khilafat movement.

25. Colonel Munro, for instance, felt that by helping the Syrian Christians he would secure "the support of a respectable body of Christian subjects, connected with the mass of the people by a community of language, occupations and pursuits, and united to the British Government by the stronger ties of religion and mutual safety." Colonel Munro, "Minutes to the Madras Government" quoted in Gladstone (1984, 64).

26. See Lemarchand (1983, 55) for a similar description of the situation in Africa.

27. This is not to imply that there is necessarily a conscious understanding of the unfolding of these processes at the time they take place.

28. See Jeffrey (1993, 43–44) where he lists in tabular form the different marriage and inheritance legislations passed in Kerala beginning in 1896. According to him, the matrilineal joint-family system collapsed because it could not adapt to the requirements of a cash economy. Seeing the prosperity of the patrilineal groups with smaller families like the Syrian Christians, prominent Nayars began to advocate family reform.

29. They converted several from the slave castes in this period. These converts, however, were not absorbed into the Syrian Christian society but were called "Backward Class Christians" and thus conversion did not significantly change their caste and social status.

30. The Madras Government (Kerala was under its administration) was inundated by petitions from the missionaries (Jeffrey 1976). It must be noted here that there are Keralite historians who contest the interpretation of Jeffrey's that it was pressure from the colonialists that led to the abolition of slavery in the two southern states. (Personal conversation and correspondence with Dr. Gangadhara Menon, one such historian.)

31. It was abolished in 1843 in Malabar, 1854 in Cochin, and in 1855 in Travancore.

32. In 1859, what has since been called the "breast cloth disturbance" broke out in South Kerala with a section of the low castes emboldened by the support of the missionaries agitating for the right of their women to wear breast cloths.

33. In 1936, the Temple Entry Proclamation was made, which permitted all Hindus, irrespective of caste status, the right to enter temples.

34. Although they were still not permitted into government schools in this period, the Ezhavas sent an increasing number of their children to mission schools. Thus, between 1875 and 1891 literacy among them increased from 3.15 percent to 12.1 percent (Jeffrey 1976, 146).

35. See Washbrook (1982, 143) for a description of the all-India picture.

36. Since voting in South Kerala (as in many other parts of the world) was on the basis of the amount of taxes paid, the Brahmins and Nayars predominated. Starting from 1932 the other major groups—the Ezhavas, the Muslims, and the Christians—organized themselves and submitted petitions asking for increased and proportional representation in the legislature and a widening of the franchise. When these demands were not conceded, an abstention movement was launched with the leaders asking voters not to exercise their franchise. In 1936, the government yielded to the demand.

37. In 1918, the Syrian Christians formed the Civil Rights League, claiming to represent the Christians, lower-caste Hindus, and the Muslims, to demand equal rights in public offices (Mathew 1989).

38. Thus 60 percent of the Ezhavas (this formed the bulk of the support of the communists since the Ezhavas were the largest community in Kerala with 22 percent of the population), 75 percent of the Harijans, 25 percent of the Nayars, and 10 percent of the Catholics and Syrian Christians supported the communists according to a survey conducted in 1960 (Nossiter 1982, 134).

39. Muslim men tied their mundu (a long piece of cloth covering the body from waist to ankles) on the left (Hindus tied them on the right), and this was kept in position by a waist string. Small cylinders of metal containing texts from the Koran were attached to the waist string. The men kept their hair very closely cropped. Muslim women generally wore a mundu of dark blue cloth, kept in place with a broad, intricately carved silver belt, a white loose blouse, and a scarf around their head. They wore earrings in the lobes of their ears (as did women of other groups), but in addition, Muslim women also wore earrings (up to a dozen) on the helix of their ears (see Innes 1951).

40. A term introduced by M. N. Srinivas (1968, 6), Sanskritization refers to the adoption of the rituals and practiced of Sanskritic Hinduism practices by the upper castes.

41. For instance, like the Brahmins, a newborn baby was fed with powdered gold mixed in honey; in the eleventh month after its birth the baby was ceremoniously fed with boiled rice for the first time. Like the Brahmins, the marriage ceremonies stretched over four days. In addition many of the Brahmanical marriage traditions such as the use of the *mantrakodi* (the bridal veil), the drawing of threads from the latter to suspend the tali, and many of the marriage rituals were observed by the Nazranis. This similarity also extended to death ceremonies, and the Christians also kept the legal defilement for ten to eleven days from the death of someone in the family and the several feasts kept in memory of the dead (Podipara 1973, 107).

42. Podipara writes, "The father was supreme in the family. Grown-up children would never sit in the presence of their fathers . . . Children consider it a sacred duty to help their aged parents" (1973, 107).

43. See S. G. Pothan (1963) for a more contemporary account of Syrian Christian practices.

CHAPTER 4   *The Middle Eastern Migration from Kerala*

1. Eighteen percent of the total labor force (Kerala Economics and Statistics Division 1987, 4).
2. 1986 figures (Franke and Chasin 1989, 11).
3. Sometimes they took up employment as domestic workers. In some ways, this was advantageous to both workers and employers. Workers benefited since houses were rarely subjected to police checks for illegal migrants and because domestic work also offered migrants the chance to obtain a more secure job through the influence of the employer. Employers found it profitable since domestic workers were not bound by a formal contract and were willing to work for lower wages.
4. According to the Government Survey, 56 percent of the migrants studied went through the help of relatives and friends and 19 percent through unlicensed agencies (Kerala Economics and Statistics Division 1987, 7).
5. Another aspect of the migration procedure was the halt at Bombay. Most of the migrants (particularly the poorer ones) flew out from Bombay instead of from Trivandrum (the capital of the state) since the former route was cheaper (e.g., at the time of fieldwork, the airfare from Bombay to Dubai was Rs. 3,334 one way compared with Rs. 4,500 for the Trivandrum-Dubai sector. The train or bus fare from Trivandrum to Bombay was only around Rs. 250). In addition, the primary agent was usually located in Bombay (the people the migrants were in direct contact with are generally the subagents) so often migrants were taken there to wait for the formalities to be completed and the visa to come through. Many stayed there for months and then returned empty handed.
6. Usually, food and accommodation would be provided in such circumstances.
7. Thus, there were questions on type of job, monthly earnings, monthly or annual remittances (see Commerce Research Bureau 1978; Government of Kerala 1987; Prakash 1978; Radhakrishnan and Ibrahim 1981). Again, Ashwini Saith in his article on the impact of the Kuwait crisis on Kerala makes the following calculation: "Assuming that 75 per cent of the total of 181,000 Indians in Iraq and Kuwait were workers . . . and that every worker on average sent home a monthly remittance of Rs. 3,000 . . . the figure for the loss of remittances would be approximately US $270 million per year" (Saith 1992, 108). Although Isaac (1993) discusses different types of Gulf migrants, he too falls into the trap of equating the "salaries" of the migrants with their total monetary gain from the migration.
8. The Commerce Research Bureau thus had the following categories: Land, Buildings, Jewelry, Radio, Car, Scooter, Cycle, Tape-recorder, Refrigerator, Total [value of these assets] (Commerce Research Bureau 1978, 25).
9. The government of Kerala conducted a survey in 1987 which covered all the fourteen districts of the state (two-stage stratified sample) and studied 1,467 remittance receiving households, 690 households with no foreign remittances, and 411 households with Gulf returned persons.
10. Statistics from the survey are presented by Banerjee, Jayachandran, and Roy (1997).
11. The survey results are discussed by Zachariah, Mathew, and Rajan (1999 and 2000).
12. Gulati and Mody 1983, 19. These figures are very close to those obtained by the National Family Health Survey conducted in 1992 and by the Kerala Migration Study in 1998.

13. Banerjee, Jayachandran, and Roy (1997, 8–9) report similar findings from the National Family Health Survey conducted in 1992.

14. The report warns that migrants were in general very reluctant to talk about financial aspects and that therefore the figures mentioned in the survey should be taken as very conservative estimates. The data presented should therefore be examined with this caution in mind. The average monthly household income of the migrant families was Rs. 1943 as compared with Rs. 930 of the nonmigrant families. Migrant families had 0.47 hectares of land compared to 0.27 hectares for nonmigrant families. With respect to the utilization pattern of the remittances by the migrant households: between 1982 and 1986, 48.5 percent had gone for the purchase of land and the construction of buildings, 7.3 percent for ornaments, 6.4 percent for education, 8.2 percent remained as savings in financial institutions, and 2.3 percent was invested in business (Government of Kerala 1987, 24). Note that these are averaged across the entire migrant sample and thus do not capture community variation in expenditure patterns.

15. Just as an illustration: the Reserve Bank of India only included amounts above Rs. 10,000 sent from abroad as constituting remittances. But as I discovered in the course of my study, most of the money came in smaller amounts for monthly household expenditure. Thus there is no doubt that official figures grossly underestimate the actual remittances. Again, in areas like Veni, most of the remittances were sent through illegal channels, which were not included in the official estimates.

16. Personal conversation with Thomas Isaac of the Centre for Development Studies, Trivandrum, Kerala. The ESCAP study notes that remittances contributed 40 percent of the GDP of the state and 50 percent of that of the high migrant districts though no particular year is mentioned (ESCAP 1987, 74).

17. According to local economists, the construction boom and the increase in consumption had mainly benefited the building contractors and the producers of consumer items, most of whom were located outside Kerala. Because of this, Kerala's major grievance was that the Indian government was not doing enough to help in the repatriation of the returnees to Kerala though the benefits of the migration had accrued to the nation as a whole.

18. However, the Kerala Migration Study of 1998 concludes that migration (both within India and outside India) "considerably eased the unemployment problem in the state." According to the study, the number of people who were unemployed declined by 32 percent as a result of migration and the unemployment rate by about three percentage points to about 11 percent (Zachariah, Mathew, and Rajan 2000, 28).

19. The rapid increase in the wage rates for construction workers is due to the big boost to house construction given by the Gulf remittances.

20. There was a big increase in the number of houses built between 1975 and 1980, though in the subsequent period, this increase tapered off. There was a big difference between the high-migrant and low-migrant districts in the degree of increase (Nair 1989, 349).

21. In the early 1980s Kerala was the scene of the unprecedented growth of private financing institutions. These institutions were characterized by their extremely high rate of interest (from 39.5 percent to 42 percent for loans and 24 percent for deposits), which were given unofficially (the rates shown on the promissory note were 12 percent and 9 percent, respectively). The large amounts of funds brought in by

the Gulf migrants was one (although not necessarily the most important) factor for the mushrooming of these institutions at the peak of the Gulf migration and in the high-migrant areas like Trichur. However, the reign of these institutions proved to be short lived. Many started collapsing during 1984, and by 1987 the majority of them had ceased their operations. The reasons for the collapse are complicated, but here again, the steep fall in the Gulf remittances consequence on the oil price crash of 1983 is an important factor (Prakash 1987).

The other institution whose development (though fortunately not crash) hinged partly on the Gulf phenomenon in the state was the Cochin Stock Exchange. This was established only in 1978 but registered a phenomenal growth in its first decade, and in the nineties was the biggest stock exchange in South India and the fourth largest in the country (next only to Bombay, Calcutta, and Delhi). Here again, some of the credit for its rise must go to remittances from the Gulf (Mohan and Raman 1990).

22. This article introduces a symposium on the economic performance of Kerala, and many other contributors echo the same themes. (See *Economic and Political Weekly* 1990.)

23. There is evidence to indicate that the per capita annual expenditure on consumption was higher than the official per capital income (between 1983 and 1994, the two figures were Rs. 1,857 and Rs. 1,761, respectively). According to Kannan (1990, 1952), "This excess of expenditure of income in 1983–1984 is most likely to have been due to the impact of remittances." This is because income coming from outside the state does not enter into the calculation of state income.

24. This came through very strongly as I talked to people during the course of my fieldwork.

25. When I went into a hut of a poor daily laborer, the woman told me with great sorrow that her child had lost his appetite and was not even eating his daily quota of cookies. She had started buying him cookies (viewed as a delicacy) despite the great expense, feeling that it was the best food she could get for him.

26. Varghese (1982, 223) describing the changes brought about in a village in central Travancore as a consequence of the Gulf migration says, "They consume luxury items like bread, biscuits, cakes, cheese, chicken and mutton and thus all the shopkeepers are anxious to get their patronage."

27. This account is based on discussions with some local Malayalam professors and other scholars.

28. For accounts of the syndrome in Pakistan, see Abbasi and Mohammed (1986, 190–191), Appleyard (1989, 29), and Ahmed (1988, 183).

CHAPTER 5   *Ethnicity and Migration in Veni*

1. The rest of the population was Hindu. However, the Hindus generally lived together in small settlements, so if such localities were excluded, the rest of the areas were around 90 to 95 percent Muslim.

2. The ratio of Mappilas to the total Hindu population in Malabar was 1:2 (Panikkar 1989, 54).

3. Even their medical needs were almost entirely met by these specialists. Charms were dispensed by religious leaders. The Tangals would also give patients words of the

Koran inscribed on a leaf for them to swallow. Childbirth was at home and attended to by the ritual midwife, the wife of the barber.

4. Villagers who completed the Haj pilgrimage added "Haaji" to their names.
5. K. V. Joseph (1997, 9) has noted that there was a large outmigration from the Malabar region from this period.
6. The Muslims of Kerala were relatively cut off from North Indian Islam, which is culturally quite different from the Islam of the Mappilas.
7. Friday services served as a meeting point of the men of the local community. It was also an affirmation of their unity and faith. The Sunni mosques generally conducted the ritual prayers in Arabic. Even the sermon was in Arabic and was a ready-made and standardized address affirming the greatness of Allah and his prophet. Since very few of the population were fluent in the language the actual content of the message probably escaped them.
8. The word *nercha* literally means vow or oath. It has come to be used to designate Mappila festivals connected with particular saints since people would make vows in the name of the saint during these celebrations.
9. Undoubtedly, their heritage of official harassment and oppression is an important contributory factor.
10. As Miller points out (1992, 289), "A special Mappila literary achievement is Arabic-Malayalam, a blend of a Malayalam grammatical base, Arabic script and Malayalam plus some Arabic, Tamil, Urdu and Persian vocabulary."
11. I am not referring to individual relationships, which of course could vary, but to the relationship as normatively defined in the community in question. These definitions constrain individual relationships but do not determine them.
12. As mentioned, the local Muslim population was a product of this interaction.
13. A professor in a Muslim college near Veni told me: "Young boys are just waiting to go. Barely do they turn eighteen (the minimum age for the migration) and they try to go over in one way or another. They have lots of friends and relatives there with whom they can stay, so it is not much of a problem even if they do not get a job straight away."
14. This income would be supplemented by the vegetables, fruits, and coconuts grown around the house.
15. During the time of my fieldwork, salaries were highest in the United Arab Emirates (around Rs. 3,000) and lowest in Saudi (around Rs. 2,000).
16. Distant relatives were paid back first. Very close relatives often never got back the money but of course received the direct and indirect benefits of the migration, if it was successful.
17. Such rotating credit institutions are common among migrant and immigrant communities in different parts of the world.
18. Wearing a headscarf would not have been a solution but would only have made matters worse. In that region, only Muslim women wore scarves, and it was seen as a symbol of Islamic identity. Thus, it would not have been proper for me as a non-Muslim to adopt a Muslim practice. Had I pretended to be a Muslim as some people suggested, I would not have been able to do the kind of work that I did, since it would have been seen as totally inappropriate for a Muslim woman.
19. The health workers told me that at first the villagers were convinced that they had come to kill their children (with the vaccinations and injections). When their children

did not die, they decided that the medicines given to the children were to make them sterile. According to the paramedical workers, such suspicions had been finally put to rest only in the past few years.

20. These cards provided each household with a certain quantity of basic provisions such as rice, lentils, sugar, and oil at a subsidized price.

21. According to the Kerala Migration Study, 77 percent of the women in emigrant households in the district used contraceptives (often birth-control pills brought from abroad by the migrant) compared to only 55 percent of nonmigrant households. The authors argue that this, together with the long absences of male migrants, had brought down the fertility rates in the area (Zachariah, Mathew, and Rajan 2000, 7).

22. I was told that there were six orphanage subcommittees in different countries in the Gulf to collect money for the institution.

23. According to the Kerala Migration Study, the average age at marriage of women (marriages that took place after 1990) was lower in migrant families (18.3 years) than in nonmigrant families (19.8 years) (Zachariah, Mathew, and Rajan 2000, 6).

24. As mentioned in the introduction, I did some fieldwork in a nonmigrant village in the region which was to serve as a control group, so that the general changes affecting the region at large could be separated from the changes brought about as a result of the migration. I also made briefer visits to several other nonmigrant areas.

25. Stichter (1985) and Engelbrektsson (1978) also document this effect of migrant remittances.

26. The Christians fit into a different occupational niche in the Middle East and thus had little social contact with the Mappila and Hindu workers.

27. They had also started wearing underclothing, which apparently they had not done earlier.

Chapter 6   *Ethnicity and Migration in Cherur*

1. The society for the propagation of Sri Narayana's teachings.

2. The rules of inheritance were modified and there were regional variations in the subsequent descent rules (Fuller 1976). From the villagers I gathered that in the interim period, during the middle decades of the century, the property of the mother (family property) would be divided among her children and the children of her daughters. Thus, if a woman had two daughters and one son and one of the daughters had two children, the property would be divided into five shares with three shares going to the daughter with children and one share each going to the younger daughter and the son. (In the traditional matrilineal system, property passed from uncle to nephew—mother's brother to sister's son.) The property of the father (individual property) could in theory be disposed of in any way he wished.

3. Thus, all marriages and deaths had to be registered with this organization, and with the fee provided at this time, the organization would send a notice to all the Ezhava families, publicizing the event.

4. The going rate for Gulf grooms had fallen since the mid-eighties, relative to a person with a good government job.

5. At the time of my fieldwork, hospital charges were generally fairly reasonable, even in private hospitals and were certainly nowhere near those in the United States.

6. It must be noted that such behavior was possible only after 1924, when the law per-

mitting partition of land came into effect. In the traditional system as mentioned, the land belonged to the taravad as a whole and could be sold only with the permission of all its members, and thus such transactions were relatively rare.

7. The earlier pattern when there were no such ceremonies was that the gifts would be given at the time of the wedding, and any money given would go to the boy's family.

8. In practice this was part of the dowry of the girl but in theory, the term *dowry* in this area referred to cash (and expensive consumer items) given to the bridegroom or his family at the time the marriage was contracted. In addition to the gold (and cash which may or may not be given), the girl got a share of the family property. Here again, in theory the property was to be divided equally between the children, but in practice in most poor and middle-class homes most of it ended up going to the daughters for their dowries.

9. Cross-cousins were, however, merely the preferred category of spouses. In practice, the choice of the actual spouse depended on the circumstances such as age, availability, and interfamilial relationships.

10. In fact, it is even hypothesized that one of the reasons for the better position of women in Kerala (and South India in general) is that cross-cousin marriages were fairly widely prevalent (Dyson and Moore 1983).

    Structurally, there is another major difference between the two types of marriage patterns. Intermarriage between relatives, or restricted exchange, creates smaller, close-knit subgroups within the larger community and also serves the function of keeping property holdings within this group. Hypergamy and hypogamy are, however, means of forming alliances with powerful strangers (see Levi-Strauss 1969).

11. A wealthier family would prefer to obtain a bridegroom who was wealthy and educated. This they were able to do by giving a larger dowry.

12. This is transcribed from a long conversation I had with some Ezhava women in Muttam, Cherur, regarding marriage practices and ceremonies.

13. Undeniably it is also partially because of the relatively high salary as well as the permanent (pension benefits) and steady nature of the income that the latter is expected to be able to earn. But income per se is not the main reason (since Gulfites and businessmen could earn more). What is more important is the fact that income earned through the use of education is seen as prestigious or honorable income.

14. In relative terms, the economic position of the Harijans had improved when compared to that of the Nayars. In fact, in Cherur there were some Nayar families who were almost as poor as many of the Harijans and who also depended on casual labor. They were very bitter about the additional benefits that the Harijans enjoyed.

15. I have indicated that about 90 percent of the households that I surveyed in Muttam were migrant households in that one or more of its members *or close relatives* were in the Middle East. However, this figure cannot be compared directly to the figures from Veni, because, in Veni, I classified a household as "migrant" only if a member of the household was or had been in the Middle East. This was because I obtained a lot of the survey data from the registers of the health workers and the balawadi teachers.

CHAPTER 7   *Ethnicity and Migration in Kembu*

1. According to the Valiyapally records, this was due to attacks by hordes of low-caste tribal groups.
2. This data, collected from interviews with the villagers, is corroborated by K. V. Joseph (1988, 43), who writes that the majority of the migrants to Malaya from central Travancore were Syrian Christians. They worked as clerks, supervisors, junior officers, teachers, businesspersons, and government servants.
3. It is therefore no coincidence that it was the Christians who were instrumental in starting the first banks and joint stock companies in the state.
4. The Latin Catholics as converts from the fishing caste were usually regarded as having a position in between the Syrians and the Backward Caste Christians, but since Kembu was in the interior there were very few Latins in the area.
5. Joseph (1988, 43) notes that the outbreak of the Second World War put an abrupt stop to the migration to Southeast Asia. This was followed by the migration of educated people and professionals to Africa, the United States, Europe, and the Middle East. These migrants were predominantly Christians from the central Travancore area.
6. Ex-military men constituted a large proportion of the migrants in the period soon after the war. When they found themselves without jobs, they applied to the oil companies in the Middle East, with the advantage of a better education than many Indians at that time.
7. In the pre–1986 period, the banks used to issue loans against the employment contract document and a surety of land. However, in many instances the document was not genuine or the employer did not stick to the salary specified on the contract. Thus, there were many cases of defaulting and for this reason, the government stopped permitting such loans.
8. Many of the migrants from this area preferred to use the travel agencies in the nearest town (fifteen miles away) since they were larger and had contacts with more airlines.
9. Estimates based on discussions with the owner of the travel agency, community leaders, and my household survey.
10. Religiosity, in Kembu, unlike the case of Veni where there was a strong emphasis on charity, primarily involved being an active and regular member of the local church.
11. A term of respect for older men, in this case, her husband.
12. However, I was told that there were no reported cases of dowry-abuse of brides in the region, unlike in other parts of the country.
13. As mentioned, Syrian Christians were accorded the status of high-caste Nayars. However, as one bitter "Pulaya" Christian pointed out to me, converts of any caste other than the Harijans (Ezhavas, for instance) were accepted as Syrian Christians.
14. The pastor of the corresponding Syrian Christian denomination would take the service in such churches on one Sunday a month. Lay preachers from the Backward Class community would lead on other Sundays.
15. Some of the Backward Class Christians in the area seemed to be in the process of mobilizing to try to improve their status. A Depressed Classes Federation (including both the Harijans and the Backward Class Christians) had been formed to promote their cause. One young man who said he was an office bearer in the Federation was very voluble about the injustice of the Christian caste division. "Christ's mis-

sion was mainly among the poor and the outcastes and he worked to remove such stigmas. Yet the Syrians who profess to be such devout Christians treat us so shamefully. What kind of Christianity is that?" A little later in the conversation he added, "Agriculture and the food it produces is vital for everyone and yet the people who do the actual agricultural work have the lowest status in society. Is that right?"

CHAPTER 8   *The Ethnic Kaleidoscope and International Migration Revisited*

1. See Hochschild (1989), who makes this point about the United States.
2. For instance, see the discussion of the "new racism" (Balibar and Wallerstein 1991, 17–28; Bhatt 1997; Gilroy 1991).

GLOSSARY

Arabis	Arabs. Also refers to a small group of Kerala Muslims who claim to be descendants of Arabs
Auto-rickshaw	Three-wheeler taxi
Avarna	Unclean or untouchable caste
Backward Class Christians	Christians belonging to the former slave castes
Balawadi	Preschool
Brahmin	Priestly caste
Burkha	A loose garment covering the entire body with a veiled opening for the eyes, worn by some Muslim women
Chitty	Rotating credit association
Coolie	Term for unskilled laborer who does a variety of jobs
Ezhavas	Lower-caste Hindus in southern Kerala
Haaji	Honorary name adopted by men who completed the Haj pilgrimage
Haj	Pilgrimage to Mecca
Harijan	Literally "children of God." Gandhi coined this term to refer to the former slave castes
Hypergamy	Type of marriage in which the man is from a higher-status family or group
Hypogamy	Type of marriage in which the man is from a lower-status family or group
Jacobite	A Syrian Christian denomination
Jeevitha reethi	Lifestyle

Kanji	Rice gruel
Katcha huts	Houses with mud walls and thatched roofs
Kshatriya	Warrior caste
Latin Catholics	Malayalee Catholics who follow the Latin liturgy and come under the Pope
Madrasa	Religious education school of the Muslims
Mahila Sabha	Women's council
Malabari	Literally, "person from Malabar." Refers to the mass of Mappila Muslims
Malayalam	The language spoken in Kerala state in south India
Malayalee	Person whose ancestral language is Malayalam
Mappilas	Muslims in northern Kerala
Marthomites	A reformed Syrian Christian denomination
Maulavi	Priest or officiary at the mosque
Maulud	Occasions when there are antiphonal readings from the Koran
Mujahid	Muslim sect
Mukkuvar	Fisherfolk
Nambudiris	Kerala Brahmins
Nayar	Upper-caste Hindus in Kerala
Nazranis	Term for Syrian Christians in the precolonial period
Nercha	Literally "vow" or "oath." Refers to special Mappila festivals
Nikkah	Muslim marriage contract
Olah	Coconut frond
Olah work	Weaving coconut fronds for thatching roofs
Oppana	Dance of Mappila women
Ossans	Muslim barbers in northern Kerala
Panchayat	Rural administrative unit consisting of a few villages
Pavan	Unit of gold, about eight grams
Pucca houses	Houses with concrete walls and tiled roofs
Pulaya	Former slave caste
Pusalars	"New" Muslims or converts from the fisherfolk

SNDP	Sri Narayana Dharma Paripalana (Yogam); society for the preservation of the moral law of Sri Narayana. Ezhava organization established by Sri Narayana
Sambandham	"Agreement" marriages of the Nayars
Sanskritization	Term coined by M. N. Srinivas to refer to the process whereby the lifestyle, customs, and rituals of a higher caste were adopted
Savarna	"Pure" or upper caste
Scheduled Castes	Official designation for former slave castes
Sooji	Literally, "needle." Refers to injections
Sri	Honorific title
Sridhanam	Dowry
Sudra	Service caste
Sunni	Muslim sect
Syrians	Christian group in Kerala that used to follow a Syriac liturgy
Tali	Marriage pendant
Tangals	Elite group of Malayalee Muslims that traced its ancestry to the Prophet
Taravad	Matrilineal joint family of the Nayars. Also refers to the type of houses that the Nayar joint family traditionally lived in
Tindal Jati	Caste that pollute from a distance
U.A.E.	United Arab Emirates
Vaisya	Business caste
Valiyapalli	Big church
Yagas	Complex rites with sacrifices
Zamorin	King of the kingdom of Calicut in north Kerala

REFERENCES

Abbasi, N., and I. Mohammed. 1986. "Socio-Economic Effects of International Migration on Pakistani Families." In F. Arnold and N. M. Shah, eds., *Asian Labor Migration: Pipeline to the Middle East*. Boulder, Colo.: Westview Press.

Abella, M. 1992. "The Troublesome Gulf: Research on Migration to the Middle East." *Asian and Pacific Migration Journal* 1:145–167.

Abella, M., and Y. Atal., eds. 1986. *Middle East Interlude: Asian Workers Abroad*. Bangkok: UNESCO Regional Office.

Aceves, J. 1971. *Social Change in a Spanish Village*. Cambridge, Mass.: Schenkman Publishing Company.

Adams, R. H. Jr. 1991. "The Effects of International Remittances on Poverty, Inequality and Development in Rural Egypt." Research Report 86. (May.) Washington, D.C.: International Food Policy Research Institute.

Addleton, J. S. 1992. *Undermining the Centre: The Gulf Migration and Pakistan*. Karachi: Oxford University Press.

Ahmad, I. 1973. "Endogamy and Status Mobility among the Siddiqui Sheikhs of Allahabad, Uttar Pradesh." In I. Ahmad, ed., *Caste and Social Stratification among the Muslims*. New Delhi: Manohar.

Ahmed, A. J. 1986. "Death in Islam: The Hawkes Bay Case." In A. S. Ahmed, ed., *Pakistani Society: Islam, Ethnicity and Leadership in South Asia*. Karachi: Oxford University Press.

Aiya, N. 1906. *Travancore State Manual, Vols. 1, 2 & 3*. Trivandrum: Travancore Government Press.

Aiyappan, A. 1944. *Iravas and Culture Change*. Madras: Madras Museum.

————. 1965. *Social Revolution in a Kerala Village*. New York: Asia Publishing House.

Alba, R. 1990. *The Transformation of White America*. New Haven, Conn.: Yale University Press.

————. 1992. "Ethnicity." In E. F. Borgatta and M. L. Borgotta, eds., *Encyclopedia of Sociology*. New York: Macmillan.

Alexander, K. C. 1968. *Social Mobility in Kerala*. Poona: Deccan College Publishing.

Allen, P. S. 1973. *Social and Economic Change in a Depopulated Community in Southern Greece*. Ph.D. Thesis. Anthropology, Brown University, Providence, R.I.

Alvarez, J. H. 1967. *Return Migration to Puerto Rico*. Berkeley: University of California, Institute of International Studies.

Amjad, R., ed. 1989. *To the Gulf and Back*. Geneva: ILO.

Appadurai, A. 1996. *Modernity at Large: Cultural Dimensions of Globalization*. Minneapolis: University of Minnesota Press.

Appleyard, R. T., ed. 1988a. *International Migration Today: Vol. 1, Trends and Prospects*. Paris: UNESCO.

————. 1988b. "General Introduction." In R. T. Appleyard, ed., *International Migration Today: Vol. 1, Trends and Prospects*. Paris: UNESCO.

————. 1988c. "International Migration in Asia and the Pacific." In R. T. Appleyard, ed., *International Migration Today: Vol. 1, Trends and Prospects*. Paris: UNESCO.

————. 1989. "International Migration and Developing Countries." In R. T. Appleyard, ed., *The Impact of International Migration on Developing Countries*. Paris: Development Centre of the Organization for Economic Co-operation and Development (OECD).

Arnold, F., and N. M. Shah, eds.1989. *Asian Labor Migration: Pipeline to the Middle East*. Boulder, Colo.: Westview Press.

Asad, T. 1970. *The Kababish Arabs*. London: C. Hurst.

Ayyar, A. L. K. 1926. *The Anthropology of the Syrian Christians in Malabar*. Ernakulam: Cochin Government Press.

Bailey, F. G. 1963. "Closed Social Stratification in India." *Archives of European Sociology* 4.

Balan, J. 1988. "Selectivity of Migration in International and Internal Flows." In Charles Stahl, ed., *International Migration Today, Vol. II*. Paris: UNESCO.

Balibar, E., and I. Wallerstein. 1991. *Race, Nation, Class: Ambiguous Identities*. London and New York: Verso.

Balmer, R. 1994. "American Fundamentalism: The Ideal of Femininity." In J. S. Hawley, ed., *Fundamentalism and Gender*, 47–62. New York: Oxford University Press.

Banerjee, S. K., V. Jayachandran, and T. K. Roy. 1997. "Has Emigration Influenced Kerala's Living Standard: A Micro Level Investigation." Paper presented at the T. N. Krishnan Memorial Seminar on Development Experience of South Indian States. September 7–9, Centre for Development Studies, Trivandrum.

Banks, M. 1996. *Ethnicity: Anthropological Constructions*. New York: Routledge.

Barnett, S. 1977. "Identity, Choice and Caste Ideology in Contemporary South India." In K. David, ed., *The New Wind: Changing Identities in South Asia*. Netherlands: The Hague.

Barth, F. 1969. "Introduction." In Fredrik Barth, ed., *Ethnic Groups and Boundaries: The Social Organization of Cultural Difference*. Boston: Little, Brown.

Bartky, S. L. 1988. "Foucault, Femininity and the Modernization of Patriarchal Power." In Irene Diamond and Lee Quinby, ed., *Feminism and Foucault: Reflections on Resistance*, 61–88. Boston: North Eastern Press.

Basch, L., N. G. Schiller, and C. S. Blanc. 1994. *Nations Unbound: Transnational Projects, Postcolonial Predicaments and Deterritorialized Nation-States*. Amsterdam: Gordon and Breach.

Battistella, G. 1991. "Gulf Returnees: Profile of a Crisis." *Asian Migrant* 4 (1): 25–29.

Bayly, C. A. 1985. "The Pre-History of 'Communalism'? Religious Conflict in India 1700–1860." *Modern Asian Studies* 19:177–203.

Bayly, S. 1989. *Saints, Goddesses and Kings*. Cambridge, U.K.: Cambridge University Press.

Behar, R., and D. Gordon, eds. 1996. *Women Writing Culture.* Berkeley and Los Angeles: University of California Press.

Bell, D. 1975. "Ethnicity and Social Change." In N. Glazer and D. Moynihan, eds., *Ethnicity: Theory and Experience.* Cambridge, Mass.: Harvard University Press.

Bell, D., P. Caplan, and W. J. Karim, eds. 1993. *Gendered Fields: Women, Men and Ethnography.* London and New York: Routledge.

Bennett, J., W. 1975. *The New Ethnicity: Perspectives from Ethnology.* St. Paul, Minn.: West Publishing Co.

Bennett, L. 1983. *Dangerous Wives and Sacred Sisters: Social and Symbolic Roles of High Caste Women in Nepal.* New York: Columbia Press.

Bhai, T. 1987. *Changing Patterns of Caste and Class Relations in South India.* Delhi: Gian Publishing House.

Bhatt, C. 1997. *Liberation and Purity: Race, New Religious Movements and the Ethics of Postmodernity.* Bristol, Pa., and London: UCL Press.

Bloch, H. Lee. 1984. "Emigration, Cultural Conservatism and Change in a Polish Village." In O. Lynch, ed., *Culture and Continuity in Europe.* Delhi: Hindustan Publishing Corporation.

Bloch, R. H. 1978. "Untangling the Roots of Modern Sex Roles: A Survey of Four Centuries of Change." *Signs* 4:237–252.

Bohning, W. R. 1975. "Some Thoughts on Emigration from the Mediterranean Basin." *International Labor Review* 3:251–277.

Bonacich, E. 1972. "A Theory of Ethnic Antagonism: The Split Labor Market." *American Sociological Review* 37:547–560.

———. 1973. "A Theory of Middleman Minorities." *American Sociological Review* 38:583–594.

Bourdieu, P. 1977. *Outline of a Theory of Practice.* Cambridge, U.K.: Cambridge University Press.

———. 1984. *Distinction: A Social Critique of the Judgement of Taste.* Cambridge, Mass.: Harvard University Press.

———. 1990. *In Other Words: Essays toward a Reflexive Sociology.* Palo Alto, Calif.: Stanford University Press.

Bovenkerk, F. 1974. *The Sociology of Return Migration: A Bibliographic Essay.* The Hague: Martinus Nijkoff.

Brandes, S. H. 1975. *Migration, Kinship and Community: Tradition and Transition in a Spanish Village.* New York: Academic Press.

Brass, P. 1974. *Language, Religion and Politics in North India.* London and New York: Cambridge University Press.

Brass, P. R. 1991. *Ethnicity and Nationalism: Theory and Comparison.* New Delhi: Sage Publications.

Brettel, C. B. 1986. *Men Who Migrate, Women Who Wait.* Princeton, N.J.: Princeton University Press.

Brien, O. 1986. "Towards a Reconstitution of Ethnicity: Capitalist Expansion and Cultural Dynamics in Sudan." *American Anthropologist* 88:898–907.

Brown, K. M. 1994. "Fundamentalism and the Control of Women." In J. S. Hawley, ed., *Fundamentalism and Gender*, 175–201. New York: Oxford University Press.

Brubaker, R. 1985. "Rethinking Classical Theory: The Sociological Vision of Pierre Bourdieu." *Theory and Society* 14:723–744.

Caplan, L., ed. 1987. *Studies in Religious Fundamentalism*. Albany: State University of New York Press.

Castles, S., and M. J. Miller. 1993. *The Age of Migration: International Population Movements in the Modern World*. New York: Guilford Press.

Chen, T. 1940. *Emigrant Communities in South China*. New York: Secretariat, Institute of Pacific Relations.

Chhachi, A. 1991. "Forced Identities: The State, Communalism, Fundamentalism and Women in India." In D. Kandiyoti, ed., *Women, Islam and the State*, 144–175. Philadelphia, Pa.: Temple University Press.

Chiswick, B. R. 1978. "The Effect of Americanization on the Earnings of Foreign-Born Men." *Journal of Political Economy* 86:897–921.

Choucri, N. 1983. "Migration to the Middle East: Transformation and Change." *Middle East Review* xvi:16–27.

Cohen, R. 1988. *The New Helots: Migrants in the International Division of Labour*. Hants, England: Gower Publishing Company.

Collier, J. F., and S. J. Yanagisako. 1987. *Gender and Kinship*. Palo Alto, Calif.: Stanford University Press.

Collins, H. 1991. *The HarperCollins Dictionary of Sociology*. New York: HarperCollins Publishers.

Colson, E. 1968. "Contemporary Tribes and the Development of Nationalism." In J. Helm, ed., *Essays on the Problems of the Tribe*. Seattle: University of Washington Press.

Commerce Research Bureau. 1978. *Emigration, Inward Remittances and Economic Growth of Kerala*. Bombay: NKM International House.

Conzen, K. N., D. A. Gerber, E. Morawska, G. E. Pozzetta, and R. J. Vecoli. 1992. "The Invention of Ethnicity: A Perspective from the U.S.A." *Journal of American Ethnic History* 12:3–41.

Cornelius, W., et al. 1976. "Dynamics of Migration: International Migration." Occasional Monograph Series. 5 (2). ICP Work Agreement Reports. Washington, D.C.: Smithsonian Institution.

Cronin, C. 1970. *The Sting of Change: Sicilians in Sicily and Australia*. Chicago: University of Chicago Press.

Dale, S. F. 1980. *Islamic Society on the South Asian Frontier: The Mappilas of Malabar*. Oxford, U.K.: Clarendon Press.

D'Souza, V. S. 1978. "Status Groups among the Moplahs on the South-West Coast of India." In I. Ahmad, ed., *Caste and Social Stratification among Muslims in India*, 41–56. New Delhi: Manohar Publications.

De Vos, G. 1975. "Ethnic Pluralism, Conflict and Accommodation." In G. De Vos and L. Romanucci-Ross, eds., *Ethnic Identity: Cultural Continuities and Change*. Palo Alto, Calif.: Mayfield Publishing Company.

De Vos, G., and L. Romanucci-Ross, eds. 1975. *Ethnic Identity: Cultural Continuities and Change*. Palo Alto, Calif.: Mayfield.

Deutsch, K. W. 1966. *Nationalism and Social Communication: An Inquiry into the Foundations of Nationality*. Boston, Mass.: M.I.T. Press.

Dhruvarajan, V. 1989. *Hindu Women and the Power of Ideology*. New Delhi: Vistaar Publications.

Dib, G. 1988. "Laws Governing Migration in Some Arab Countries." In R. T. Appleyard, ed., *International Migration Today: Vol. I, Trends and Prospects*. Paris: UNESCO.

DiMaggio, P. 1991. "Social Structure, Institutions and Cultural Goods: The Case of the United States." In P. Bourdieu and J. S. Coleman, eds., *Social Theory for a Changing Society*, 133–155. Boulder, Colo.: Westview Press.

Dirks, N. 1989. "The Invention of Caste." *Social Analysis* 25:42–52.

Douglass, W. A. 1975. *Echalar and Murelega: Opportunity and Rural Exodus in Two Spanish Basque Villages*. New York: St. Martin's Press.

Dumont, L. 1970. *Homo Hierarchicus: The Caste System and Its Implications*. Chicago: Univerisity of Chicago Press.

Durand, J., W. Kandel, E. Parrado, and D. S. Massey. 1996. "International Migration and Development in Mexican Communities." *Demography* 33:249–264.

Durand, J., and D. S. Massey. 1992. "Mexican Migration to the United States: A Critical Review." *Latin American Research Review* 27:3–42.

Dyson, T., and M. Moore. 1983. "On Kinship Structure, Female Autonomy and Demographic Behavior in India." *Population and Development Review* 9:35–60.

Eades, J. 1987. *Migrants, Workers and the Social Order*. London and New York: Tavistock Publications.

Economic and Political Weekly. 1990. "Kerala Economy at the Crossroads, Parts I and II." *Economic and Political Weekly*, September 1 and September 15.

Eelens, F., T. Schampers, and J. D. Speckmann, eds. 1992. *Labour Migration to the Middle East: From Sri Lanka to the Gulf*. London: Kegan Paul.

Eikelman, D. F., and J. Piscatori. 1990. "Social Theory in the Study of Muslim Societies." In D. F. Eikelman and J. Piscatori, eds., *Muslim Travellers: Pilgrimage, Migration and the Religious Imagination*. Berkeley and Los Angeles: University of California Press.

Engelbrektsson, U.-B. 1978. *The Force of Tradition: Turkish Migrants at Home and Abroad*. Goteborg, Sweden: Acta Universitatis Gothoburgensis.

Enloe, C. H. 1973. *Ethnic Conflict and Political Development*. Boston: Little, Brown.

Epstein, A. L. 1978. *Ethos and Identity: Three Studies in Ethnicity*. London: Tavistock.

ESCAP (Economic and Social Commission for Asia and the Pacific). 1986. "Returning Migrant Workers: Exploratory Studies." Bangkok: United Nations.

———. 1987. "International Labour Migration and Remittances between the Developing ESCAP Countries and the Middle East." Bangkok: United Nations.

Farley, R. 1994. *The New American Reality: Who We Are, How We Got Here, Where We Are Going*. New York: Russell Sage.

Findley, S. E. 1987. *Rural Development and Family Migration: A Study of Family Choices in the Philippines*. Boulder, Colo.: Westview Press.

Foucault, M. 1979. *Discipline and Punish: The Birth of a Prison*. New York: Vintage Publishers.

Fox, R. 1985. *Lions of the Punjab: Culture in the Making*. Berkeley and Los Angeles: University of California Press.

Franke, R. W., and B. Chasin. 1989. *Kerala: Radical Reform as Development in an Indian State*. San Francisco, Calif.: Institute for Food and Development Policy.

Frankel, F. 1990. "Conclusion: Decline of a Social Order." In F. Frankel and M.S.A. Rao, eds., *Dominance and State Power, Vol. II*. Delhi: Oxford University Press.

Fuller, C. J. 1976. *The Nayars Today*. Cambridge, U.K.: Cambridge University Press.

Ganesh, K. N. 1989. *Kerala State Gazetteer, Vol. 3*. Trivandrum: Superintendent, Government Presses.

Gans, H. 1962. *The Urban Villagers: Group and Class in the Life of Italian Americans.* New York: Free Press.

―――. 1979. "Symbolic Ethnicity: The Future of Ethnic Groups and Cultures in America." *Ethnic and Racial Studies* 2:1–20.

―――. 1992. "Second Generation Decline: Scenarios for the Economic and Ethnic Futures of Post–1965 American Immigrants." *Ethnic and Racial Studies* 15:173–192.

Gardner, K. 1995. *Global Migrants, Local Lives: Travel and Transformation in Rural Bangladesh.* Oxford, U.K.: Clarendon Press.

Geertz, C. 1969. "The Integrative Revolution." In Clifford Geertz, ed., *Old Societies and New States.* New York: Free Press.

―――. 1973. *The Interpretation of Cultures.* New York: Basic Books.

Gibson, M. A. 1988. *Accommodation without Assimilation: Sikh Immigrants in an American High School.* Ithaca, N.Y.: Cornell University Press.

Gilani, I. S. 1986. "Pakistan." In Manolo Abella and Yogesh Atal, eds., *Middle East Interlude: Asian Workers Abroad.* Bangkok: UNESCO Regional Office.

―――. 1988. "Effects of Emigration and Return on Sending Countries: The Case of Pakistan." In C. Stahl, ed., *International Migration Today: Vol. II.* Paris: UNESCO.

Gilroy, P. 1991. *There Ain't No Black in the Union Jack: The Cultural Politics of Race and Nation.* Chicago: University of Chicago Press.

Gitmez, A. S. 1988. "The Socio-Economic Reintegration of Returned Migration: The Case of Turkey." In C. Stahl, ed., *International Migration Today: Vol. II.* Paris: UNESCO.

Gladstone, J. W. 1984. *Protestant Christianity and People's Movements in Kerala.* Kerala United Theological Seminary, Trivandrum: Seminary Publications.

Glazer, N., and D. Moynihan, eds. 1975. *Ethnicity: Theory and Experience.* Cambridge, Mass.: Harvard University Press.

Gmelch, G. 1980. "Return Migration." *Annual Review of Anthropology* 9:135–159.

Gogate, S. 1986. "India." In M. Abella and Y. Atal, eds., *Middle East Interlude: Asian Workers Abroad.* Bangkok: UNESCO Regional Office.

Goldring, L. 1992. *Diversity and Community in Transnational Migration: A Comparative Study of Two Mexico-U.S. Migrant Circuits.* Ph.D. thesis. Rural Sociology, Cornell University, Ithaca, N.Y.

Gordon, M. 1964. *Assimilation in American Life.* New York: Oxford Univerisity Press.

Gough, K. 1961. "Nayar: North Kerala." In D. M. Schneider and K. Gough, eds., *Matrilineal Kinship.* Berkeley and Los Angeles: University of California Press.

Government of Kerala (Economics and Statistics Division). 1982. "Survey on Housing and Employment, 1980." Trivandrum: Government of Kerala.

―――. 1987. "Report of the Survey on the Utilization of Gulf Remittances in Kerala." Trivandrum: Government of Kerala.

Granovetter, M. 1985. "Economic Action and Social Structure: The Problem of Embeddedness." *American Journal of Sociology* 91:481–510.

Grebler, L., J. W. Moore, and R. C. Guzman. 1970. *The Mexican-American People: The Nation's Second Largest Minority.* New York: Free Press.

Greenberg, S. 1980. *Race and State in Capitalist Development.* New Haven, Conn.: Yale University Press.

Gulati, I. S., and A. Mody. 1983. "Remittances of Indian Migrants to the Middle East: An Assessment with Special Reference to Migrants from Kerala State." Working Paper 182, Centre for Development Studies, Trivandrum, Kerala.

Gulati, L. 1983. "Impact of Male Migration to the Middle East on the Family: Some Evidence from Kerala." Working Paper 176, Centre for Development Studies, Trivandrum, Kerala.

———. 1987. "Coping with Male Migration." *Economic and Political Weekly*. October 31:WS41–WS46.

———. 1993. *In the Absence of Their Men: The Impact of Male Migration on Women.* New Delhi: Sage Publications.

Gulick, J. 1955. *Social Structure and Culture Change in a Lebanese Village.* New York: Wenner-Gren Foundation for Anthropological Research Inc.

Gunatilleke, G., ed. 1986. *Migration of Asian Workers to the Arab World.* Tokyo: United Nations University.

Gupta, A., and J. Ferguson. 1992. "Beyond 'Culture': Space, Identity and the Politics of Difference." *Cultural Anthropology* 7:6–23.

Gurak, D. T., and Fe Caces. 1992. "Migration Networks and the Shaping of Migration Systems." In M. M. Kritz, L. L. Lim, and H. Zlotnick, eds., *International Migration Systems: A Global Approach*, 150–176. Oxford, U.K.: Clarendon Press.

Hardacre, H. 1993. "The Impact of Fundamentalisms on Women, the Family and Interpersonal Relations." In M. E. Marty and S. R. Appleby, eds., *Fundamentalism and Society*, 129–150. Chicago: University of Chicago.

Harker, R., C. Mahar, and C. Wilkes, eds. 1990. *An Introduction to the Work of Pierre Bourdieu: The Practice of Theory.* New York: St. Martin's Press.

HarperCollins. 1991. *HarperCollins Dictionary of Sociology.* New York: HarperCollins Publishers.

Hawley, J. S., ed. 1994. *Fundamentalism and Gender.* Oxford, U.K.: Oxford University Press.

Hochschild, A. R. 1989. *The Second Shift: Working Parents and the Revolution at Home.* New York: Viking.

Horowitz, D. L. 1985. *Ethnic Groups in Conflict.* Berkeley and Los Angeles: University of California Press.

Hugo, G. J. 1981. "Village-Community Ties, Village Norms, and Ethnic and Social Networks: A Review of Evidence from the Third World." In G. F. DeJong and R. W. Gardner, eds., *Migration Decision Making: Multidisciplinary Approaches to Microlevel Studies in Developed and Developing Countries*, 186–225. New York: Pergamon Press.

Huguet, J. W. 1989. "International Labour Migration from the ESCAP Region." In R. T. Appleyard, ed., *The Impact of International Migration on Developing Countries*, 93–108. Paris: OECD.

Ignatiev, N. 1995. *How the Irish Became White.* New York: Routledge.

Inden, R. 1990. *Imagining India.* Oxford, U.K.: Oxford University Press.

Indian Express. 1990. "Air India Winds Up Evacuation." In *Indian Express*. October 12, p. 1.

Innes, C. A. 1951. *Malabar.* Madras: Superintendent, Government Press.

Isaac, T.T.M. 1993. "Economic Consequences of the Gulf Crisis: A Study of India with Special Reference to Kerala." In Piyasiri Wickramasekara, ed., *The Gulf Crisis and South Asia: Studies on the Economic Impact*, 59–102. New Delhi: UNDP/ILO(ARTEP).

Jeffrey, P. 1979. *Frogs in a Well: Indian Women in Purdah.* London: Zed Press.

Jeffrey, R. 1976. *The Decline of Nayar Dominance: Society and Politics in Travancore, 1847–1908*. New Delhi: Vikas Publishing House, Inc.

———. 1993. *Politics, Women and Well-Being: How Kerala Became a Model*. Delhi: Oxford University Press.

Jenkins, R. 1997. *Rethinking Ethnicity: Arguments and Explorations*. Thousand Oaks, Calif.: Sage Publications.

Joseph, K. V. 1988. *Migration and Economic Development of Kerala*. Delhi: Mittal Publications.

———. 1997. "Patterns of Migration from Kerala during the Pre-Independence Period." Paper presented at the T. N. Krishnan Memorial Seminar on Development Experience of South Indian States in a Comparative Setting, September 7–9, Centre for Development Studies, Trivandrum.

Juergensmeyer, M. 1993. *The New Cold War? Religious Nationalism Confronts the Secular State*. Berkeley and Los Angeles: University of California Press.

Kallen, E. 1982. *The Western Samoan Kinship Bridge: A Study in Migration, Social Change and the New Ethnicity*. Leiden: E. J. Brill.

Kannan, K. P. 1990. "Kerala Economy at the Crossroads?" *Economic and Political Weekly* 25:35–36 (September 1–8), 1951–1956.

Kearney, M. 1986. "From the Invisible Hand to Visible Feet: Anthropological Studies of Migration and Development." *Annual Review of Anthropology* 15:331–361.

———. 1986. "Integration of the Mixteca and the Western U.S. Mexico Region Via Migratory Wage Labor." In I. Rosenthal-Urey, ed., *Regional Impacts of U.S.-Mexico Relations*. La Jolla: Center for U.S.-Mexico Relations, University of California, San Diego.

Keyes, C. F., ed. 1981. *Ethnic Change*. Seattle: University of Washington Press.

King, R., ed. 1986. *Return Migration and Regional Economic Problems*. Kent, Great Britain: Croom Helm Ltd.

King, R., and A. Strachan. 1983. *Return Migration: A Sourcebook of Evaluative Abstracts*. Oxford, U.K.: Oxford Polytechnic.

Klijn, A.F.J. 1962. *The Acts of Thomas*. Leiden, Netherlands: E. J. Brill.

Koilparambil, G. 1979. *Caste in the Catholic Community in Kerala: A Study of Caste Elements in the Inter-Rite Relationships of Syrians and Latins*. Ph.D. thesis, Sociology, Loyola College of Social Sciences. Trivandrum, Kerala.

Koovakal, G. 1982. "Development of Theology among Mappila Muslims." In C. W. Troll, ed., *Islam in India: Studies and Commentaries, Vol. I*. New Delhi: Vikas Publishing House.

Kopytoff, I. 1990. "Women's Roles and Existential Identities." In P. R. Sanday and R. G. Goodenough, eds., *Beyond the Second Sex*. Philadelphia: University of Pennsylvania Press.

Koya, M.S.M. 1983. *Mappilas of Malabar*. Calicut: Sandhya Publications.

Kubat, D., ed. 1984. *The Politics of Return*. New York: Center for Migration Studies.

Kumar, G. 1989. "Gender, Differential Mortality and Development: The Experience of Kerala." *Cambridge Journal of Economics* 13:517–539.

Kurian, G. 1961. *The Indian Family in Transition: A Case Study of Kerala Syrian Christians*. Netherlands: Gravenhage, Mouton and Institute of Social Studies.

Kurian, R. 1978. *Patterns and Effects of Emigration from Kerala*. M.Phil. thesis, Centre for Development Studies. Trivandrum, Kerala.

Kurien, P. A. 1992. "Sojourner Migration and Gender Roles: A Comparison of Two Ethnic Communities in Kerala, India." In J. S. Emlen, ed., *Continuity and Change: Women at the Close of the Twentieth Century*, 43–61. Occasional Paper No. 12. Thomas J. Watson Jr. Institute for International Studies, Providence, R.I.

————. 1994a. "Colonialism and Ethnogenesis: A Study of Kerala, India." *Theory and Society* 23:385–417.

————. 1994b. "Economy in Society: Consumption, Investment and Exchange Patterns among Three Emigrant Communities in Kerala, India." *Development and Change* 25:757–783.

————. 1998. "Becoming American by Becoming Hindu: Indian Americans Take Their Place at the Multi-cultural Table." In R. S. Warner and J. G. Wittner, eds., *Gatherings in Diaspora: Religious Communities and the New Immigration*. Philadelphia, Pa.: Temple University Press.

————. 1999. "Gendered Ethnicity: Creating a Hindu Indian Identity in the U.S." *American Behavioral Scientist* 42:642–664.

Kurup, K.K.N. 1981. *William Logan: A Study in the Agrarian Relations of Malabar*. Calicut, Kerala: Sandhya Publications.

Laitin, D. D. 1985. "Hegemony and Religious Conflict: British Imperial Control and Political Cleavages in Yorubaland." In P. Evans, D. Rueschemeyer, and T. Skocpol, eds., *Bringing the State Back In*. Cambridge, U.K.: Cambridge University Press.

Lal, B. B. 1983. "Perspectives on Ethnicity: Old Wine in New Bottles." *Ethnic and Racial Studies* 6:154–173.

Lawrence, B. B. 1989. *Defenders of God: The Fundamentalist Revolt against the Modern Age*. San Francisco: Harper and Rowen.

Leach, R. E. 1960. *Aspects of Caste in South India, Ceylon and North-West Pakistan*. Cambridge, U.K.: Cambridge University Press.

————. 1965 (1954). *Political System of Highland Burma*. Boston: Beacon Press.

Lemarchand, R. 1983. "The State and Society in Africa: Ethnic Stratification and Restratification in Historical and Comparative Perspective." In D. Rothchild and V. A. Olorunsola, eds., *State Versus Ethnic Claims: African Policy Dilemmas*. Boulder, Colo.: Westview Press.

Levi-Strauss, C. 1969. *The Elementary Structures of Kinship*. Boston: Beacon Press.

Levitt, P. 1995. *The Transnationalization of Civil and Political Change: The Effect of Migration on Institutional Ties between the U.S. and the Dominican Republic*. Ph.D. thesis, Urban Studies and Planning, Massachusetts Institute of Technology, Boston.

Lewis, B. 1993. *Islam and the West*. Oxford, U.K.: Oxford University Press.

Lieberson, S. 1985. "Unhyphenated Whites in the United States." *Ethnic and Racial Studies* 8:159–180.

Logan, W.M.C.S. 1981. *Malabar*. Trivandrum: Charitham Publishers.

Lorber, J., and S. A. Farrell. 1991. *The Social Construction of Gender*. Newbury Park, Calif.: Sage Publications.

MacLeod, J. 1994. *Ain't No Makin' It: Aspirations and Attainment in a Low-Income Neighborhood*. Boulder, Colo.: Westview Press.

Mandelbaum, D. G. 1970. *Society in India*. Berkeley and Los Angeles: University of California Press.

Marriott, M., ed.1955. *Village India*. Chicago: University of Chicago Press.

Marthoma Valliyapalli, of "Kembu" 1987. *225 Anniversary Souvenir*. Edavaka Publication.

Marty, M. E., and S. R. Appleby, eds. 1991. *Fundamentalisms Observed*. Chicago: University of Chicago.

———, eds. 1993a. *Fundamentalism and Society*. Chicago: University of Chicago.

———, eds. 1993b. *Fundamentalisms and the State*. Chicago: University of Chicago.

Massey, D. S., R. Alarcon, J. Durand, and H. Gonzalez. 1987. *Return to Aztlan: The Social Process of International Migration from Western Mexico*. Berkeley and Los Angeles: University of California Press.

Massey, D. S., L. Goldring, and J. Durand. 1994. "Continuities in Transnational Migration: An Analysis of Nineteen Mexican Communities." *American Journal of Sociology* 99:1492–1533.

Massey, D. S., J. Arango, G. Hugo, A. Kouaouci, A. Pellegrino, J. E. Taylor. 1993. "Theories of International Migration: A Review and Appraisal." *Population and Development Review*, 19 (3) (September): 431–466.

Mathai, P. P. 1987. "Fading Gulf Boom Problem for Kerala." *Times of India*, Bombay, February 8.

Mathew, E. T., and P.R.G. Nair. 1978. "Socio-Economic Characteristics of Emigrants and Emigrant Households." *Economic and Political Weekly* 13:1141–1153.

Mathew, G. 1989. *Communal Road to a Secular Kerala*. New Delhi: Concept Publishing Company.

Mayer, A. C. 1952. *Land and Society in Malabar*. London: Oxford University Press.

Mazrui, A. 1985. "Francophone Nations and English-Speaking States: Imperial Ethnicity and African Political Formations." In D. Rothchild and V. Olorunsola, eds., *State Versus Ethnic Claims: African Policy Dilemmas*, 25–43. Boulder, Colo.: Westview Press.

Mckay, J. 1982. "An Exploratory Synthesis of Primordial and Mobilizationist Approaches to Ethnic Phenomenon." *Ethnic and Racial Studies* 5:395–420.

Meillasoux, C. 1975. *Maidens, Meal and Money: Capitalism and the Domestic Community*. Cambridge, U.K.: Cambrige University Press.

Menachery, G. 1973. *The St. Thomas Christian Encyclopedia of India*. Madras: B.N.K. Press Pvte Ltd.

Menon, D. M. 1994. *Caste, Nationalism and Communism in South India: Malabar, 1900–1948*. Cambridge, U.K.: Cambridge University Press.

Menon, I. D. 1981. *Status of Muslim Women in India: A Case Study of Kerala*. New Delhi: Uppal Publishing House.

Menon, S. 1967. *A Survey of Kerala History*. Kottayam, India: National Book Center.

———. 1979. *Social and Cultural History of India: Kerala*. Sterling, New Delhi.

Mernissi, F. 1975. *Beyond the Veil: Male-Female Dynamics in a Modern Muslim Society*. Cambridge, Mass.: Schenkman Publishing Company.

Miller, E. 1954. "Caste and Territory in Malabar." *American Anthropologist* 56:410–420.

Miller, R. E. 1992. *Mappila Muslims of Kerala: A Study in Islamic Trends*. Sangam Books: London.

Milner, M. J. 1994. *Status and Sacredness: A General Theory of Status Relations and an Analysis of Indian Culture*. New York and Oxford, U.K.: Oxford University Press.

Mohan, K.T.R., and K. R. Raman. 1990. "Of Cochin Stock Exchange and What It Means." *Economic and Political Weekly* 25 (1) January 6.

Mohanty, C. T., A. Russo, and L. Torres. 1991. *Third-World Women and the Politics of Feminism*. Bloomington: Indiana University Press.

Morales, R., and F. Bonilla. 1993. "Restructuring and the New Inequality." In R. Morales and F. Bonilla, eds., *Latinos in a Changing U.S. Economy*, 1–27. Newbury Park, Calif.: Sage Publications.

Morauta, L. 1984. *Left behind in the Village: Economic and Social Conditions in an Area of High Outmigration*. Boroko, Papua, New Guinea: Institute of Applied Social and Economic Research.

Morawska, E. 1990. "The Sociology and Historiography of Immigration." In V. Yans-McLaughlin, ed., *Immigration Reconsidered: History, Sociology and Politics*. New York and Oxford, U.K.: Oxford University Press.

Nagel, J. 1994. "Constructing Ethnicity: Creating and Recreating Ethnic Identity and Culture." *Social Problems* 41:152–176.

Nair, K.K.R. 1986. *Kerala State Gazetteer, Vol. 1*. Kakkanad, Cochin, Kerala: Text Book Press.

Nair, P.R.G. 1983. "Asian Migration to the Middle East: Emigration from Kerala." Working Paper 180. Centre for Development Studies, Trivandrum, Kerala.

———. 1986a. "Asian Migration to the Arab World: Migration from Kerala." Unpublished Report. Centre for Development Studies, Trivandrum, Kerala.

———. 1986b. "India." In G. Gunatilleke, ed., *Migration of Asian Workers to the Arab World*. Tokyo: United Nations University.

———. 1987a. "Incidence, Impact and Implications of Migration: Migration to the Middle East from Kerala, India." Unpublished Report. Centre for Development Studies, Trivandrum, Kerala.

———. 1987b. "Enhancement of Household Capacity in the Post Migration Phase, Kerala." Unpublished Report. Centre for Development Studies, Trivandrum, Kerala.

———. 1989. "Incidence, Impact and Implications of Migration to the Middle East from Kerala." In Amjad Rashid, ed., *To the Gulf and Back*, 343–364. New Delhi: ILO (ARTEP).

———. 1996. "Rehabilitation of Return Gulf Migrants in Kerala: Issues and Options." Paper presented at the conference on Kerala's Development Experience, National and Global Dimensions. December 9–11, New Delhi.

Nambiar, A.C.K. 1995. *The Socio-Economic Conditions of Gulf Migrants*. New Delhi: Commonwealth Publishers.

Namboodiripad, E.M.S. 1984. *Kerala Society and Politics: An Historical Survey*. New Delhi: National Book Centre.

Narayan, K. 1993. "How Native Is a 'Native' Anthropologist?" *American Anthropologist* 95:671–686.

Nash, M. 1989. *The Cauldron of Ethnicity in the Modern World*. Chicago, Ill: University of Chicago Press.

Nayyar, D. 1994. *Migration, Remittances and Capital Flows: The Indian Experience*. Delhi: Oxford University Press.

Neilson, F. 1985. "Ethnic Solidarity in Modern Societies." *American Sociological Review* 50:133–149.

Newcomer, P. 1972. "The Nuer Are Dinka." *Man* 7:5–11.

Nossiter, T. J. 1982. *Communism in Kerala: A Study in Political Adaptation*. Berkeley and Los Angeles: University of California Press.

———. 1988. *Marxist State Governments in India: Politics, Economics and Society*. London: H. B. Pinter.

O'Brien, J. 1986. "Toward a Reconstitution of Ethnicity: Capitalist Expansion and Cultural Dynamics in Sudan." *American Anthropologist* 88:898–907.

Omi, M., and H. Winant. 1986. *Racial Formation in the United States: From the 1960's to the 1980's.* New York: Routledge & Kegan Paul.

Oommen, M. A. 1991. "Land Reforms and Economic Change: Experiences and Lessons from India's Kerala State." Unpublished Paper.

Ortner, S. B. 1974. "Is Female to Male as Nature Is to Culture?" In M. Rosaldo and L. Lamphere, eds., *Women, Culture and Society.* Stanford, Calif.: Stanford University Press.

Ortner, S. B., and H. Whitehead, eds. 1981. *Sexual Meanings.* Cambridge, U.K.: Cambridge University Press.

Osella, F., and C. Osella. 2000a. *Social Mobility in Kerala: Modernity and Identity in Conflict.* London: Pluto Press.

———. 2000b. "Migration, Money and Masculinity in Kerala." *Journal of the Royal Anthropological Institute* 6:117–133.

Owen, R. 1985. *Migrant Labour in the Gulf.* London: Minority Rights Group.

Owens, R. L., and A. Nandy. 1977. *The New Vaisyas.* New Delhi: Allied Publishers.

Pandey, R. 1986. *The Caste System in India: Myth and Reality.* New Delhi: Criterion Publications.

Panikkar, K. N. 1989. *Against Lord and State.* Delhi: Oxford University Press.

Papademetriou, D. G., and L. P. Martin, eds. 1991. *The Unsettled Relationship: Labor Migration and Economic Development.* Westport, Conn.: Greenwood Press.

Park, R. E. 1950. *Race and Culture.* Glencoe, Ill.: Free Press.

Parker, A., M. Russo, D. Summer, and P. Yaeger, eds. 1992. *Nationalisms and Sexualities.* New York and London: Routledge Press.

Parry, J. P. 1979. *Caste and Kinship in Kangra.* London: Routledge & Kegan Paul.

Parry, J., and M. Bloch. 1989. "Introduction: Money and the Morality of Exchange." In J. Parry and M. Bloch, eds., *Money and the Morality of Exchange,* 1–32. Cambridge, U.K.: Cambridge University Press.

Patterson, O. 1975. "Context and Choice in Ethnic Allegiance." In N. Glazer and P. Moynihan, eds., *Ethnicity: Theory and Practice,* 305–349. Cambridge, Mass.: Harvard University Press.

Peach, C. 1994. "Three Phases of South Asian Emigration." In J. M. Brown and R. Foot, eds., *Migration: The Asian Experience,* 38–55. New York: St. Martin's Press.

Perlmann, J. 1988. *Ethnic Differences: Schooling and Social Structure among the Irish, Italians, Jews and Blacks in an American City, 1880–1935.* Cambridge, U.K.: Cambridge University Press.

Phadnis, U. 1990. *Ethnicity and Nation Building in South Asia.* New Delhi: Sage Publications.

Philpott, S. B. 1973. *West Indian Migration: The Montserrat Case.* London: Athlone Press, University of London.

Pillai, A.K.B. 1987. *The Culture of Social Stratification: The Nayars.* Acton, Mass.: Copley Publishing Group.

Pillai, V.T.K. 1940. *The Travancore State Manual.* Trivandrum, Kerala: V. V. Press Branch.

Piore, M. J. 1979. *Birds of Passage.* Cambridge, U.K.: Cambridge University Press.

Pitt, D. 1970. *Tradition and Economic Progress in Samoa.* London: Oxford University Press.

Podipara, P. 1973. "Hindu in Culture, Christian in Religion, Oriental in Worship." In G. Menachery, ed., *The St. Thomas Christian Encyclopedia of India, Vol. 2.* Madras: B.N.K. Press.

Portes, A., and R. Rumbaut. 1996. *Immigrant America: A Portrait.* Berkeley and Los Angeles: University of California Press.

Portes, A., and J. Sesenbrenner. 1993. "Embeddedness and Immigration: Notes on the Social Determinants of Economic Action." *American Journal of Sociology* 98:1320–1350.

Pothan, S. G. 1963. *The Syrian Christians of Kerala.* Bombay: Asia Publishing House.

Prakash, B. A. 1978. "Impact of Foreign Remittances: A Case Study of Chavakkad Village in Kerala." *Economic and Political Weekly,* July, 1107–1111.

———. 1987. "Kerala's Private Financing Firms: Rise and Fall." *Fortune India* 37–39.

———, ed. 1994. *Kerala's Economy: Performance, Problems and Prospects.* New Delhi: Sage Publications.

———. 1998. "Gulf Migration and Its Economic Impact: The Kerala Experience." *Economic and Political Weekly,* December 12. Internet Edition.

Price, P. 1989. "Ideology and Ethnicity under British Imperial Rule: 'Brahmans,' Lawyers and Kin-Caste Rules in Madras Presidency." *Modern Asian Studies* 23:151–177.

Radhakrishnan, C., and P. Ibrahim. 1981. "Emigration, Inward Remittance and Economic Development." *Manpower Journal* 16:15–52.

Radhakrishnan, P. 1989. *Peasant Struggles, Land Reforms and Social Change: Malabar, 1836–82.* Newbury Park, Calif.: Sage Publications.

Ragin, C. C. 1987. *The Comparative Method: Moving beyond Qualitative and Quantitative Strategies.* Berkeley and Los Angeles: University of California Press.

Rashid, A., ed. 1989. *To the Gulf and Back.* New Delhi: ILO (ARTEP).

Redfield, R. 1941. *The Folk Culture of Yucatan.* Chicago: University of Chicago Press.

Reimers, C. W. 1985. "A Comparative Analysis of the Wages of Hispanics, Blacks and Non-Hispanic Whites." In G. J. Borjas and M. Tienda, eds., *Hispanics in the U.S. Economy,* 27–75. Orlando, Fla.: Academic Press.

Richards, A. 1969. *The Multicultural States of East Africa.* Montreal, Canada: McGill-Queens University Press.

Robertson, R. 1992. *Globalization: Social Theory and Global Culture.* Newbury Park, Calif.: Sage Publications.

Robinson, F. 1974. *Separatism among Indian Muslims.* Cambridge, U.K.: Cambridge University Press.

Roosens, E. 1989. *Creating Ethnicity: The Process of Ethnogenesis.* Newbury Park, Calif.: Sage Publications.

Rosaldo, M. 1974. "Women, Culture and Society: A Theoretical Overview." In M. Rosaldo and L. Lamphere, eds., *Women, Culture and Society.* Palo Alto, Calif.: Stanford University Press.

Rozario, S. 1992. *Purity and Communal Boundaries: Women and Social Change in a Bangladeshi Village.* London: Zed Books.

Rudolph, L., and S. Rudolph. 1967. *The Modernity of Tradition: Political Development in India.* Chicago: University of Chicago Press.

Rueschemeyer, D., and P. Evans. 1985. "The State and Economic Transformation: Toward an Analysis of the Conditions Underlying Effective Intervention." In D.

Rueschemeyer, T. Skocpol, and P. Evans, eds., *Bringing the State Back In*. Cambridge, U.K.: Cambridge University Press.

Rueschemeyer, D., T. Skocpol, and P. Evans, eds. 1985. *Bringing the State Back In*. Cambridge, U.K.: Cambridge University Press.

Rumbaut, R. 1994. "The Crucible Within: Ethnic Identity, Self-esteem and Segmented Assimilation among Children of Immigrants." *International Migration Review* 28:748–794.

Said, E. W. 1978. *Orientalism*. New York: Random House.

Saith, A. 1992. "Absorbing External Shocks: The Gulf Crisis, International Migration Linkages and the Indian Economy, 1990 (with special reference to the impact on Kerala)." *Development and Change* 23:101–146.

Samuel, V. T. 1977. *One Caste, One Religion, One God: A Study of Sree Narayana Guru*. New Delhi: Sterling Publishers.

Sangari, K., and S. Vaid, eds. 1990. *Recasting Women: Essays in Indian Colonial History*. New Brunswick, N.J.: Rutgers University Press.

Sapiro, V. 1993. "Engendering Cultural Differences." In C. Young, ed., *The Rising Tide of Cultural Pluralism: The Nation-State at Bay?*, 36–54. Madison: University of Wisconsin Press.

Saradamoni, K. 1980. *Emergence of a Slave Caste: Pulayas of Kerala*. New Delhi: People's Publication.

Sarkar, S. 1989. *Modern India, 1885–1947*. New York: St. Martin's Press.

Sassen-Koob, S. 1978. "The International Circulation of Resources and Development: The Case of Migrant Labor." *Development and Change* 9:509–545.

Schermerhorn, R. A. 1978. *Ethnic Plurality in India*. Tucson: University of Arizona Press.

Schiller, N. G., L. Basch, and C. Szanton-Blanc, eds. 1992. *Towards a Transnational Perspective on Migration: Race, Class, Ethnicity and Nationalism Reconsidered*. New York: New York Academy of Sciences.

Seccombe, I. J. 1988. "International Migration in the Middle East: Historical Trends, Contemporary Patterns and Consequences." In R. T. Appleyard, ed., *International Migration Today: Vol. 1, Trends and Prospects*. Paris: UNESCO.

Serageldin, I., et al. 1983. *Manpower and International Labour Migration in the Middle East and North Africa*. New York: Oxford University Press (for the World Bank).

Shankman, P. 1976. *Migration and Underdevelopment: The Case of Western Samoa*. Boulder, Colo.: Westview Press.

Shils, E. 1957. "Primordial, Personal, Sacred and Civil Ties." *British Journal of Sociology* 8:130–145.

Shils, E. A., and H. A. Finch. 1949. *Max Weber on the Methodology of the Social Sciences*. Glencoe, Ill.: Free Press.

Shoemaker, R. 1976. "Colonization and Urbanization in Peru: Empirical and Theoretical Perspectives." In D. Guillet and D. J. Uzzel, eds., *New Approaches to the Study of Migration*, 163–175. Houston, Tex.: Rice University.

Singh, J. P. 1992. "Migration in India: A Review." *Asian and Pacific Journal* 1 (1): 169–192.

Slater, R. P., J. R. Watson, and R. N. Tripathy, eds. 1989. *In the Shadow of the Gulf: Case Studies of Poverty Alleviation in Kerala*. Hyderabad, India: National Institute of Rural Development.

Smelser, N. 1976. *The Sociology of Economic Life*. New Jersey: Prentice Hall.

Smith, A. 1981. *The Ethnic Revival.* Cambridge, U.K.: Cambridge University Press.

Smith, A. D. 1986. *The Ethnic Origins of Nations.* Oxford, U.K.: Basil Blackwell.

So, A. Y. 1990. *Social Change and Development: Modernization, Dependency and World Systems Theory.* Newbury Park, Calif.: Sage Publications.

Srinivas, M. N., ed. 1960. *India's Villages.* Bombay: Asia Publishing House.

————. 1968. *Social Change in Modern India.* Berkeley and Los Angeles: Univerisity of California Press.

Stahl, C. 1988. *International Migration Today.* Paris: UNESCO.

Steinberg, S. 1981. *The Ethnic Myth: Race, Ethnicity and Class in America.* New York: Atheneum Press.

Stichter, S. 1985. *Migrant Laborers.* Cambridge, U.K.: Cambridge University Press.

Stinner, W. F., K. de Alburquerque, and R. S. Bryce-Laporte, eds. 1982. *Return Migration and Remittances: Developing a Caribbean Perspective.* Washington, D.C. Research Institute on Immigration and Ethnic Studies, Smithsonian Institution.

Sturtevant, W. 1971. "Creek into Seminole." In E. B. Leacock and N. O. Lurie, eds., *North American Indian in Historical Perspective.* New York: Random House.

Summers, A. 1975. *Damned Whores and God's Police: The Colonization of Women in Australia.* Ringewood: Penguin Books.

Takaki, R. 1979. *Iron Cages: Race and Culture in Nineteenth-Century America.* Seattle: University of Washington Press.

Tambiah, S. J. 1973. "Dowry and Bridewealth, and the Property Rights of Women in South Asia." In J. Goody and S. J. Tambiah, eds., *Bridewealth and Dowry.* Cambridge, U.K.: Cambridge University Press.

Taylor, J. E. 1986. "Differential Migration, Networks, Information and Risk." In O. Stark, ed., *Research in Human Capital and Development,* Vol. 4, *Migration, Human Capital and Development,* 147–171. Greenwich, Conn.: JAI Press.

Tharakan, M. 1984. "Socio-Economic Factors in Educational Development: The Case of Nineteenth-Century Travancore." Working Paper 190. Centre for Development Studies, Trivandrum, Kerala.

Tipps, D. C. 1973. "Modernization Theory and the Comparative Study of Societies: A Critical Perspective." *Comparative Studies of Society and History* 15:199–226.

Tuan, M. 1999. *Forever Foreigners or Honorary Whites: The Asian Ethnic Experience.* New Brunswick, N.J.: Rutgers University Press.

UNESCO. 1984. *Women in the Villages, Men in the Towns.* Paris: UNESCO.

United Nations. 1982. *International Migration Policies and Programs: A World Survey.* New York: United Nations Publication.

Van Den Berghe, P. L. 1981. *The Ethnic Phenomenon.* New York: Elsevier Press.

Van Velsen, J. 1960. "Labor Migration as a Positive Factor in the Continuity of Tonga Tribal Society." *Economic Development and Cultural Change* 8:265–278.

Varghese, T. C. 1970. *Agrarian Change and Economic Consequences: Land Tenures in Kerala, 1850–1960.* Bombay: Allied Publishers.

————. 1982. *Slow Flows the Pampa.* New Delhi: Concept Publishing Company.

Varshney, A. 1998. "Why Democracy Survives: India Defies the Odds." *Journal of Democracy* 9:36–50.

Vatuk, S. 1996. "Identity and Difference or Equality and Inequality in South Asian Muslim Society." In C. J. Fuller, ed., *Caste Today,* 227–262. Delhi: Oxford University Press.

Virtanen, K. 1979. *Settlement of Return.* Helsinki: Finnish Historical Society.

Visvanathan, S. 1989. "Marriage, Birth and Death: Property Rights and Domestic Relationships of the Orthodox/Jacobite Syrian Christians of Kerala." *Economic and Political Weekly* June 17, 1341–1346.

———. 1993. *The Christians of Kerala: History, Belief and Ritual among the Yakoba.* Madras: Oxford University Press.

Visweswaran, K. 1994. *Fictions of Feminist Ethnography.* Minneapolis: University of Minnesota Press.

Washbrook, D. A. 1982. "Ethnicity and Racialism in Colonial Indian Society." In R. Ross, ed., *Racism and Colonialism: Essays on Ideology and Social Structure.* The Hague: Martinus Nijhoff Publishers.

Waters, M. C. 1990. *Ethnic Options: Choosing Identities in America.* Berkeley and Los Angeles: University of California Press.

———. 1999. *Black Identities: West Indian Immigrant Dreams and American Realities.* New York: Russell Sage.

Watson, J. L. 1975. *Emigration and Chinese Lineage.* Berkeley and Los Angeles: University of California Press.

———. 1977. *Between Two Cultures: Migrants and Minorities in Britain.* Oxford, U. K.: Basil Blackwell.

Weber, M. 1958. *The Religion of India: The Sociology of Hinduism and Buddhism.* Glencoe, Ill.: Free Press.

———. 1963. *The Sociology of Religion.* Boston: Beacon Press.

———. 1978. *Economy and Society, Vol. 1.* Berkeley and Los Angeles: University of California Press.

Weiner, M. 1985. "On International Migration and International Relations." *Population and Development Review* 11:3 (September), 441–455.

Wickramasekara, P., ed. 1993. *The Gulf Crisis and South Asia: Studies on the Economic Impact.* New Delhi: UNDP/ILO (ARTEP).

Woocock, G. 1967. *Kerala: A Portrait of the Malabar Coast.* London: Faber and Faber.

World Bank. 1981. "Labor Migration from Bangladesh to the Middle East." Washington, D.C.: World Bank.

Yancey, W., E. Ericksen, and R. Juliani. 1976. "Emergent Ethnicity: A Review and Reformulation." *American Sociological Review* 41:391–403.

Zachariah, K. C., E. T. Mathew, and S. I. Rajan. 1999. "Impact of Migration on Kerala's Economy and Society." Working Paper 297. Centre for Development Studies, Trivandrum, Kerala.

———. 2000. "Socio-Economic and Demographic Consequences of Migration in Kerala." Working Paper 303. Centre for Development Studies, Trivandrum, Kerala.

Zelizer, V. 1989. "The Social Meaning of Money: 'Special Monies.'" *American Journal of Sociology* 95:342–377.

Zhou, M., and C. L. Bankston III. 1998. *Growing Up American: How Vietnamese Children Adapt to Life in the United States.* New York: Russell Sage.

INDEX

Addleton, Jonathan, 40
Africa, 1, 35, 48
Aiyappan, A., 46
Arabs, 43, 77, 111; as employers, 100; as
   migration sponsors, 63, 64–65, 85;
   Muslim, 31, 47, 79, 94, 101
Asia, South, 1

Bahrain, 142
Bailey, Reverend, 134
Bangladesh, 29, 31, 39, 81
Barth, Fredrik, 21, 60
Bayly, Susan, 47–48, 55, 58, 176n2,
   177nn6, 14
Bible, the, 134–35, 137
black market, 82, 85, 86, 91
Bloch, Maurice, 41–42, 104, 165
Bombay, 80, 85, 180n5
Bourdieu, Pierre, 24–26, 37, 39, 131
Brahmins. *See* Hindus, Brahmin
Brass, Paul, 35

castes, 2, 179n33; Backward Class
   (Pulaya), 16, 44, 52, 138, 157–58, 168,
   186nn4, 13–15; clothing of, 45;
   housing of, 45; Kshatriya, 45, 59;
   lower, 15, 49, 53–54, 55, 69, 116, 134,
   161, 178n32; slave, 45, 47, 66, 176n1.
   See also slavery; Sudra, 45; untouchable, 45, 46–47, 52, 54, 57; upper, 15,
   116, 124, 177n7, 179n40; Vaisya, 45.
   See also Hindus, Brahmin; Hindus,
   Harijan
caste system, 167–68, 176n2, 177n15;

abolition of, 55; changes to, 52–55,
   116–17, 121–26; in Cherur, 105, 116–
   17, 121, 123–26; crusade against, 54,
   55, 57, 106; disabilities of, 23, 48, 53,
   54, 55; divisions in, 11, 14, 22, 35–36,
   138, 157–58, 159, 160–61, 168;
   impact of migration on, 4, 101; in
   Kembu, 138, 157–58; in Kerala, 45–
   47, 48; and Sanskritization, 116–17,
   125; varna, 44–45; in Veni, 11, 77,
   100–101, 168. *See also* Hindus
Chad, 48
Cherur, 14, 15, 67, 108, 130–32, 172;
   competition in, 105–6; health care and
   health workers in, 112, 115–16, 129,
   184n5; Palam, 105, 112; Sripuram
   (locality), 105; Trivandrum (city), 14–
   15, 113, 150. *See also* Kuttur; Muttam
children, 95–96, 97, 98, 113, 130;
   education of, 96, 115, 118, 122, 130,
   163, 169; and gender discrimination,
   72, 130, 163; health of, 92, 93, 94,
   151, 183–84n19. *See also* family
Choucri, Nazli, 12
Christian churches, 31, 48, 138, 157,
   175n8, 178n18, 186n10, 186n14
Christianity, 30, 186–87n15; converts to,
   48, 49, 52, 54, 134–35, 161, 168,
   178n29, 186n13; early, 47–48, 49,
   134–35, 177n11
Christian missionaries. *See* missionaries
Christians, 179n36; Backward Class
   (Pulaya), 16, 44, 52, 138, 157–58, 168,
   186nn4, 13–15; Bangladeshi, 29; Latin

ABOUT THE AUTHOR

Prema A. Kurien is an assistant professor of sociology at the University of Southern California. Her current work focuses on religion and ethnicity among Indian immigrants in the United States. She is at work on a book titled *Multiculturalism and Immigrant Religion: The Development of an American Hinduism* for publication by Rutgers University Press.